Clean Air and Good Jobs

Clean Air and Good Jobs

---

*U.S. Labor and the Struggle
for Climate Justice*

TODD E. VACHON

TEMPLE UNIVERSITY PRESS
Philadelphia • Rome • Tokyo

TEMPLE UNIVERSITY PRESS
Philadelphia, Pennsylvania 19122
tupress.temple.edu

Library of Congress Cataloging-in-Publication Data

Names: Vachon, Todd E., 1976– author.
Title: Clean air and good jobs : U.S. labor and the struggle for climate
    justice / Todd E. Vachon.
Description: Philadelphia : Temple University Press, 2023. | Includes
    bibliographical references and index. | Summary: "Addresses the role
    that the U.S. labor movement has or could have in forging a 'just
    transition' away from dependence on fossil fuels toward a Green New Deal
    to address the dual crises of climate change and inequality"— Provided
    by publisher.
Identifiers: LCCN 2022040366 (print) | LCCN 2022040367 (ebook) | ISBN
    9781439923214 (cloth) | ISBN 9781439923221 (paperback) | ISBN
    9781439923238 (pdf)
Subjects: LCSH: Climate justice—United States. | Labor movement—United
    States. | Energy transition—United States. | Green New Deal—United
    States. | Climatic changes—Government policy—United States.
Classification: LCC GE230 .V34 2023 (print) | LCC GE230 (ebook) | DDC
    333.791/5—dc23/eng20230126
LC record available at https://lccn.loc.gov/2022040366
LC ebook record available at https://lccn.loc.gov/2022040367

Printed in the United States of America

9 8 7 6 5 4 3 2 1

Dedicated to "The Popular Wobbly"
and all those fighting for a more just, democratic,
and sustainable future.

Contents

Preface

A Prequel to the Green New Deal

On November 13, 2018, more than two hundred youth activists flooded House Minority Leader Nancy Pelosi's office to demand that the U.S. government establish a "select committee to develop legislation for a total economic mobilization to transition our country toward a 100 percent renewable energy economy—as the IPCC has tasked every nation to do" (Corbett 2018). Joined by Representative-Elect Alexandria Ocasio-Cortez, the protesters were demanding a "Green New Deal" to address the growing crises of climate change and runaway inequality in America. "I just want to let you all know how proud I am of each and every single one of you for putting yourselves and your bodies and everything on the line to make sure we save our planet, our generation, and our future. It's so incredibly important," Ocasio-Cortez told the activists, fifty-one of whom were arrested for unlawfully demonstrating at Pelosi's office (Corbett 2018).

This iconic moment appears to be the start of the movement for a Green New Deal, which has already transformed the nature and limits of policy debate in the Democratic Party and the nation and, if successful, would lead to a significant transformation of the American government, economy, and society. But years of effort helped bring this moment to pass and may help determine whether it is just a flash in the pan or the start of a period of transformation. One little-known aspect of that effort is the subject of this book: The movement of climate activists within the U.S. labor movement, which I refer to as the labor–climate movement (LCM), helped lay the groundwork for the Green New Deal by building a base within labor for supporting climate protection as a vehicle for good jobs and the reconstruction of American society.

Three months after the youth sit-in at Pelosi's office, on February 7, 2019, Ocasio-Cortez and Senator Ed Markey introduced House Resolution 109 "Recognizing the duty of the Federal Government to create a Green New Deal" (U.S. Congress 2019). The resolution called for a ten-year national mobilization to "achieve net-zero greenhouse gas emissions through a fair and just transition for all communities and workers" (5). While the resolution is a vision piece rather than actual legislation, it stands out from previous climate mitigation plans brought before Congress because of its focus on jobs, workers' rights, unions, climate justice, and the need for a just transition. It calls for the creation of "high-quality union jobs that pay prevailing wages, hire local workers, offer training and advancement opportunities, and guarantee wage and benefit parity for workers affected by the transition" (U.S. Congress 2019, 12). It also calls for the inclusion of communities and unions in the process of developing climate change mitigation plans: "The Green New Deal must be developed through transparent and inclusive consultation, collaboration, and partnership with frontline and vulnerable communities, labor unions, worker cooperatives, civil society groups, academia, and businesses" (U.S. Congress 2019, 10).

The first union to endorse the resolution was Local 32BJ of the Service Employees International Union (SEIU), a union representing 175,000 office cleaners, maintenance workers, security officers, engineers, door attendants, porters, window cleaners, and food service workers. However, despite the great deal of attention given to workers, unions, and worker voices, the resolution was not met with resounding support from the whole of the U.S. labor movement. On March 8, the powerful Energy Committee within the national American Federation of Labor and Congress of Industrial Organizations (AFL-CIO), primarily comprising energy unions representing more than 300,000 building trades and utility workers, issued a public letter acknowledging the problem of climate change but went on to state, "We will not accept proposals that will cause immediate harm to millions of our members and their families. We will not stand by and allow threats to our members' jobs and their families' standard of living go unanswered" (AFL-CIO Energy Committee 2019). In the months and years that followed, various unions and labor federations at all levels took turns either supporting or resisting the Green New Deal.

At the same time, activists within the growing climate justice movement cautiously supported the Green New Deal resolution. Groups such as the Climate Justice Alliance (CJA), which promote a transition away from extractive systems of production, consumption, and political oppression toward resilient, regenerative, and equitable economies, maintained that the Green New Deal must focus on addressing inequities along the lines of race and gender as well as class. As with some in labor, the CJA initially critiqued the Green New Deal resolution process for its apparent lack of consultation with grassroots organizers and members of frontline communities during its development, but in the end the group proclaimed support for it. In particular, climate justice activists supported the plan to create good job alternatives for the 6.4 million workers currently employed in the energy sector so long as the transition was also just for communities that live on the front lines of extractive and toxic polluting industries.

While the Green New Deal resolution itself is new, the apparent division it reveals within the U.S. labor movement over how best to confront the climate crisis has been growing for many years. We have seen it on display at other key historic junctures, such as the battles over the Keystone XL and Dakota Access pipelines, when Ocasio-Cortez says she made the decision to run for office. Several unions, including Communication Workers of America (CWA), SEIU, National Nurses United (NNU), and Amalgamated Transit Union (ATU), stood with climate justice activists and opposed the pipelines, in direct opposition to the North America's Building Trades Unions (NABTU). In response, Terry O'Sullivan, general president of Laborers International Union of North America (LIUNA), stated, "These four unions have no equity in this pipeline; it will not put a single one of their members to work yet they choose to take food off of our members' tables. A central tenet of the labor movement has always been that when it comes to a project in which you have no equity at stake, you either support it or remain silent" (LIUNA 2016).

Most major media outlets are quick to pick up on the Jobs vs. the Environment narrative espoused by workers and unions supporting environmentally destructive projects such as fossil fuel pipelines and power plants. There is, of course, much truth in the claim that climate change mitigation in the form of reducing greenhouse gas (GHG) emissions threatens the jobs and livelihoods of some blue-collar workers in the fossil fuel industry. The fears of those workers who face potential job displacement, and thus the loss of a means to support their families, are real and absolutely justified given the U.S. government's less-than-stellar history of "transitioning" workers after major job-loss events. Decades of neoliberal globalization have not left blue-collar workers with many good job alternatives—at least not ones paying as much as the fossil fuel sector or offering the benefits and protections of a union contract. The same neoliberal ideology that has prevented meaningful transition programs for displaced workers and fueled the outsourcing of jobs (and pollution) to countries with lax labor and environmental laws has also resulted in the utter paucity of the U.S. welfare state. Without universal access to health insurance, for example, the stakes for workers facing job loss in America are much greater than in any other advanced capitalist democracy. College tuition is expensive and financed overwhelmingly in the form of debt by the individual student, who also bears the risk that the degree may not even translate into a well-paying job in the end. For these reasons, the Green New Deal resolution so wisely incorporated universal access to healthcare and education as well as a federal jobs guarantee into its plan to address climate change—but still the AFL-CIO remains wary, narrowly focusing on existing fossil fuel jobs rather than the greater good of the whole working class.

Less recognized than the sporadic Jobs vs. the Environment struggles is the growing participation by labor activists, union leaders, and some unions in the fight to address the climate crisis. While decarbonizing the economy threatens the jobs of a small percentage of workers, failing to do so threatens the health and well-being of all workers—and as with most unnatural disasters, the ill effects will hit those who are most vulnerable first and worst. Accordingly, LCM activists have increasingly been aligning with the climate justice movement and making the case that climate change is a working-class issue: Passing union resolutions, training union members, participating in climate marches and more recently in youth climate strikes—because no worker, no job, no community, no industry will be left unscathed by climate change.

Fortunately, the growing LCM has made great strides in bringing many unions to a more progressive stance on climate change in recent years. In fact, if not for those efforts, the labor movement might not be divided on the issue of climate protection but rather stand as a monolith of opposition. More than a decade before the Green New Deal resolution was introduced, this small minority of LCM activists began promoting the idea of a "World War II–style mobilization of the US economy" to address the climate crisis in a just way. In a 2011 Labor Day post, Joe Uehlein, founding president of the Labor Network for Sustainability, stated, "The solution for labor, as for America and indeed for the world, lies in a Green New Deal to mobilize our unused human resources to meet our increasingly desperate needs" (Uehlein 2011). Drawing from the work of the late labor leader and occupational health and safety activist Tony Mazzocchi, LCM activists went beyond mere calls for "green growth" and began demanding decarbonization of the economy with a "just transition" for workers facing job displacement as a result of such efforts. Some, having been involved with climate justice or environmental justice organizations outside of work, started to bring those concerns into their union activity. If labor as a whole can be brought to support the Green New Deal or a similar program with a strong just transition program for workers and vulnerable communities, it will have a greater chance of becoming a reality, and it will be in large part a result of the LCM. But much more work still needs to be done.

This book examines the collective actions and framing processes of the nascent LCM that refused to "remain silent" in the years leading up to the arrival of the Green New Deal resolution. What structural factors can foster or hinder union participation in efforts to protect the climate in accordance with the demands of science? How do LCM activists frame the problem and possible solutions to the dual crises of climate and inequality? How do these framing processes influence the tactics and actions taken by labor–climate SMOs? Based on extensive original research, as well as my own experiences over two decades of participation in the U.S. labor movement as a carpenter, an organizer, and a local union president, this book aims to tell the story of the workers and union leaders who have been waging a slow, but steadily growing, revolution within their unions to make labor as a whole an active and progressive champion for both workers and the environment—to become a proactive force for Clean Air and Good Jobs. Even in the wake of the failure of President Biden's Build Back Better plan and the passage of the largely market-driven solutions of the Inflation Reduction Act, the movement continues to fight to make a Green New Deal–style plan a reality by building alliances with climate justice activists, environmentalists, youth activists, and other social movement organizations (SMOs). Because, as the now-popular refrain goes, "There are no jobs on a dead planet." So, as we stand teetering at the edge of a climate change precipice, facing the end of the world as we know it, I hope this examination of the "movement within the movement" can offer some useful lessons to help us learn to fly—so we might reach the truly just and sustainable world we all so desperately want and need.

Acknowledgments

My greatest debt in this project is to the folks in the labor movement across the United States who are working tirelessly to promote labor–climate justice. Their willingness to welcome me as a participant and to discuss their political activities and aspirations made this research possible. Because they were assured they would not be identified in any way, I can only now express my gratitude for their participation.

Equally important have been my academic advisers and peers at the University of Connecticut. In particular, if it weren't for the undying commitment to student mentoring by my adviser, Michael Wallace, the marriage of my own activist efforts and scholarly interests in labor and climate change would not have manifested in this project as they have. My dissertation committee—Mary Fischer, Jeremy Pais, Brian Obach, and Lyle Scruggs—provided me with invaluable advice throughout this project. My fellow graduate worker comrades kept me sufficiently distracted by working together to organize a union and bargain a first contract and then electing me to serve as union president—all of which ultimately afforded me greater access to important field sites (and two extra years of grad school).

I owe a debt of gratitude to J. Mijin Cha, Les Leopold, Mike Merrill, Vivian Price, and Dimitris Stevis for always engaging me in such thoughtful conversations on just transitions and challenging me to think outside the box. I also wish to thank all my wonderful colleagues at Rutgers School of Management and Labor Relations and the Rutgers AAUP-AFT, and especially Will Brucher, Dorothy Sue Cobble, Patty Deitsch, Janice Fine, Rebecca Givan, Chris

Hayes, Tamara Lee, Judy Lugo, Carmen Martino, Eugene McElroy, Patrick Nowlan, Fran Ryan, Tobias Schulze-Cleven, Marilyn Sneiderman, Paula Voos, Naomi R Williams, Laura Walkoviac, and Sherry Wolf, who made me feel so welcome when I first arrived in this strange land called New Jersey. And to Debra Coyle McFadden and Cecelia Leto from the NJ Work Environment Council, my remote work partners during the dark days of the pandemic—"saving lives, protecting workers." In the final months of this project, I befriended a terrific copyeditor, Peggy Currid, to whom I owe much for so quickly and efficiently working out some dents and putting the shine on this ride on an unreasonably short timeline. And to my editor at Temple, Aaron Javsicas, who guided a naive first-time author through this process—thank you for your support and patience.

This project would not have been possible without support from my family and friends. My wonderful parents, Nelson and Bonnie—both good union members—always told me I could accomplish anything if I put my mind to it. My partner, Genea Bell, was the driving force and inspiration for my returning to school to earn a Ph.D. and who still encourages me to take risks and try new things I otherwise might not. Our three amazing kids—Marley, Toliver, and Ebba—always kept things lively as they tagged along with their dad to endless meetings, first as a student; then as an organizer, researcher, union president, and postdoc; and finally as a professor, over the course of their childhood years. My extended family, the ESP crew, kept my soul fed with good music and comradery throughout this journey. And to my friend and frequent coauthor, Allen Hyde, thanks for running that last set of models—I'm really busy this week!

At last, I would like to acknowledge three truly great individuals who have been my "shadow committee" for many years. These outsider–insiders were a great source of inspiration for making my research meaningful and keeping me focused on the potential for my work to make positive changes in the real world—if not in the writing, then in the act of participating. To Jeremy Brecher, John Humphries, and Mark Sullivan I offer my sincerest gratitude, and I look forward to future chats over coffee or beer in the very near future.

List of Abbreviations

Unions and Labor Federations

AAUP	American Association of University Professors
AFGE	American Federation of Government Employees
AFL-CIO	American Federation of Labor and Congress of Industrial Organizations
AFSCME	American Federation of State, County, and Municipal Employees
AFT	American Federation of Teachers
APWU	American Postal Workers Union
ARU	American Railroad Union
ATU	Amalgamated Transit Union
BSCP	Brotherhood of Sleeping Car Porters
CNA	California Nurses Association
CWA	Communication Workers of America
IAM	International Association of Machinists and Aerospace Workers
IBEW	International Brotherhood of Electrical Workers
ILGWU	International Ladies' Garment Workers' Union
ILWU	International Longshore and Warehouse Union
ITUC	International Trade Union Confederation
IUOE	International Union of Operating Engineers
IWW	Industrial Workers of the World
LIUNA	Laborers International Union of North America

NABTU	North America's Building Trades Unions
NEA	National Education Association
NNU	National Nurses United
NYSNA	New York State Nurses Association
OCAW	Oil, Chemical and Atomic Workers
SEIU	Service Employees International Union
SMART	International Association of Sheet Metal, Air, Rail and Transportation Workers
TWU	Transport Workers Union
UA	United Association of Plumbers and Pipefitters
UAW	United Auto Workers
UBC	United Brotherhood of Carpenters
UE	United Electrical, Radio and Machine Workers of America
UFCW	United Food and Commercial Workers
UMWA	United Mine Workers of America
UNITE-HERE	Union of Needletrades, Industrial, and Textile Employees–Hotel Employees and Restaurant Employees
USW	United Steelworkers
UTU	United Transportation Union
UWUA	Utility Workers Union of America

Other Organizations

BGA	BlueGreen Alliance
CJA	Climate Justice Alliance
JMA	Jobs to Move America
JTA	Just Transition Alliance
LUPE	Labor Unions for Public Energy (pseudonym)
NECA	National Electrical Contractors Association
SSSP	Society for the Study of Social Problems
SPEC	State Partnership for Employment and Climate (pseudonym)
USE	Unions for Sustainable Energy (pseudonym)

Government and Intergovernmental Agencies

BLM	Bureau of Land Management
BLS	Bureau of Labor Statistics
DOE	Department of Energy
EPA	Environmental Protection Agency

ILO	International Labour Organization
IPCC	Intergovernmental Panel on Climate Change
IRENA	International Renewable Energy Agency
NASA	National Aeronautics and Space Administration
NOAA	National Oceanic and Atmospheric Administration
OJT	Office of Just Transition
OSHA	Occupational Safety and Health Administration
WTO	World Trade Organization

Other Abbreviations

BCG	Bargaining for the Common Good
COP	Conference of the Parties
IRA	Inflation Reduction Act
LCM	Labor–Climate Movement
NAFTA	North American Free Trade Agreement
PLA	Project Labor Agreement
SMO	Social Movement Organization

Clean Air and Good Jobs

1

"The Biggest Threat to Our Humanity"

Climate Change and the Emerging
Labor–Climate Movement

The New York City subway system moves over 5.3 million people per day across 660 miles of tracks beneath the city. It links to four other commuter rail systems, bringing an additional one million people into the city from the suburbs and smaller regional cities such as Stamford, Connecticut; White Plains, New York; and Newark, New Jersey, each day. The system connects workers to jobs, consumers to goods and services, and students to schools, and it underpins the over $4.6 billion dollars of economic activity in the city each day. It also accounts for more than half of the seventy thousand jobs in the Metropolitan Transit Authority, which runs New York's public transit system. That is why, on the evening of Sunday, October 28, 2012, New York's decision to suspend all subway service in anticipation of Superstorm Sandy was not taken lightly. This decision proved wise because the storm arrived with a vengeance on October 29, rendering the subway system nonoperational until Thursday, November 1.

Beyond paralyzing the subway, the storm caused unprecedented destruction throughout the Northeast as 80 mph winds and record storm surges wreaked havoc across the East Coast, flooding roads, destroying homes, leaving more than eight million without power across seventeen states, and causing fires like the one that burned down the community of Breezy Point in Queens. Over one hundred deaths were attributed to the storm. As with previous extreme storms such as Hurricane Katrina, which hit the Gulf Coast in 2005, or later storms like Hurricane Maria, which ravaged Puerto Rico in 2017, it was the working class and poor—the frontline communities—who were hit first and worst. Nine years later, New York and New Jersey were devastated again by Hurricane Ida while still continuing to shore up transit infrastructure ruined by Sandy, with repairs on some lines not even forecast to begin until 2022. The storm's damage to the New York City subway alone was estimated to cost $5 billion to repair. National Oceanic and Atmospheric Administration (NOAA) places the total cost of the storm at $70.2 billion—possibly the costliest to ever hit the region (National Centers for Environmental Information, n.d.). The storm was the most devastating event to hit New York City since the terrorist attacks of September 11, 2001.

Steve Downs, a member and local leader of Transport Workers Union (TWU) Local 100, described to me how more than 1,500 members of his union had worked around the clock after the storm to get service back up and running in just a few days, exceeding even the most optimistic predictions. "Transit workers always play a special part in the functioning of the city," he said, "but they really stepped up and did extra during this time; in less than optimal conditions, with no shelters, in the elements, working double overtime, including people who had their own personal concerns, who had lost their homes and had uncertainty of where their family was going to be at night".

Some workers stayed on the job for three or four straight days, pumping out over fifty miles of flooded tunnels, reconnecting electricity, checking signals, and operating a continuous cycle of shuttle buses across the major bridges into and out of Manhattan to keep the city moving while the nine flooded tunnels connecting the island to the mainland were cleaned out and repaired. "In 108 years [of operation]," stated Joe Lhota, chairman of the Metropolitan Transit Authority, "our employees have never faced a challenge like the one that confronts us now [in the wake of the storm]."

At their union's national convention on September 23, 2013—nearly a year after the storm—many transportation workers shared their stories of loss, of bravery by fellow members who had saved their lives, and of the union's tremendous relief efforts, which brought donations in from other locals around the country to help the New York and New Jersey members after the storm. More than one thousand of the union's members lived in the storm-ravaged Coney Island area of Brooklyn. Many had their homes wiped out by the storm, and others had over eight feet of water in their homes in the days following the storm. They had lost electricity, they had lost their winter clothes just before the season was about to change, and many had lost everything they owned. "Just to drive down these streets and see their homes being emptied out and all the debris and the broken water lines and how they were affected," one member recounted in a video played at the convention. "It was like, you know, I'm not old enough to say I lived through the Great Depression, but I think I've seen it. These people are standing in line for a daily meal."

The New York State Nurses Association (NYSNA) also coordinated relief efforts after the storm, including organizing volunteer efforts by their members who visited the hardest-hit communities to provide care. They opened up a deployment site that operated out of the organization's RV on Staten Island, sending teams of registered nurses door-to-door to determine people's needs and provide much-needed care to many residents affected by the storm. As health professionals, the nurses dealt directly with the people affected by the health consequences of climate change. At a rally, Nella Pineda-Marcon, chair of the union's Committee on Climate and Environmental Justice, stated, "We nurses are all too familiar with the fact that climate change wreaks havoc on our weather, and extreme weather events create public health emergencies" (NYSNA 2018).

Bruce Hamilton, a leader in the ATU with members in New Jersey, said living through Sandy had opened the eyes of their membership and some of their local leaders. The highly diverse memberships of the New York and New Jersey transportation unions had many members whose neighborhoods were among the worst hit by the storm but who also had histories of racial, economic, and environmental injustices—all issues the members had brought into their union work. Sandy dramatically revealed that the issue of climate change was just another injustice their unions should confront and that it was, in fact, inextricably connected with the issues of economic and social justice the union was already confronting daily. Many locals formed union climate justice committees. At the national level, the ATU went so far as to adopt a resolution titled "Opposing Fossil Fuel Dependency." Bruce said that "Sandy made it clear that climate change was real and that it was a worker issue, a union issue."

Similarly, Henry Garrido, executive director of American Federation of State, County, and Municipal Employees (AFSCME) District Council 37 in New York City, said at a rally, "Our workers were at the forefront manning shelters, evacuating people, preparing hospital beds, and rescuing people every day" during and after Sandy. "Labor," he went on, "must stand for more than working conditions. We must stand for more than contracts. We must stand for environmental justice—otherwise, we will become irrelevant." The issue of climate change, he stated, is "the biggest threat to our humanity. We can no longer afford to put our heads in the sand" (Brecher 2015).

However, not all unions were singing "Kumbaya" about climate justice. In the lead-up to Sandy and the two years following the storm, the nation's major construction unions, known as the building trades, were fighting fiercely against environmentalists, liberal politicians, and several unions, including the TWU, over the proposed Keystone XL oil pipeline. For the construction unions, the pipeline project represented a huge employment opportunity for their members, who were still facing high levels of unemployment in the wake of the Great Recession. For environmentalists, Indigenous people, climate justice advocates, and several other unions, it represented a tremendous step in the wrong direction in the battle against climate change. LIUNA's Terry O'Sullivan stated, "It's repulsive, it's disgusting, and we're not going to stand idly by. . . . Unions and environmental groups that have no equity in the work have kicked our members in the teeth. And anger is an understatement as to how we feel about it. We're not sitting at the same table as people that destroy our members' lives." He went so far as to propose using his union's political influence to block funding for public transportation projects and promised to oppose any future bailouts of the auto industry, indicating resentment for the United Auto Workers (UAW), which had signed a statement supporting President Obama's decision to block the pipeline project.

Neither were leaders of the United Mine Workers of America (UMWA) jumping up to support a transition to renewable energy. The long-term decline in coal jobs, caused overwhelmingly by automation and market forces such as the rise of cheaper natural gas as an alternative fuel source, left many coal communities economically devastated. The workers and their unions, however, blamed the devastation not on the forces of capitalism but rather on the government—in particular, the Environmental Protection Agency and its pollution and emission regulations. This anger led in part to the success of Donald Trump's presidential campaign in traditionally Democratic areas of Appalachia, where he held "Trump Digs Coal" rallies and promised to undo environmental regulations and bring coal jobs back.

However, for Steve and tens of thousands of other workers who were victims of Sandy and other climate catastrophes in recent years, the question remained: "But what about the devastation *we* have experienced as a result of burning too many fossil fuels?" Not just the direct impact of any particular storm "but the increasing health problems for the kids, the asthma and allergies, the dangerous heat days on the job, and the risk of more extreme storms [from the long-term changes being made to the climate]." All those problems disproportionately impact workers from historically marginalized communities that have been dealing with environmental injustices for decades and are now confronted with climate injustice as well.

Environmental justice activists who have been organizing for decades to address the legacies of industrial pollution and environmental racism were quick to connect the dots between Sandy and climate injustice. For example, UPROSE, a community organization in Brooklyn, convened and hosted a community meeting in Sunset Park on December 19, 2012, to listen to and engage with community members about their experiences during and after the storm. Sharing stories of neighbors helping neighbors and describing some of the unexpected problems and challenges families encountered, meeting participants declared, "We are the First Responders!" This meeting led to the creation of the Climate Justice Center, which has been working to develop community strategies to address the problems identified and make the community more sustainable and resilient for residents, workers, and businesses in the face of increasingly severe and more frequent extreme weather that not only harms human health and well-being but also has significant economic implications.

In a piece titled "Hurricane Sandy by the Numbers," *Time* magazine reported that the estimated dollar value of the lost business activity as a result of Sandy was $25 billion (Webley 2012). Over fifty-seven thousand utility workers came from thirty states and Canada to New York to assist in restoring power to the city. Sandy was so devastating that it forced the closing of the New York Stock Exchange for two days, the first time it had been closed for two consecutive days because of weather since the Blizzard of 1888. The storm, as measured by the diameter of tropical storm–force sustained wind, was 820 miles across when it slammed into the New Jersey coast—more than double the landfall size of Hurricanes Isaac and Irene combined. New York City had a gasoline rationing system in effect for fifteen days and New Jersey for eleven days, with customers lined up at the pumps awaiting their allotted gas rations to power their electrical generators (if they were fortunate enough to have acquired one before the stores sold out in the run-up to the storm).

The New York State Department of Labor estimated the storm had wiped out thirty thousand jobs (McGeehan 2012). As with previous climate disasters in other cities, Sandy disproportionately harmed the most vulnerable. Approximately eighty thousand public housing residents in 402 buildings lost power, heat, and hot water—and power was not restored in many of the buildings for more than two weeks. One week after the storm, Green Party presidential candidate Jill Stein laid out her signature campaign plank in an interview on PBS: "The Green New Deal," she said, "calls for emergency action now, like we did after World War II, as if we had been attacked. Because we have been attacked by storms, drought, and flooding. In the process of building up green energy, we can put millions of people back to work" (Ponsot 2012).

While it is difficult to attribute any one weather event to climate change, climate scientists typically talk about the increased propensity for extreme storms as a result of the underlying changes in the climate caused by global warming. Warmer ocean temperatures and air temperatures, melting Arctic ice, rising sea levels, and shifting ocean and air currents can all lead to larger, slower-moving storms that carry more water and maintain their intensity much longer. If left unchecked, climate change may pass a critical threshold, or tipping point, after which a tiny change can completely alter the state of the system, inciting catastrophes ranging from widespread drought to an overwhelming rise in the sea level (Russill and Nyssa 2009). In sum, the perceptions of the 78 percent of respondents in a Quinnipiac poll following the storm who "believe we are experiencing large storms such as Sandy and Irene more frequently as a result of climate change" were correct (Webley 2012). Climate change cannot be said to have "caused" Superstorm Sandy, but it did increase its likelihood and its intensity. And as the members of the New York City transportation, nurses, and public sector unions know all too well, those effects of climate change on weather can have devastating consequences for working people, both on the job and in their communities.

Changing Climate, Changing Society

Twenty-four years before Superstorm Sandy, on June 23, 1988, a hot and humid day in Washington, DC, NASA climate scientist James Hansen explained to Congress, and the world, that the heat-trapping gases emitted by the burning of fossil fuels were pushing global temperatures higher. His remarks that day marked the official opening of "the age of climate change." In the years since Hansen's testimony, the scientific community has affirmed that climate change is a serious cause for concern (Oreskes 2004, 1686). Over 97 percent of scientists agree that climate change is real, that it is caused overwhelmingly by the burning of fossil fuels, and that we are already feeling its effects right now (U.S. Global Change Research Program 2017). Each day, the seemingly mundane actions of billions of human beings, from turning on the lights to driving to work to cooking their meals, release billions of tons of greenhouse gases (GHGs) into the atmosphere, including more than thirty billion tons of carbon dioxide (CO_2) per year (IPCC 2014; Levin 2018). These gases linger, accumulate, and trap heat inside the atmosphere, causing the average temperature of the planet to rise. The science of global warming is nothing new and is simple. The solution? Seemingly simpler—reduce GHG emissions into the atmosphere. The act of pursuing that solution? Perhaps the biggest challenge ever faced by humanity.

To reduce GHG emissions enough to slow global warming and prevent catastrophic climate change, humans must significantly reduce their burning of fossil fuels, and we must do it rapidly. In 2016, atmospheric concentrations of carbon dioxide surpassed 400 parts per million, which has caused a planetary warming of roughly 1°C (33.8°F) above preindustrial temperatures, when

CO_2 was estimated to be at just 280 parts per million (NOAA 2017). An average temperature rise of two degrees Celsius has been identified by scientists, including the authors of the United Nations Intergovernmental Panel on Climate Change (IPCC) report that informed the Paris Climate Accord, as a point at which most climate change becomes damaging (IPCC 2014). To keep global warming below that mark, global GHG emissions will need to be reduced to less than 50 percent of 1990 levels by 2050 and be on a path to zero emissions. To put that in perspective, it means there is room in the atmosphere to burn or vent less than one-quarter of all known oil, natural gas, and coal reserves (Allen et al. 2009).

The transition away from fossil fuels and toward 100 percent renewable energy can take many forms, or as scholars of institutions would say, there are several "modes of change" (Mahoney and Thelen 2010; Streeck and Thelen 2005; Thelen 2009). Given the political landscape of America, an abrupt "puncture," or radical shift within a short period of time, seems somewhat unlikely but is not beyond the realm of possibility. More likely is some sort of incrementalist approach, such as layering or displacement. *Layering* involves the addition of renewable infrastructure on top of the existing fossil fuel–based energy system. This approach, which is codified in the Inflation Reduction Act of 2022 (IRA), is already under way—and indeed is generally supported by the same building trades unions that have been promoting oil pipelines such as the Keystone XL—but unfortunately, without phasing out fossil fuel infrastructure, layering will do little to reduce emissions, and the disparate impacts of climate change and pollution on environmental justice communities will continue. *Displacement*, on the other hand, involves the elimination of fossil fuels—a distinction that marks the divide between the unions supporting and those opposing new fossil fuel infrastructure. Displacement can happen in two primary ways: attrition and intentional change. Through attrition, old fossil infrastructure lives out its life span while only new green infrastructure is built, ultimately displacing all fossil fuels. Depending on the age of all existing infrastructure, this process may take too long to meet the scientifically recommended targets and do little to avoid possibly preventable climate injustices in the near term. Intentional change involves the planned phaseout of all fossils and replacement with renewables on a timeline informed by science. This sort of change can be pursued through regulations, market incentives, or direct government involvement in the energy sector.

Unfortunately for the climate, there has been little progress in reducing GHG emissions in the thirty years since James Hansen's touchstone presentation on global warming. Much to his chagrin, the global levels of annual GHG emissions have increased by 30 percent in the intervening years, as have the corporate profits of the major oil companies. "He's a tragic hero," said Naomi Oreskes of Hansen in an interview with *The Guardian* newspaper in 2018: "He's cursed to understand and diagnose what's going on, but unable to persuade people to do something about it. We are all raised to believe knowledge is power, but Hansen proves the untruth of that slogan. Power is power" (Milman 2018).

Fossil fuels remain the primary source of electricity, heat, and transportation for most of the world's population, constituting 95 percent of transportation and 67 percent of electricity generation in the United States (Institute for Energy Research 2012; U.S. DOE 2017b). Their extraction, transportation, and sale on the market are also a source of tremendous profit for corporations, power for wealthy elites, and gainful employment for workers. Total profits for oil, gas, and coal companies operating in the United States and Canada were $257 billion in 2014 (Oil Change International 2015). At the start of 2017, over one million workers were employed in coal, oil, and natural gas extraction, transportation, and electricity generation in the United States (U.S. DOE 2017a). These levels of revenue generation and job creation in a capitalist economy—especially one governed by the logic of free market fundamentalism—translate into a tremendous base of support for fossil fuels continuing to be the primary source of energy. A radical reduction of fossil fuel use would equate to nothing less than, to borrow Polanyi's phrase, a "great transformation" of the economy, the likes of which has not been seen since the Industrial Revolution, which ushered in the current era of wide-scale fossil fuel use (Polanyi 1944). Some argue that any attempt to drastically curb fossil fuel use will undermine the economy and leave us cold and in the dark. Others remind us of the perils of not rapidly and significantly reducing fossil fuel use—melting Arctic ice; rising sea levels; increased incidents of extreme weather such as droughts, flooding, wildfires, blizzards, hurricanes, and superstorms like Sandy; and the mass extinction of countless species, possibly including humans (Klein 2014; Kolbert 2014; McKibben 1989).

Many pose these two outcomes as an either-or situation in which people must choose between a thriving economy and a healthy planet but cannot have both. This line of reasoning is rooted in the dominant free market ideology of contemporary American capitalism, which largely eschews any government intervention in markets, and which explains the over-reliance on tax incentives as the primary vehicle for addressing climate change in the IRA. Fortunately, these two extreme situations need not be the only possible outcomes. The physical world is a complicated system—and the social world is no simpler—but scientific research, both physical and social, can inform our individual and collective decisions about how to confront the tremendous challenge we now face. The key tasks for physical scientists are to measure GHG emissions and global temperatures, determine the relationships between these variables, evaluate the atmospheric and climatic limits, and devise technologies to reduce or replace fossil fuel consumption. The task reserved for social science is to understand the ways in which people and societies form an integral and differentiated part of the Earth's delicate ecosystem, both creating the problem of climate change and simultaneously holding the key to its solution (Hackmann, Moser, and St. Clair 2014). Social scientists must dissect the societal, economic, political, and cultural dimensions of climate change and climate change mitigation, a process that will include identifying and understanding the sources of resistance to the changes necessary for society to avoid the most devastating effects of runaway climate change and the steps that can be taken to counteract this resistance. These "pillars of support" for business as usual include the workers and unions in the fossil fuel industry; however, they stand in contrast to the ongoing struggle by progressive union and climate justice activists to build broad support for a transition to renewable energy that confronts the climate crisis and addresses historical environmental injustices. It is this movement, which I refer to as the labor–climate movement (LCM) and which was born of the experiences by workers such as those in New York City after Sandy, that animates the pages and chapters that follow.

Confronting the Major Pillars of Support for the Fossil Fuel Regime

Social movements scholar Gene Sharp uses the term "pillars of support" to describe "institutions and sections of the society that supply the existing regime with sources of power required for maintenance and expansion of its power capacity" (2005, 12). According to Sharp, all nonviolent action is rooted in an understanding that power ultimately depends on the cooperation and obedience of large numbers of people acting through the institutions that constitute the power structure within a given field; these institutions are the pillars of support. Some of these pillars, such as the military, the police, and the courts, are coercive, compelling obedience through force or the threat thereof, while other pillars, like the media, education system, and religious institutions, support the system through their influence over culture and popular opinion. Others still, such as corporate profits and employment opportunities, support the system through their built-in economic incentives for shareholders, managers, and workers within the capitalist system.

From this perspective, power is contingent on the support of key institutions, themselves vulnerable to popular action or withdrawal of consent from the general population. Once people decide they no longer accept the status quo, they engage in collective action framing to develop, propose, and seek to mobilize consensus around particular solutions (Benford and Snow 2000; Goffman 1974; Snow et al. 1986). Through the act of resistance, the balance of power shifts. Even the powerless can overcome great obstacles and achieve social change if members of the broader polity contribute resources—both material and cultural—to social movement attacks on powerful targets (Jenkins and Perrow 1977).[1]

When considering the problem of climate change and the elimination of the entrenched fossil fuel regime, we can identify five major pillars of support: the fossil fuel industry, fossil-using industries, individual consumers, politicians, and fossil fuel workers and their unions. All of these pillars are underpinned by a powerful free market ideology that dictates what can and cannot be on the table for political discussion (Wright and Rogers 2015). In particular, government intervention in the market in order to solve collective problems—including climate change—is akin to heresy from this ideological perspective. As we shall see, undermining any one of these pillars of support requires climate protection advocates to pose some form of challenge to the underlying market ideology.

The first and most obvious pillar of support for continued fossil fuel use is the fossil fuel industry itself, whose primary product happens to be the cause of global climate change. Stated differently, true climate protection will require the abolition of fossil fuel use, essentially rendering the industry's primary product worthless.

The second pillar of support for continued fossil fuel use—industries that use fossil fuel—comprises the myriad of other industries that rely on a cheap and abundant supply of fossil fuels to manufacture their own products, either as an energy source to power factories or as a raw ingredient in the production process, such as in the manufacture of plastics. For many of these industries, gas and oil fuel their end products: cars, trucks, tractors, and recreational vehicles such as motorcycles, campers, all-terrain vehicles, and boats, as well as power tools such as chain saws, lawn mowers, leaf blowers, and wood chippers.

The third pillar of support is the individual fossil fuel consumer. Because 86 percent of Americans commute to work by car, there is a huge base of support for cheap and abundant gasoline (Florida 2011). Just think of the last time the governor in your state attempted to raise the gas tax to repair the potholed roads; it likely did not go over too well with voters.

The fourth pillar of support is politicians. Not all flavors of politician are supporters of the fossil fuel industry—some Democrats are even its presumptive enemies—but the elected officials who do support the industry are influential, and they receive tremendous economic support from fossil fuel companies. In fact, candidates who choose to run on a bold platform of GHG reductions are almost guaranteed to face a challenge from a competitor funded by the deep-pocketed fossil fuel industry, which is why so many elected leaders who purportedly support climate solutions by promoting green growth are not backing more proactive measures such as the Green New Deal.

The fifth and final pillar is workers and unions—the focus of this book. Workers in general occupy a historically unique position when it comes to the crisis of climate change because workers not only rely heavily on the use of fossil fuels to sustain their standard of living when away from work but also contribute to global warming when completing the daily tasks associated with their employment. Whether they drive trucks, manufacture petroleum-based products, operate power plants, operate a cash register in a retail store, or care for the elderly, workers to varying degrees are contributing to climate change by the very act of doing their jobs within our current political–economic structure.

Jeremy Brecher has referred to this conundrum as "climate alienation," an extension of the Marxian concept of the alienation of labor (Brecher 2017; Marx and Engels 2009). For Karl Marx, "alienation" refers to a condition in which workers labor not for their own individual and collective ends but rather for those who control their labor. Although workers are autonomous, self-realized human beings, as economic entities their goals and activities are dictated by the bourgeoisie—who own the means of production—in such a way as to extract from them the greatest amount of surplus value possible. In other words, the alienation of labor leads workers to willingly engage in their own exploitation. Climate alienation represents a particular form of the alienation of labor in the contemporary era: workers produce through their own labor the GHGs that are destroying the climate they depend on for life. In other words, they are using their human capacities for their own destruction. Climate alienation, argues Brecher, is a feature of the way we work, day by day.

Climate alienation is also a feature of the collective political action of working people, making them a key pillar of support for fossil fuels as they tolerate or even promote the use of their labor in ways that lead to climate destruction. Through their unions and the broader labor movement, many workers have served as the strongest cheerleaders for fossil fuel companies, often siding with employers they have previously struggled against for better wages and working conditions, by now joining them to oppose environmental regulations that would reduce air pollution and GHG emissions.

For example, the UMWA protested the Obama administration's Clean Power Plan, which set a goal of reducing GHG emissions to 68 percent of 2005 levels by the year 2030. This reduction would represent 870 million tons less carbon pollution in the atmosphere. Citing the attack on their jobs, seven thousand union mine workers rallied and marched through the streets of Pittsburgh to protest the new rules before bringing their message to the doorstep of the Environmental Protection Agency (EPA) in Washington, DC. Along with the International Brotherhood of Electrical Workers (IBEW), which represents coal power plant operators, the UMWA joined the coal industry and the attorneys general of several coal-producing states in a lawsuit against the EPA claiming that the Clean Power Plan represented an unlawful overreach of authority. The conservative majority of the Supreme Court, with two new Trump appointees, sided with the industry in its 2022 *West Virginia vs. EPA* decision, stating that the EPA cannot put state-level caps on carbon emissions under the 1970 Clean Air Act. Importantly, these unions and others on the powerful AFL-CIO Energy Committee wield disproportionate influence within the labor movement. As we discuss in Chapter 3, they represent the position of incumbents in the labor–climate field, which means their views tend to be heavily reflected in the dominant organization of the field.

Of the five pillars, this final one most clearly demonstrates the power of the hegemonic free market ideology that dominates modern political discourse in the United States; that is, workers in those industries generally see the false choice of deciding between having a healthy environment and having a good job as just another mundane feature of the natural order of the world. I refer to this as the "Jobs vs. the Environment" master frame, and it underpins the existing ensemble of discourses, identities, and practices that organize consent to the existing capitalist political arrangements in society (Gramsci 1971). However, dominant frames such as this are constantly being challenged, with greater or lesser degrees of success, because framing is ultimately a power struggle over who gets to define the situation—the use of collective agency to confront entrenched structural power. In the case of jobs and the environment, the emerging counterframe is "Clean Air and Good Jobs." This counterframe fundamentally challenges the dominant capitalist free market ideology by envisioning an expansion of democracy beyond the formal political realm and into matters of the economy to provide for a just and sustainable society for all. It is portrayed vividly in Naomi Klein's recent book and movie *This Changes Everything: Capitalism vs. The Climate* (Klein 2014; Lewis 2016), which states not only that capitalism will not save us from climate change but that it is in fact the cause of the problem and that the real solution will require breaking every rule in the free market playbook. The counterframe is also at the heart of the Green New Deal resolution introduced to the U.S. Congress by Representative Alexandria Ocasio-Cortez and Senator Ed Markey in 2019 (U.S. Congress 2019).

Successfully confronting the climate crisis will require challenging each of the five pillars of support as well as the dominant neoliberal ideology underpinning them. Massive investments in green infrastructure and green products will of course create tens of thousands of jobs—many of them unionized—but supporting green growth alone will not reduce GHG emissions or achieve climate justice. Fossil fuels must be phased out, which will require overcoming climate alienation and the debilitating Jobs vs. the Environment narrative that frames most contemporary discussions of work and climate change. The research conducted in this book focuses on the emerging LCM, a movement within U.S. labor to undermine the fifth column of support—workers and unions—in hopes of ultimately replacing the fossil fuel regime with a Green New Deal or equivalent large-scale plan to decarbonize the economy that will also protect workers and vulnerable communities. Their goal is to discredit the Jobs vs. the Environment master frame that elicits the complicity of workers with their own climate alienation and to supplant it with the more liberating Clean Air and Good Jobs counterframe to address "the biggest threat to our humanity."

The mainstream environmental movement has focused on nature conservation and pollution reduction since the 1960s and has increasingly become an advocate for reducing carbon emissions in the past two decades. The movement has faced serious and legitimate criticisms for often ignoring the real consequences their efforts would have on workers. Also, the lack of understanding, historically, by most mainstream environmental groups of the racialized experience of pollution led to the rise of the environmental justice movement in the 1970s and 1980s and more recently the climate justice movement to promote equity in climate solutions. Many in labor have come to support green growth in the form of infrastructure investment in renewable energy and energy efficiency, as was the case with the IRA of 2022, but most continue to avoid the issue of closing fossil fuel plants and addressing environmental justice concerns. The LCM seeks to build bridges between all of these movements by centering worker and community voices in shaping the transition away from fossil fuels, although the task will not be easy. For example, many in labor mistrust environmentalists on the basis of previous experiences of protesters demanding their workplaces be closed. Many in the climate justice movement remain skeptical of those in labor because of past experiences with building trades and fossil fuel unions supporting the construction and operation of polluting plants in predominantly minority neighborhoods.

Although weakened in recent decades, labor still represents the most influential, organized political voice of the working class in the country. And compared with many other movements, their ability to turn out voters in key elections is a real source of power and influence. Union workers, like everyone else, will be affected by climate change, especially those from historically marginalized communities. At the same time, their members' livelihoods may also be affected by measures taken to mitigate climate change. The extent to which they will act to protect the narrow job interests of some workers in the fossil fuel sector or the broader class interests of all workers, including those from disproportionately affected communities, is uncertain and depends largely on the actions taken by activists within the movement to change labor's narrative, and thus action, around climate change.

As we can see, the overlapping nature of the pillars of support has led some unions to adopt the Jobs vs. the Environment frame to defend jobs in the fossil fuel industry while simultaneously promoting a green growth agenda. Others who embrace the Clean Air and Good Jobs frame have divergent solutions for how best to achieve this goal and align more closely with the growing climate justice movement. The difference is due in part to the structural features of our economy, particularly the industries in which they work and their unique organizational forms—what I refer to in Chapter 3 as their position within the labor–climate spectrum. This ongoing struggle over collective action framing within labor will ultimately influence the types of climate legislation unions will support. Will it be a green growth approach of layering that does not directly confront the fossil fuel regime? Will it be a set of safety-net protections for workers in the event of job displacement? Or will it be a proactive Green New Deal that displaces fossil fuels, creates jobs, and promotes climate justice?

High-profile cases like the historic struggle between timber workers and defenders of the spotted owl in the Pacific Northwest have reinforced the Jobs vs. the Environment narrative, creating the misperception that unions are opposed to environmental protection measures (Brecher 2014; Foster 1993). However, there are countless instances of cooperation between labor and the environmental movement as well, including joint support for environmental legislation such as the Clean Air and Clean Water Acts that led to the formation of the EPA (Dewey 1998; Obach 2004). The part of the spotted owl saga that is not well-known publicly is that unions and environmentalists ultimately came together and cooperated to conserve areas of the old-growth forests designated for spotted owl protection while allowing responsible logging activities to continue in the region (Associated Press 1989).

Such historical examples offer great insight into the prospects for the emerging LCM to achieve its goal of building a working-class environmental movement within U.S. labor that is aligned more closely with the demands of the growing climate justice movement. The internal resistance represented by LCM activists engaged in collective action framing contests within unions currently suggests a fracture in the fifth pillar and a potential crumbling of labor support for the fossil fuel regime. But that future is neither imminent nor inevitable. As history has shown, the labor movement itself can serve as a battleground for some of the most pressing issues of a given era, and it is littered with failures along with its successes.

Motivation for This Research

Since its inception, the history of climate change research has been solidly rooted in the physical and natural sciences, with the social sciences largely ignored and absent from major national and international reports (Bjurström and Polk 2011). This is both perplexing and injurious, considering that human activity has been identified as the leading contributor to the GHG emissions that have contributed to the global warming process since the Industrial Revolution (IPCC 2014)—so much so that the current era has been termed the Anthropocene to acknowledge the extent to which human activity has become interconnected with natural forces such that the fate of one is interconnected with the fate of the other (Zalasiewicz et al. 2010).

Despite their early exclusion, the social science community has been increasingly contributing to the study of climate change. Because the key drivers of human-caused, or anthropogenic, climate change are rooted in the daily routines of social life and the social organization of modern societies, sociology uniquely offers important theoretical and methodological insights for assessing climate change, climate change mitigation, and climate adaptation. Acknowledging this fact, the major professional organization for sociologists, the American Sociological Association, formed the Task Force on Sociology and Global Climate Change in 2010. The task force then published an edited volume titled *Climate Change and Society: Sociological Perspectives*, which proposes a framework for the ways in which sociologists can help understand the societal origins of climate change as well as how various social, political, economic, and cultural factors are likely to affect efforts to address climate change (Dunlap and Brulle 2015).

In sum, Dunlap and Brulle contend that sociology brings two distinct and advantageous approaches to the study of climate change: it is well equipped to study the social structures, institutions, and cultural values that contribute to climate change and that can either help or hinder efforts to address it; and it is a critical discipline that is relatively untethered to contemporary hegemonic political–economic belief systems such as market fundamentalism or neoliberalism.[2] An additional and related consideration is the rise of "public sociology," or the increasingly deliberate effort by some sociologists in recent years to engage the public beyond the academy on sociological issues of public concern. As sociologist Michael Burawoy (2004) notes, sociology has a particular interest in the defense of civil society—including unions and voluntary associations—that is beleaguered by the encroachment of markets and states. In the case of labor and climate change, civil society is the best terrain for the defense of humanity—a defense that can be aided by a critical, public sociology.

In the chapters that follow, I examine the social dynamics and framing processes of the "movement within the movement" that began pushing American labor to take a strong stand on climate change in the years leading up to the introduction of the Green New Deal resolution in early 2019. The research is motivated by my experiences as a local union officer and as an active member of various unions throughout my life (including the American Federation of Teachers [AFT], LIUNA, UAW, and United Brotherhood of Carpenters [UBC]). In addition, as the founding president of the Graduate Employee Union, UAW Local 6950 at the University of Connecticut, I knew that climate change, among many other issues, was something our members cared about. After reaching out to members through one-on-one organizing, we formed a Social, Environmental, and Economic Justice Committee. From there we began our work on climate justice issues at the university level, then the state level, and ultimately the national level, which brought me into contact with other union leaders and activists from around the United States who were pursuing similar goals. In sum, these activists were trying to get their unions, state labor confederations, and the national union confederation (the AFL-CIO) to recognize climate justice as a core labor issue that the movement would throw its organizing and advocacy strength behind.

To be sure, the labor movement has a long history of supporting working-class interests that go beyond the often narrow and immediate interests of just their members, from promoting minimum wage laws and other social safety-net measures to pushing for health and safety standards for all workers. LCM activists contend that climate change poses a real threat to workers' livelihoods, health, and safety—in particular for the least well-off—and thus is a working-class issue. Further, they acknowledge that the changes necessary to address climate change go beyond just supporting green growth and will certainly cost some people their jobs in the fossil fuel industry and energy sector as we reduce GHG emissions and pursue climate justice. Rather than expending tremendous resources and effort to save jobs that are doomed to expire eventually, these activists are urging labor to be proactive by advocating for strong measures such as those included in the Green New Deal to assist workers through a planned period of transition before their jobs are eliminated. They also understand that a transition away from fossil fuels means a transition into some other renewable fuel sources, which would be a source of new jobs that could be organized and could possibly provide an opportunity to undo past injustices along the lines of race and gender.

On a more personal level, this research is also motivated by my sincere desire to help inform ongoing efforts to save the planet from climate catastrophe. As an avalanche of scientific evidence attests, climate change is real, it is caused by human activity, we are already experiencing its effects, and it is the greatest threat and challenge humankind has ever faced. As a father of three children, I am deeply concerned about the habitability of the world we will leave for them and their children as they grow up. In his second inaugural address, just before the end of the Civil War, Abraham Lincoln said, "There is no greater injustice than to wring your profits from the sweat of another man's brow." If he were alive today, Lincoln's words might be repurposed to fit the contemporary era: "There is no greater injustice than to wring your profits from the habitability of the Earth your children and grandchildren will inherit." The scale of intergenerational injustice that we are all witnessing is almost incomprehensible until you consider that counteracting such temporal wrongs requires sacrifice in the present. And given the dominant free market ideology governing much of the world today and the corresponding individualistic culture of material consumption, the profit interests of capitalist corporations selling those consumer goods outweigh the promise of life, liberty, and a livable planet for future generations. Unless we can find a means of successfully challenging this ideology, a way of "changing everything," to paraphrase Naomi Klein (2014), future generations face certain environmental catastrophe, or at the least, a considerably less desirable planet on which to toil and live.

Primary Research Questions and Methods

The primary question guiding this study of the nascent LCM is this: How, in the face of great structural obstacles, can social actors, through collective action framing processes, move the position and ultimately the actions of an entire movement? The accompanying narrative is that (1) there is a political–economic structure underpinning the positions of many unions; but (2) through the act of framing, social actors are using their agency to attempt to redefine the situation and shift the ideological perspective of workers and unions to see alternative paths forward; (3) it is in the contestation over the definition of just transition that the nature of the alternative path is being shaped; and (4) the results of such contests ultimately influence the ability of LCM activists to shift labor away from the Jobs vs. the Environment frame and toward support for sustainability, jobs, and climate justice.

To interrogate this narrative, I formulate specific questions in three key areas: questions regarding political–economic structure, questions regarding social agency, and questions that examine the interplay of structure and agency. For the sake of this book, "structure" is defined simply as the stable patterns of interaction among the members of a society, institution, or organization. "Agency" refers to the capacity of individuals to act independently and make their own free choices. Structure and agency are often codetermined; that is, structural factors can influence and limit the decisions of agents, while at the same time, the actions of agents can sometimes reshape social structures. The particular questions raised in the remaining chapters are the following:

- What key structural features of the capitalist political economy and the U.S. labor movement lead some unions to adopt the Jobs vs. the Environment master frame, alienating themselves from the climate and serving as a key pillar of support for the fossil fuel industry?
- How do the activists who have formed an LCM within the labor movement come to understand climate as a labor issue, rejecting the Jobs vs. the Environment frame and instead promoting the counterframe of Clean Air and Good Jobs?
- What solutions to the dual crises of climate and inequality do LCM activists offer? Whom do they target? And what tactics do they deploy to achieve the goal of Clean Air and Good Jobs?
- How does their collective understanding of the problem and possible solutions interact with the existing political landscape to either help or hinder their efforts to achieve the goal of Clean Air and Good Jobs?

To answer these questions, I engage in a three-pronged qualitative analysis consisting of participant observation; semi-structured, in-depth interviews; and content analysis of original source documents.

For the participant observation component of data collection, I was actively and openly involved with three labor–climate social movement organizations (SMOs) from October 2014 through August 2018: one at the state level, one at the national level, and one international organization.[3] I gained access to each organization through my role as president of my local union. I also conducted fifty semi-structured interviews (thirty-four between 2014 and 2018, during my participant observation period, and sixteen between 2019 and 2022) with key participants from the three labor–climate SMOs examined in this study.[4] Interviews ranged from sixty to ninety minutes with several targeted follow-up interviews lasting up to four hours. All interview participants were recruited from the three SMO sites of my participant observation, and they included a combination of top leaders as well as rank-and-file participants of the organizations. The one restricting criterion for inclusion in this study was past or present regular participation in one of the three labor–climate SMOs—single-time or first-time activists were excluded from participation. Apart from public comments made by organizational leaders, the names of all participants were replaced with pseudonyms, with the ultimate goal of confidentiality for every research participant.[5] The content analysis involved a close reading of all SMO publications, including policy papers, newsletters, and official statements by the three organizations.[6]

The timing of the participant observation proved to be fortuitous because it encapsulated the years leading up to the introduction of the Green New Deal resolution in Congress. Interviews and content analyses in the following years captured the ways in which movement participants adapted to the changing political opportunity structure brought on not only by the introduction of the Green New Deal vision but also by the onset of the COVID-19 pandemic and the transition from the Trump to the Biden administration, marking perhaps the greatest opportunity yet to address climate change. In sum, the book marshals two forms of data to carry the narrative forward: anonymized case observations in the middle chapters and tangible examples in the later chapters. The first form of data is needed to protect confidentiality while offering qualitatively rich insights into labor–climate activism, and the second form of data is used to situate the efforts of the anonymized cases within familiar political terrain.

Studying the Labor-Climate Movement: Three Case Sites

Three organizations were selected for this study, each representing a different geographic level of operation. The actual names of the three SMOs have been replaced with pseudonyms to help protect the privacy of participants. The first is a state-level organization, which I call the State Partnership for Employment and Climate (SPEC). The second is a national-level organization, which I call Unions for a Sustainable Economy (USE). The third is an international organization, which I call Labor Unions for Public Energy (LUPE).

These three SMOs were selected on the basis of a variety of criteria, including their relationship to one another (i.e., some cooperation and overlap of participants), their geographic diversity (state/local, national, international), and my ability to participate in all three organizations contemporaneously. Most important, they are prototypical labor–climate organizations, as judged by two defining criteria: independence from established labor leadership and a focus on decarbonization. First, these three organizations are not controlled by established leaders of the labor movement or any particular union, but rather they represent grassroots, cross-union initiatives with a focus on influencing the direction of labor as a whole from within.

Second, the three organizations selected for this study have taken a strong stance on climate change, demanding meaningful reductions in carbon emissions—not just supporting green jobs or carbon capture technologies, as other groups, such as the Apollo Alliance and the BlueGreen Alliance, have done historically. In fact, the LCM arose as a response to the inadequacy of merely supporting green investments, infrastructure, and manufacturing to create jobs without also taking on the more difficult task of eliminating fossil fuels, which has real job-loss implications. As illustrated in Figure 1.1, the LCM is situated within the sphere of the "blue–greens," a broader group within labor that supports green growth but does not push for emission-reduction targets. Together with the blue–greens, they are situated within the labor movement

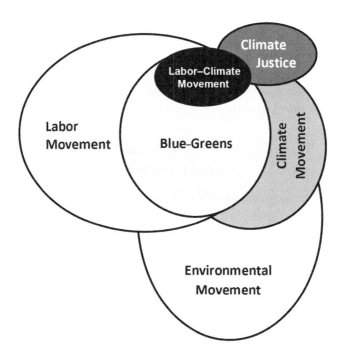

Figure 1.1 The Labor-Climate Movement in Relation
to Associated Movements

as a whole, which has some overlap with the environmental movement and the climate movement.[7]

Importantly, the LCM also overlaps partially with the growing climate justice movement, positioning it in a central and potentially strategic location for helping to build a broad-based coalition of labor, environmental, and climate activists fighting for climate solutions that center the needs of both workers and vulnerable communities. The concept of climate justice acknowledges that climate change has differing social, economic, and health impacts on under-privileged populations. Climate justice activists, rooted in Indigenous, African American, Latinx, Asian Pacific Islander, and poor white communities on the front lines of the climate crisis, share legacies of colonialism along with racial and economic oppression and strive to have these inequities addressed head-on in all climate change mitigation and adaptation strategies. Like the environmental justice movement that arose in response to the mainstream environmental movement's lack of focus on issues of justice, or its occasional active promotion of injustice through "not in my backyard" (NIMBY) campaigns, climate justice movement organizations such as the Climate Justice Alliance (CJA) arose in response to the broader climate movement's lack of attention to racial and gender inequities embedded in climate change and its potential solutions.

While not the focus of the current study, the climate justice movement does interact frequently with the LCM and is touched on sporadically throughout this book. The key point at which the two movements either align or diverge is in the demands that are made around transitioning the economy away from fossil fuels. In particular, the question is whether labor's plan will center equity, addressing past social, economic, and environmental injustices along the lines of race, class, and gender, or focus exclusively on protections for fossil fuel union members, often at the expense of underprivileged communities. As we indicate in later chapters, many in the LCM share the goals of the climate justice movement and even participate in both movements, while others remain focused largely on protecting unionized workers only.

Each of the three labor–climate SMOs examined in this research is made up of participants from the labor movement, including leaders of local, state, and regional unions acting in official and unofficial capacities and rank-and-file union members concerned with climate change as a labor issue. Many individuals are also involved in local environmental, climate, or climate justice organizations in addition to their unions. In some instances, unions participated in the SMOs as organizational affiliates or partners on particular campaigns. The history, mission, and organizational structure of each SMO, as well as the nature of my involvement with each organization, is sketched out below.

State Partnership for Employment and Climate

SPEC, the state-level organization, was formed in 2012 as a partnership between a faith-based environmental justice organization and representatives from several labor unions in a northern state. The foundational meeting occurred after the close of the state's AFL-CIO convention in 2012, when several labor, environmental, climate, and faith leaders agreed to continue a discussion about labor and climate that had begun earlier. In its mission statement, SPEC states that it "seeks to strengthen collaboration among [the state's] labor, environmental, and religious groups in advocating for public policies that address urgent concerns about climate change while creating good-paying jobs right here in our state." It goes on to say its goal is "to build a worker-oriented environmental movement organizing to secure a fair and just transition that protects not only the environment but also the livelihoods threatened by both climate change and the steps taken toward mitigation and adaptation."

At the time I left the field, SPEC comprised fourteen affiliated organizations, including six labor organizations, four environmental organizations, three faith-based organizations, and one community group. Beyond the official affiliates, many other organizations and individuals—including other labor organizations—participated loosely in SPEC over the period I was in the field. The affiliated organizations paid dues to support the work of the organization and selected one liaison to serve as the intermediary between their organization and SPEC. During my time of participation, I served as the liaison for my union and attended various SPEC meetings and events, including press conferences, public engagement events, and lobby days. As mentioned earlier, my participation in SPEC predates the initiation of this research, and my interaction with the organization inspired this project.

SPEC is governed by a Steering Committee consisting mostly of participants who attended the group's foundational meeting. The organizational liaisons, such as I, served as a second tier of governance. In union terms, the Steering Committee is analogous to the executive board of a union, and the liaisons are the shop stewards who handle much of the on-the-ground organizing, attend all meetings or events, and provide valuable input in decision-making. SPEC has just one part-time, paid staff organizer, and most of the management of the organization typically takes place by biweekly conference calls by members of SPEC's Steering Committee.

SPEC also holds regular meetings at least twice each year to bring together the Steering Committee, liaisons, and other supporters to discuss specific events or campaigns the various constituencies agree to work on together. The Steering Committee then takes these ideas to its semiannual strategic planning sessions to set priorities for the next six months. The activist agenda that is adopted at these meetings is determined by the interests of participating organizations and the ability of the different constituencies to find common-ground issues in pursuit of the organizational mission of addressing climate change and creating jobs. Two examples of campaigns include one supporting a state program to make public buildings more energy efficient using in-state, unionized labor to do the construction work and another promoting legislation to reduce and cap the fixed electricity rates charged by the two monopoly electric companies in the state. These and other examples are discussed in further detail in Chapter 6.

Unions for a Sustainable Economy

The national-level organization, USE, did not have a formal affiliation process for unions to join and pay dues as SPEC did during my time in the field. Rather, supportive unions were encouraged to vote or pass resolutions stating that they agreed with the set of guiding principles laid out by USE on its website. Lacking membership dues, USE secures most of its funding through competitive grants. However, near the end of my observation period, the organization rolled out an individual and organizational member drive to gain financial commitments from individual participants and make membership more formal, but no such affiliation structure was established for unions or other organizations during the years of my participant observation. Unlike SPEC, USE had three or four part-time staff members who handled everything from administration and organizing to graphic design, website management, research, and writing.

USE was founded in 2009 by a group of labor activists, spearheaded by a former leader in the top rung at the AFL-CIO, to confront labor's negligence on the issue of climate change as well as the apparent inattention by environmentalists to the economic issues of jobs and income inequality. The following excerpt from the organization's mission statement provides further detail:

> We believe that workers and environmentalists must be engaged together in order for our society to address the dual deepening crises of both climate and income inequality. We further believe that the environmental movement should have a jobs program of its own and should not leave the jobs piece up to labor. We believe that the labor movement should become a part of the solution to the climate crisis and have a climate program of its own because it is in their core self-interest, rather than leaving climate protection up to the environmental movement. In other words, we believe both movements need to move beyond

simply trying to understand and even honor each other's core missions and begin to internalize how their missions are truly intertwined.

One of the cofounders explained to me in an interview that the organization was based on an understanding that long-term sustainability cannot be achieved without combining three elements:

- Environmental protection, in particular addressing climate change by cutting carbon emissions dramatically
- Economic fairness, in particular addressing income inequality and the lack of good jobs
- Social justice, in particular eliminating prejudice and structural racism and defending human rights, civil rights, and democracy

USE is governed by a ten-person board that meets regularly by phone or videoconference. The group typically organizes semiannual or annual in-person meetings with participants. These meetings are organized by steering committees of participants who meet monthly or biweekly via conference calls to plan gatherings that typically focus on the labor–climate connection. Finally, USE hosts regular teleconference meetings as well as frequent webinars with dozens of individual activists from various participating unions across the United States. Participants in calls engage in dialogue and develop strategies to promote the mission of the organization. As with so many SMOs, the nature of particular campaigns, including the messaging, strategies, and tactics deployed by USE, depend in large part on who shows up, but the vision of the founders always serves as the guiding light for all actions. The principal founder and current president, who has a strong background in the labor movement, is highly respected and viewed by participants as a strong role model for other national-level leaders who must gather the courage to take a stand on climate change.

Being a national organization, USE drew a pool of labor leaders and activists from a diverse set of unions and geographic regions in the country. That being said, there often was more participation by leaders and members of unions from the states of the East and West Coasts than states in either the Midwest or the South. At the first national in-person meeting, there were about 65 participants from unions on the East and West Coasts. The second meeting was attended by over 130 participants, with a few more attendees from the South and Midwest, but participants were still predominantly from the Northeast and the West Coast. Both of these meetings were held on the East Coast, near

Washington, DC. The third and last major meeting I attended was held in a midwestern state and brought greater involvement from that region, attracting more than 300 participants, including a contingent of leaders and activists from the climate justice movement.

As with SPEC, I participated in USE on behalf of my local union, but in this case, there was no official title such as "liaison." During my time in the field, I helped build support for national campaigns at the local level in my state and within my union. I also served on the planning committees that worked to design and organize participation for the two national in-person meetings mentioned above. I also coauthored a newspaper editorial highlighting the findings of some research commissioned by the organization, which found that investments in renewables in a particular state would create more jobs than further investments in fossil fuels.

Labor Unions for Public Energy

The third organization, LUPE, describes itself as an international initiative "to advance democratic direction and control of energy in a way that promotes solutions to the climate crisis, energy poverty, the degradation of both land and people, and responds to the attacks on workers' rights and protections." The organization formed in 2012 as a result of a three-day global trade union roundtable about energy transition organized by a labor scholar at an American university. Seventy trade unionists and policy experts from nineteen countries, including several preeminent U.S. climate scientists, participated in the roundtable. The attendees responded to a call decrying "the existence of a global climate emergency, marked by the unimpeded use of fossil fuels, the growing power and political influence of oil, coal and gas companies, and the inadequacy of present market-based approaches to energy transition." At the time, the governments of the world had failed to negotiate a global climate agreement under the United Nations Framework Convention on Climate Change (the Paris Climate Accord would come three years later, in 2015). At the end of the three-day meeting, the group articulated the need for democratic direction and control of energy.

Following the roundtable, unions from around the world were invited to join LUPE and designate a representative to serve on its advisory group. Although I did not attend the foundational meeting, I did become the representative for my union on the advisory group once I became involved in 2014. At the time I exited the field, there were forty-seven participating unions or union confederations from eighteen different countries. Although LUPE is international, I focus primarily on U.S. labor participation in the organization, which consisted of twelve unions. LUPE is led in large part by an executive director and three staff members, who coordinate quarterly videoconference meetings as well as various in-person meetings around the world—usually two or three per year in the United States—to help participating unions and activists advance the mission of the organization. The direction of LUPE is largely guided by the core staff members but is informed by input from representatives on the advisory group, with one caveat: the participants have acknowledged that they believe democratic control of the energy sector is key to addressing the problems of climate change and jobs. It is important to note that previous research has found that unions around the world have generally engaged earlier and more deeply with the issue of climate change than their counterparts in the United States; thus, it should not be a surprise that participants in this SMO espouse the most radical solutions to the climate crisis of the three organizations examined in this study (Farnhill 2014, 2016; Hampton 2015; Hyde and Vachon 2019; Räthzel and Uzzell 2013; Snell and Fairbrother 2010).

Outline of the Chapters

Following this introduction, Chapter 2 provides key historical insights into labor's relationship to environmental issues in the United States—offering a macrostructural understanding of the fundamental relationship between capitalist political economy and the environment. Key to this issue are the ideas of job consciousness and class consciousness, which animate competing perspectives on the purpose and goals of the labor movement. These perspectives manifest themselves in the two opposing ideal typical categories of U.S. unions: "pure and simple" business unions and social movement unions.

Chapter 3 builds from the discussion of the historical structural features of labor–environmental relations that was started in Chapter 2 by offering a snapshot of the present in what I call the labor–climate spectrum. The labor–climate spectrum is an illustration that situates unions, classified by their industry, along a spectrum based on their stance on the issues of climate change and justice. This heuristic device offers insight into the relative positions of unions on the issue of climate change, which will be useful for understanding the formation, goals, and tactics of the LCM as well as the tensions that embolden this movement within a movement. The spectrum builds a bridge between the structural factors of labor–climate relations described in Chapter 2 and the social actions of movement participants seeking to effect change by altering the narrative around labor and climate justice. The spectrum also allows for a rudimentary assessment of the effectiveness of LCM activists in their efforts to move labor as a whole toward supporting climate justice. Chapters 2 and 3 will be especially informative for readers that may be less familiar with U.S. labor and environmentalism.

Chapters 4, 5, and 6 move the discussion away from the structural factors that shape labor–climate relations and shift the focus to the collective action framing processes and tactics engaged in by movement actors during my years in the field, 2014–2018. If we think of Chapters 2 and 3 as describing a game board and establishing the positions of various pieces on that board, then Chapters 4 through 6 can be seen as describing players' actions that move the pieces, both on the existing board and in efforts to change the board altogether. In particular, those chapters will explore the negotiation of meanings by movement activists as they define the social problem they are confronting, identify the key targets of the movement, and construct possible solutions.

In sum, LCM participants define the problem in the following ways:

- Unmitigated climate change poses a serious threat to all people, but particularly workers and people from vulnerable "frontline communities," including communities of color, Tribal communities, poor and working-class communities, deindustrialized communities, and depopulated rural communities.
- Most mitigation strategies currently under consideration pose a threat to the livelihoods and well-being of workers and their communities.
- The culture of the mainstream environmental movement is not considering working-class interests in their efforts to address climate change and is often pushing for mitigation strategies that would hurt workers, reinforce existing environmental injustices, and invigorate the Jobs vs. the Environment master frame.
- To its own peril, the culture of the labor movement as a whole has prevented it from actively fighting for real solutions to climate change that incorporate working-class interests, and in many cases unions continue to serve as a major pillar of support for fossil fuels.

From this diagnosis, LCM activists identify three direct targets to which they attribute blame—the state, the culture of the mainstream environmental movement, and the culture of the labor movement itself—and a number of indirect targets, including capital.[8]

The common solution offered by LCM activists is a "just transition" to a more sustainable economy. However, while the solution was regularly conveyed by participants from all three of the organizations studied, the exact meaning of "just transition" was contested because multiple distinct frames could be identified, ranging from relatively moderate to transformatively radical in their prognosis. I name the three frames protective just transition, proactive just transition, and transformative just transition.[9]

The first frame, protective just transition, most closely mirrors the original concept of just transition put forth by the labor–environmental activists who coined the term in the 1990s when considering how best to build worker support for the closing of plants that were causing harm to worker and community health and safety. The protective frame focuses on providing a safety net for fossil fuel workers and their local communities when they lose their jobs as a result of the shift away from coal and oil to renewable energy sources. The second, proactive just transition, provides similar protections for workers and communities but also envisions a large-scale World War II–style mobilization to decarbonize the whole economy, with unions being part of a "social partnership" to draft a Green New Deal that would create millions of good, green jobs while phasing out fossil fuel use in an orderly manner. An open question within this frame is the extent to which the demands will overlap with those of the climate justice movement in seeking to remedy past harms and injustices along the lines of race and gender or whether it will be focused solely on helping displaced workers and creating new jobs as part of the decarbonization process.

The third, transformative just transition, incorporates the elements of the first two frames and also challenges the fundamental and intertwined logics of capitalism, racism, and patriarchy by insisting that to be successful, the transition to sustainable energy requires public ownership and control of the energy sector. It further demands that the transition must incorporate remedies to the previous inequalities, such as environmental and racial injustices, that have been embedded in the for-profit energy system (Sweeney and Treat 2018). This transformative vision of just transition mirrors Naomi Klein's central thesis in *This Changes Everything* (2014). As noted earlier, the point at which the LCM and the climate justice movement intersect is within the contested definition of a just transition. There is room within both the proactive and the transformative frames for addressing historical social injustices, but the transformative frame aligns most closely with the definition of "just transition" put forth by most climate justice activists. In addition to these three frames, I also identify one counterframe I call oppositional, which captures the resistance to just transition by some unions and workers who see it as merely shorthand for job loss.

Chapter 6 explores the tactical repertoires of the three LCM organizations in this study as they pursued collective action against the state, mainstream environmentalists, and the labor movement. In that chapter, I describe all of the actions undertaken by each SMO during my time in the field to give the reader a sense of the tactical repertoire of each and then examine one signature campaign for each group. Finally, I explore how the selection of targets, vulnerabilities of these targets, political opportunity structures for the targets, choice of collective action frames, and choice of tactics are interrelated. In sum, I find that the selection of targets and in particular the vulnerabilities of the targets and the existing political opportunity structure can shape the tactics used by movements (McAdam 1982; Tarrow 1983; Walker, Martin, and McCarthy 2008). However, I also find an interesting interplay between collective action frames, political opportunities, and tactics. In particular, I identify the possibility of a frame-shifting process in which SMOs not only modify their tactical repertoires in response to changing opportunity structures but also shift their framing to find the optimal alignment of framing, opportunity, and tactics for particular campaigns.

Chapter 7 looks closely at the shifts in the political opportunity structure for the LCM that occurred between 2018 and 2022. My fieldwork, which I elaborate on in Chapters 4–6, was very well timed as it led up to the introduction of the Green New Deal resolution in Congress, the onset of the COVID-19 pandemic, the unprecedented protests for Black lives, and the defeat of Donald Trump in the 2020 presidential election, all of which radically reshaped the political terrain on which the LCM operates and helped to facilitate the passage of the insufficient, but important IRA of 2022. Building from the analyses of participant observation data in previous chapters, in Chapter 7 I examine how LCM activists responded to these changes in the opportunity structure and explore the question of whether the movement has had any success in pursuing its goals of moving labor to a more pro-climate position and forging support for a just transition within the labor and environmental movements as well as in public policy formation.

The conclusion, Chapter 8, summarizes and synthesizes the key findings of this study by characterizing the modes of change pursued by LCM activists and envisioning three possible futures facing the LCM that correspond with the just transition frames presented in the book. The main findings of the book are related back to the story in the preface to consider the rationale for the inclusion of economic and social protections, including a jobs guarantee, unionization rights, and universal healthcare, into the Green New Deal resolution as sponsored by Representative Ocasio-Cortez and Senator Markey (U.S. Congress 2019). The Green New Deal and other similar plans are imagined as a space of contention—between opposition, limited support in the form of green growth, and full-throated support for a just transition to a regenerative economy—but also as a powerful vehicle with the potential for moving labor as a whole from the protective to the proactive and perhaps ultimately to the transformative frame for just transition.

The Journey Begins

The experiences of workers in the aftermath of Superstorm Sandy in 2012 and so many other extreme weather events, such as Hurricanes Harvey, Irma, and Maria in 2017—which ravaged parts of Florida and Texas and caused catastrophic damage to the island of Puerto Rico—are leading many to see the real effects of climate change on their livelihoods and well-being. Heat waves, rising sea levels, droughts, loss of biodiversity, and wildfires all affect the lives of working people. This book explores the efforts of LCM activists, within their unions, communities, and society, to reframe the problem and take action to promote a Green New Deal or something similar that will produce a climate-safe future for all working people by both creating good jobs *and* reducing GHG emissions. This effort will require educating and organizing not only fellow union members and leaders but also a critical mass of all working people and building solidarity with activists from the environmental and climate justice movements. Given the tremendous power of the fossil fuel industry, with several pillars of support—including politicians and parts of the labor movement itself—and the underlying dominant neoliberal ideology in American society, this is no small task. Labor's checkered history pertaining to environmental issues, driven largely by a structural tension between the need to protect jobs and the need to protect workers, between job consciousness and class consciousness, provides both challenges and opportunities for LCM activists using their agency to win over the hearts and minds of fellow union members and leaders to turn a key pillar of support for fossil fuels into a powerful advocate for Clean Air and Good Jobs.

In what follows, I take the reader on a journey that explores the structural challenges faced by this movement as well as the social processes within the movement to increase our understanding of how various political actors can best construct linkages among economic, social, and environmental reform agendas; which strategies are most successful for building broad support; and which forms of alliances are most conducive to supporting a rapid transition to a sustainable economy before the world passes a climate tipping point. Where will this journey take us? Toward a broad transformation of our economy and society that addresses the immediate concerns of workers and frontline communities while making the climate safe and habitable for future generations? Such a transition will not come easily: it requires both the moral and political will to build coalitions, create new centers of power, generate broad public support, and, when necessary, compensate victims of economic shifts. It is my hope that the knowledge this research offers can help build the broad-based, durable political consensus necessary to win a comprehensive climate protection policy that prioritizes providing a habitable Earth with an equitable economy for current and future generations first.

2

From Donora to Dakota

A Mixed History of Labor–Environmental
Relations in the United States

When antinuclear activists opposed the building of the Three Mile Island nuclear plant (later the scene of a serious nuclear accident), a local union distributed a bumper sticker reading "Hungry and Out of Work? Eat an Environmentalist!" In the late 1970s and early 1980s, nuclear power plant construction sites from Seabrook Station in New Hampshire to Diablo Canyon in California were ground zero for labor–environmental struggles. Labor–environmental conflict has arisen around not only nuclear energy but also coal mining, "smart growth" restrictions on development, and many other issues locally, regionally, and nationally.

The oversimplified Jobs vs. the Environment narrative has been the mantra of the mainstream media when it comes to unionized workers and environmental issues (Kojola 2015; Vachon and Brecher 2016). However, environmental and labor groups are often divided internally on such issues. For example, many environmental groups joined with labor in opposing the North American Free Trade Agreement (NAFTA) in 1993–1994, but others supported it. United Steelworkers (USW) supported the Kyoto Protocol on global warming in 1997, while UMWA and others opposed it and eventually persuaded the AFL-CIO to do so as well (Brecher 2008). While the AFL-CIO has come to recognize the reality of climate change and generally supports green growth policies, or so-called green capitalism, it has also lobbied against incorporating the targets and timelines recommended by climate scientists in international agreements (Brecher 2013; Sweeney 2017). For example, during the negotiations that led to the historic United Nations Paris Climate Accord in 2015, the AFL-CIO opposed the inclusion of legally binding emission-reduction targets and instead supported the nationally determined, voluntary commitments that the Obama administration signed on to (and the Trump administration stepped away from and the Biden administration reentered).

In other words, labor–environmental relations in the United States are a complicated matter. As these anecdotes reveal, unions have at various times supported and at other times opposed environmental measures throughout U.S. history. But what are some of the major structural factors shaping their decision to go in one direction or the other? That is the question we begin to answer in this chapter. Just as there is not one singularly defined relationship between unions and the environment, there is also not one singular explanation; however, there have been more than enough episodes of conflict and cooperation to help identify some trends and underlying structural factors that can influence the position of labor in relation to environmental measures.

In sum, the fear of job loss by workers and the pursuit of economic growth by capital and labor alike often fuel Jobs vs. the Environment conflicts (Kazis and Grossman 1982; Schnaiberg 1980). Macrosociological theories of the environment underscore the important role that the inequality in power relations between elites and non-elites plays in shaping human–nature relations (Downey 2015). Meso-level research on labor–environmental coalition building (i.e., blue–green coalitions) finds that having overlapping interests, particularly about health and safety concerns, is often a precondition for labor–environmental cooperation (Mayer 2009; Obach 2004). Theories of the labor movement suggest that labor–environmental relations are often shaped by the microlevel culture of particular unions, with those espousing "social movement" characteristics and engaging in "whole worker organizing" being more likely to make "common good" demands that go beyond just wages and other material benefits for members (McAlevey 2018a; McCartin 2016; Waterman 1991). Using historical examples to illustrate, we can look at each of these explanations more closely to gain a better understanding of how and why labor–environmental relations, and now labor–climate relations, have had such a mixed history in the United States.

Understanding Labor Opposition to Environmental Protection

A brief review of recent history reveals four broad structural explanations for labor–environmental conflict: job protection, the lack of an adequate social safety net, the pursuit of economic growth, and constraints on democracy.

While distinct, these explanations are deeply intertwined, overlapping, and reinforcing. All are underpinned by neoliberalism—the powerful free market ideology that dominates American political–economic discourse—and reinforced by the unequal distribution of power in society that this ideology has created and continually reproduces. Neoliberalism is rooted in what Adam Smith refers to as "the hidden hand of the market," and as a dominant ideology, it dictates what can and cannot be on the table for political discussion (Harvey 2005, 20). In general, government intervention in the market in order to solve social problems—including climate change, lack of healthcare, student debt, and job loss—is akin to heresy from this perspective. For workers, this constraint on democracy often leads to a false choice between having good jobs or having a healthy environment in which to live and work. Workers in the fossil fuel industry become acutely aware of this dichotomy when federal, state, and local governments discuss solutions to the crisis of climate change that involve decarbonizing the economy. The hardships associated with job loss that result from the lack of a strong social safety net and the lack of good job alternatives for displaced workers are two examples of the ways in which the hegemonic neoliberal ideology can fuel antienvironmental activity on the part of workers and their unions.

Protecting Jobs

Unsurprisingly, Jobs vs. the Environment struggles are often fueled by workers' fears that their jobs will be eliminated as a result of the government requiring employers to meet some environmental demand. This natural fear of job loss is amplified by several intertwined, underlying features of the American political economy, including a dearth of good job alternatives for workers without a college degree, low levels of unionization in most industries, the linkage of health insurance and retirement benefits to employment, and the lack of economic diversity in many fossil fuel–producing regions of the country. These background factors, typically referred to as "structural" features of the economy, can often shape, or sometimes be shaped by, the responses of workers and organizations to economic shifts. In many cases, this particular mix of structural factors leads workers with good jobs to fight like hell to keep those jobs.

Workers' interest in protecting their jobs is also used by employers to achieve their own policy objectives, and workers are often presented as the public face of opposition to environmental protection. The struggle to protect the spotted owl from logging in the Pacific Northwest is a quintessential example. Proper regulation of logging might well have extended logging employment in the long run, but the logging companies instead held meetings on paid work time to train workers to oppose the regulations, and the administration of George H. W. Bush stoked the conflict for its political advantage (Durbin 1998).

Ultimately, as mentioned in Chapter 1, labor and environmentalists came together to protect the forests as a result of intensive organizing efforts by activists such as Judy Bari of Earth First and the Industrial Workers of the World (IWW). The common cause that Bari used to unite previously adversarial timber workers and environmentalists was the demand that timber corporations stop overcutting forests at an unsustainable rate, a practice that environmentalists opposed for ecological reasons and workers opposed because it led to layoffs and the closing of sawmills once the forests were depleted of trees (Parthun 2010).

The book *Fear at Work: Job Blackmail, Labor and the Environment* by Richard Kazis and Richard L. Grossman (1982) makes the case that ever since the establishment of environmental and workplace protections in the early 1970s, private employers have resisted further curbs on corporate conduct by threatening job destruction. The refrain has been that environmental standards, and to some extent occupational safety and health standards, wipe out existing jobs and make new ones impossible. *Fear at Work* shows in detail the use of this job blackmail to peel off trade unionists from environmentalists, making unnatural enemies of those who should be allies. This often works to the advantage of those who are opposed to both labor rights and environmental protection, allowing them to promote the Jobs vs. the Environment master frame to maximally exploit workers and nature (Brecher 2013).

Sometimes such conflicts can be reconciled. When environmentalists urged restrictions on high-sulfur coal that was causing acid rain, the UMWA opposed their proposals and even insisted that the labor–environmental Occupational Safety and Health Administration (OSHA) Environmental Network be shut down. But in 1988, UMWA spent months negotiating with Senator George Mitchell, Environment and Public Works Committee member and environmentalist from Maine, to draft a compromise acid rain bill that the union, and thus their senator (Robert Byrd of West Virginia), would support. The plan would have reduced acid rain–causing sulfur dioxide emissions by millions of tons by requiring older, dirtier plants to install smokestack scrubbers and allowing plant owners to pass the costs of these upgrades on to consumers rather than paying for them by eliminating jobs (Patashnik 2008). Despite overcoming many obstacles along the way, the bill was blocked by lobbying efforts from two key constituency groups, one from each side: the utility industry and the National Clean Air Coalition.

Sometimes, protecting the environment absolutely does entail the elimination of some jobs. For example, addressing the causes of climate change will not only radically alter the way we generate electricity, travel, heat our homes, and consume goods and services but also disrupt labor markets, employment, and work in entire industries. Replacing fossil fuels with renewable energy sources will reduce the number of jobs in the fossil fuel industry while simultaneously increasing the number of jobs in renewable power generation. Electric cars do not require oil changes but do require battery replacements. Energy-efficient buildings will require fewer oil and gas deliveries but more smart-grid technicians to maximize the efficiency of operations. Offshore wind farms do not require plant operators but do require wind turbine technicians. Unlike the *threat* of job loss by employers described above, decarbonizing the economy is guaranteed to eliminate a certain number of jobs in the fossil fuel industry.

Most research examining the effects of environmental protection legislation on employment conclude that, on average, such legislation has created more jobs than it has destroyed (Baker and Lee 2021; Goodstein 1999). Unfortunately, this fact is of little comfort to the individual workers who lose *their* jobs as a result of an environmental protection policy. These studies typically do not consider whether the new jobs require the same set of skills or are located in the same geographic region. They often ignore the quality of the new jobs compared with the jobs that are lost. The only real certainty is that many of the existing jobs in the fossil fuel industry will go away as a result of decarbonizing the economy. For labor organizations, one existing unionized job today is worth more than a million jobs promised by a politician.

Fossil fuel jobs in the existing energy sector, ranging from extraction to transportation to power plant operations, are among the highest-paying jobs that do not require a college degree. They were not always good jobs, though, and only became better in the twentieth century as workers, predominantly through unions, engaged in collective activity, including bargaining, protesting, and striking for increases in wages, benefits, and workplace safety. Wages and benefits in many of the new green jobs, particularly in the residential solar industry—the largest employer in the renewable energy sector—do not compare with those in the fossil fuel industry. For example, in 2018, the mean annual salary for a fossil fuel power plant operator was $78,030, while the mean annual salary for a rooftop solar installer was $46,010 (U.S. BLS 2018b). Jobs in reproductive labor, such as healthcare, education, and services, are likely to become a major component of a green economy, but owing to the history of patriarchy and sexism in America, these largely female-dominated occupations are typically undervalued and underpaid.

The difference in pay, benefits, and job security between these industries is due in large part to the disparity in the bargaining power of workers. In the fossil fuel sector, workers have a long history of unionization and collective bargaining. The solar sector is characterized by at-will employment for largely anti-union employers who invest heavily in union avoidance campaigns to block their employees from the right to bargain collectively for higher wages (Eidelson 2018). Through concerted action by workers, residential solar jobs could become as high paying as fossil fuel jobs over time; however, the initial experience for a worker shifting from a fossil fuel occupation to the green energy sector is likely to be an immediate reduction in salary and benefits. Organizing new workers in the private sector has become increasingly difficult for unions. The steady weakening of labor protections over the past seventy years, coupled with extreme anti-union sentiment among employers, makes new union organizing more difficult than in the years following the National Labor Relations Act of 1935, when many of the fossil fuel unions were formed.

The disparities in bargaining power between workers in the fossil fuel and renewable energy industries are indicative of the lack of good union job alternatives for blue-collar workers in general. Globalization and deindustrialization—the shipping of jobs overseas to pay lower wages and pollute more in order to maximize profits in a competitive global market—have hollowed out the middle of the labor market (Bluestone and Harrison 1982). The decline in manufacturing jobs has left few well-paying alternatives for displaced workers without a college degree. Those who still hold one of the few union jobs left in the private sector, just 6 percent of workers in 2018, are not prepared to give up those jobs for themselves or their children. They also know that most alternatives readily available to them are low-paying jobs without union representation or many fringe benefits.

Geographic factors can also exacerbate the ill effects of job loss for workers. The energy infrastructure of the nineteenth and twentieth centuries was built around supplies of fossil fuels. Coal mining requires an underground supply of bituminous, and oil drilling requires an underground supply of crude. The transition to renewable energy sources that is required to reduce GHG emissions will be built around a different set of resources. Wind power requires a steady flow of air, offshore wind requires a shoreline, and solar power requires prolonged sun exposure. These renewable resources may or may not be available in the same locations as fossil fuel resources, which means the transition away from fossil fuels to renewables could harm the economy in some localities while benefiting it in others.

These geographic considerations can inspire resistance to climate protection measures by some unions, particularly those in rural or isolated areas with less diversified economies. Numerous small cities and towns across the United States are reliant on just one fossil fuel employer for the bulk of wages and local tax revenue. For those communities, the economic impact of decarbonization could be widespread economic hardship. For workers and unions in those regions, the potential for job loss is real, and the implications could be dire (for examples, see Cha and Vachon 2021). Alternatively, unions in areas where new green infrastructure projects are likely to be built would see an increase in job opportunities.

Inadequate Social Safety Net

In addition to a dearth of good job alternatives, another major reason workers must fight so hard to protect the jobs and benefits they currently have is the general lack of social welfare benefits in American society. The United States is the epitome of what political economists refer to as a liberal market economy (Hall and Soskice 2001). Liberal market economies are defined by competitive labor markets with a high degree of managerial prerogative, limited collective bargaining, and an overall emphasis on maximizing share price in the short term. Liberal market economies are also characterized by relatively thin welfare states that reinforce the fluid labor markets used by employers to manage their relations with labor (Esping-Anderson 1990). In contrast, coordinated market economies, such as in Germany, rely on nonmarket forms of coordination, including negotiation, bargaining, and collaboration, that encourage industrial citizenship and power sharing.

As the ideal typical liberal market economy, the United States has a weak social safety net. Wage replacement for unemployed workers is smaller and lasts for a shorter duration than in most other advanced capitalist democracies. When American workers lose their jobs, they lose not only their income but also health insurance for themselves and their families. Training and education is an expensive endeavor that places nearly all of the risk, usually in the form of debt, on the individual worker, with no guarantee that the investment will lead to a job in the end. The transition for workers from one occupation to another is made easier when education is free or highly subsidized and when health insurance and other benefits exist during the interim period of unemployment. This has been cited as one of the major reasons for the difference in support for climate protection measures between workers in the European context and the American context (Hyde and Vachon 2019).

The paucity of the U.S. welfare state is even more pronounced in its programs to help workers displaced from jobs as a result of government policy. A key example is the Trade Adjustment Assistance program to assist workers harmed by international trade agreements such as NAFTA. The program is generally seen as inadequate for a number of reasons, including the limited number of workers who actually qualify for assistance, the level of assistance, and the job retraining program's inability to guarantee a job at the end of the process. Most workers who received training with the program did not end up with jobs in the fields they had trained for (Barrett 2001). Rather than smoothly transitioning to a lucrative new career, most workers lost well-paying blue-collar jobs, went through an inadequate job preparation program, and ended up with low-paying service sector work they could have landed without the program. These experiences have left many unions feeling skeptical of so-called government transition programs. The inadequacy of the U.S. social safety net, including existing transition programs, is largely a result of the neoliberal governing ideology that has avoided taxation and social spending as well as most other forms of state intervention into markets.

Promoting Economic Growth

Historically, unions have supported economic growth as a means to full employment, as a way to provide a better life for all, and as an aspect of human progress. Conversely, environmentalists are often acutely aware of the negative consequences of economic growth in the pollution of air, water, and land; the harm to human health; and the threat to the Earth's climate. A beginning at reconciling this division has been made with proposals for massive job creation through "green growth" investments (Collins 2014). For example, many unions and coalition groups that I referred to as "blue–greens" in Chapter 1 have supported local renewable energy construction projects, such as wind farms and solar farms, as well as energy efficiency projects that would create union jobs improving the insulation, heating, and cooling systems of buildings to reduce their energy use and thus GHG emissions. However, many of these same blue–green unions simultaneously oppose measures to mandate GHG emission reductions that would lead to the closure of fossil fuel operations.

These questions around job protection and economic growth bring "the political economy of the environment" into sharp focus (Rudel, Roberts, and Carmin 2011, 222). "The political economy of the environment" refers to how people control, and periodically struggle for control over, the institutions and organizations that produce and regulate the flows of materials that sustain us. A critical approach to the political economy of the environment recognizes that environmental concerns are not isolated problems resulting from particular manufacturing processes; rather, they result from complex interactions among the social, economic, and political forces that constitute the capitalist economic system—a system that is not ecologically sustainable (Schnaiberg 1980). According to the treadmill-of-production perspective, one of the dominant critical theories of the environment, businesses face constant competitive pressures in the capitalist system and thus continually seek new ways to accumulate capital, typically by expanding their operations and investing in energy-intensive but labor-saving technologies that can increase their profits (Gould, Pellow, and Schnaiberg 2004).

The three major actors in the political economy of the environment are capital, labor, and the state, and the interaction of these three actors generates a treadmill of production and consumption in which continuous economic growth is the guiding light for all decisions and policies. Capital is motivated exclusively by the pursuit of profit and thus is incapable of slowing the treadmill (Obach 2004). The government—local, state, and national—generally supports and subsidizes these activities to maintain tax revenue and legitimacy, particularly in the neoliberal era of tax cuts and austerity. Workers support economic expansion insofar as it promises to replace jobs that have been lost to the labor-saving, technological innovations of capitalists. This has often been the justification for labor support of green growth initiatives that are decoupled from the phaseout of polluting industries.

For example, the IBEW has invested heavily in green jobs training programs at its apprenticeship training centers and has thrown political support behind renewable energy projects at the local and state level while simultaneously joining UMWA in suing the federal government over President Obama's Clean Power Plan, which mandates reductions in GHG emissions by fossil fuel–burning power plants. Supporting green initiatives such as renewable energy construction, without also reducing carbon emissions by phasing out coal and natural gas facilities, means just an overall increase in economic growth and energy consumption. This green growth approach has generally been the policy formulation supported by the BlueGreen Alliance, a joint project of several unions and environmental organizations (predominantly the USW and the Sierra Club) to promote solutions that solve environmental problems and support the creation and maintenance of good jobs.[1]

Unfortunately, economic growth generally leads to greater extraction and consumption of natural resources, causing environmental degradation through intensified use of toxic chemicals, increased air and water pollution, and greater emissions of GHGs that lead to climate change (York 2004). This process has been described by John Bellamy Foster (2000) as the metabolic rift—a term coined by Karl Marx to describe the rupture in the metabolic interaction between humanity and the rest of nature emanating from capitalist production. Economic expansion also leads to growing economic and political inequality as labor-saving technologies reduce the share of the economic surplus that is distributed to workers and further concentrates power in the hands of capitalists. Thus, the irony of the treadmill is that the only group with an interest in slowing or stopping the cycle—the working class—is also compelled to support the economic growth that ravages the environment as a result of their increasing dependence on capital to maintain their livelihood—an instance of what Jeremy Brecher (2017) refers to as climate alienation.

This dependence on capital leads construction unions in general to have an "all of the above" energy policy to support all forms of job growth. Unlike most other unionized industries, construction work is sporadic, so securing a steady stream of employment opportunities for members is a primary function of the IBEW and unions representing carpenters, laborers, operating engineers, and pipefitters, as well as other building trades unions. Many fossil fuel companies leverage this dependence by offering preconstruction contracts, known as project labor agreements (PLAs), to gain union political support for projects such as oil and gas pipelines and power plants. Most renewable companies do not appeal to unions in the same way. In fact, many renewable companies, such as Elon Musk's SolarCity, are notoriously anti-union.

As we have seen in the historical examples thus far, labor has often—but not always—sided with capital in promoting the pro-growth agenda, whether green or not (Mayer 2009; Obach 2004; Vachon and Brecher 2016). It is important to note that the reduced size and influence as well as the changing composition of the U.S. labor movement may bring the assumption of labor's role in promoting the treadmill into question. It is logical to assume that workers in the fossil fuel industry will continue to support increased extraction and consumption of those fuels and that workers in manufacturing will support increasing manufacturing output, green or not, but what of the millions of unionized healthcare workers, public school teachers, and public transit operators who see environmental degradation and climate change as real threats to their quality of life and may not necessarily share in the presumed benefits of endless economic growth? These developments challenge some of the assumptions of the treadmill explanation for labor opposition to environmental protection and form the basis of questions I explore in the next chapter and throughout the remainder of this book.

Constraints on Democracy

In his 2015 book, *Inequality, Democracy, and the Environment*, Liam Downey contends that a more complete explanation of the structural relationship that exists between humans and nature must explain how elites create and use organizations, institutions, and networks to achieve their goals and how those social structures simultaneously cause environmental harm and restrict pro-environmental attitudes, values, and behaviors of non-elites, including workers. Elites are the individuals who occupy the most-advantageous positions in the key power networks of society, including economic, political, military, and ideological power networks (Mann 1988). Occupying positions of authority and influence, elites have a greater potential for directing and controlling these networks, their resources, and the people who participate in them—and thus they have a greater ability than non-elites to achieve their goals.

The main goal of most elites in a capitalist economy is accumulation of capital. To achieve this goal, capitalists universally seek to expand markets, reduce trade barriers, reduce unwanted government regulations, decrease labor costs, and reduce the costs of extracting and transporting raw materials. However, accomplishing any one of these tasks requires capitalists to overcome resistance from non-elites—namely, workers and voters in democratic societies. The fact that elites so often achieve such goals suggests an unequal distribution of power in society (Boyce 2002; Downey 2015).

From this perspective, small groups of powerful elites monopolize decision-making through undemocratic organizations, institutions, and networks and shift environmental costs onto less powerful groups. These same powerful individuals and organizations can inhibit the development and dissemination of environmental knowledge, attitudes, values, and beliefs that conflict with their interests and successfully frame what is and is not considered to be acceptable pro-environmental behavior and policy (McCright and Dunlap 2003). By controlling the framing of pro-environmental behaviors and policies, elites effectively restrict the ability of non-elites to behave in environmentally friendly ways by limiting their choices and shaping the incentives available to them.

At a broader level, Erik Olin Wright and Joel Rogers (2015) argue that democratic demands in general within a capitalist economy are necessarily constrained. The basic argument is this: because the owners of capital control investments, and investments are so important for the overall health of an economy, the satisfaction of the interests of owners of capital is a necessary condition for the satisfaction of all other economic interests in the system. In other words, if the basic interests of capitalist firms are not stably secured, then capitalist firms will not make adequate profits, which will lead to a reduction in investments in capitalist firms, which in turn leads to a decline in production and thus a decline in jobs and wages. One of the consequences of this dependence on private capitalists for jobs is that the interests of business appear to be the "general interests" of society rather than merely the "special interests" of a particular class of people. Ironically, that means the political demand for lower taxes on business is seen as being in the interest of everyone while the demand for higher wages for workers is attacked as a special interest of unions. Thus, the rules of the game of capitalist democracy ensure that in general the only acceptable political demands are those compatible with capitalist interests and a "good business climate."

Both Downey's and Wright and Rogers's theories help us to understand why workers in the fossil fuel industry so readily accept the Jobs vs. the Environment master frame. Industry elites, through their unequal access to power, can corral workers into making a false choice between jobs and the environment and thus channel the attitudes and behaviors of workers into a course of action compatible with elite interests. This constraint on democracy, as well as the fear of job loss, the lack of an adequate social safety net, and the endless pursuit of economic growth are all reinforced by the dominant neoliberal ideology that permeates American society, and together they undergird the continued support by many workers for the existing, climate-destroying fossil fuel regime. Weakening that support requires challenging neoliberal thinking and expanding democracy to include decisions about the economy.

Understanding Labor Support for Environmental Protections

Despite many instances of conflict around environmental issues, unions have often confronted corporate enemies of labor and the environment. Almost lost on the shoals of history, unions such as UAW and AFSCME helped initiate Earth Day (UAW 1970). Organizer of the first Earth Day, Dennis Hayes, recalls, "The UAW was by far the largest contributor to the first Earth Day, and its support went beyond the merely financial. It printed and mailed all our materials at its expense—even those critical of pollution-belching cars. And, of course, Walter [Reuther] then endorsed the Clean Air Act that the Big Four [auto companies] were doing their damnedest to kill or gut" (Uehlein 2010).

In reviewing the history of labor–environmental cooperation in the United States, I identify six broad means by which unions have come to support environmental measures: (1) occupational safety and health issues, (2) nature conservation, (3) environmental justice, (4) opposition to international trade agreements, (5) green growth initiatives, and (6) sustainable development. In each instance, labor adopted a counterframe that challenged the dominant Jobs vs. the Environment narrative and used collective agency to push back against existing structural constraints.

Occupational Safety and Health

Labor's involvement in promoting environmental causes has frequently been an extension of its concern with health and safety issues inside the workplace to the effects of industrial processes outside the workplace. A classic example occurred on Halloween night, 1948, in Donora, Pennsylvania, birthplace of Hall of Fame baseball player Stan Musial, when fluoride released by plants of the U.S. Steel Corporation caused a toxic cloud that killed twenty people and left hundreds more sick or dying. The "Donora death fog" led the recently formed United Steelworkers union to recognize the close connection between health and safety issues in the plant and environmental issues in surrounding communities. The union became a strong supporter of environmental protection, regarding it as an extension of the union's responsibility for the health and safety of its members. In 1963, the Steelworkers supported the first federal Clean Air Act—effectively advocating for protections for all workers, not just for the security of jobs—and, in 1990, they stated that global warming "may be the single greatest problem we face" (USW 1990).

Another classic example is the Shell Oil strike. In 1973, the Oil, Chemical and Atomic Workers (OCAW), largely as a result of the pioneering work of labor–environmental activist Tony Mazzocchi, struck five refineries owned by the notorious polluter Shell Oil, demanding a national health and safety agreement that also would have significantly reduced the dangers of environmental contamination through poor plant practices. The Sierra Club and eleven other national environmental organizations supported the strike, stating, "We have increasingly come to recognize that working people are among the hardest hit by the hazards of pollution in the workplace. We support the efforts of the OCAW in demanding a better environment, not just for its own workers, but for all Americans" (Leopold 2007). Al Grospiron, president of the OCAW, said, "Organized labor must emphatically support environmental cleanup efforts and must never get into the position of opposing such efforts on the grounds of economic hardship. . . . Our position must be that nearly all polluting facilities can be corrected without hardships to the workers and that in those few cases where corrections are not possible, new job opportunities or compensation must be provided for the workers" (Leopold 2007).

Two years later, in 1975, a group called Environmentalists for Full Employment organized to challenge fears that environmental protection would lead to job loss and to promote new jobs. In 1979, unions and environmental groups such as the Sierra Club and Friends of the Earth formed the OSHA

Environmental Network, with active coalitions in twenty-two states. It helped pass legislation that gave both workers and communities the right to know about toxic substances being used in workplaces. Both the OSHA Environmental Network and Environmentalists for Full Employment were initiated by and housed in the Industrial Union Department of the AFL-CIO, the post-merger successor to the CIO (Obach 2004).

Several good books have been written in recent years on the topic of labor–environmental coalitions. For example, Brian Mayer's 2009 book, *Blue–Green Coalitions: Fighting for Safe Workplaces and Healthy Communities*, examines three cases of labor environmental coalitions focused on issues related to toxics and health: The New Jersey Work Environment Council, the Alliance for a Healthy Tomorrow, and the Silicon Valley Toxics Coalition. Mayer contends that by focusing on health, the labor movement and the environmental movement—two of the largest social movements in America—have developed a unique collective identity through local blue–green coalitions whose combined influence has had a tremendous influence on progressive social change. According to Mayer, the issue of health has often served as a bridge between two movements who often find themselves pitted against each other to serve the interests of polluting corporate employers. Similarly, in *Environmental Unions: Labor and the Superfund*, Craig Slatin and colleagues (2016) explore the history of the intersection between workplace safety and environmental concerns and argue that organized labor played a significant role in the passage of the Superfund Amendments and Reauthorization Act of 1986 and the subsequent implementation of the Worker Training Program.

Brian Obach's earlier study of blue–green coalitions, *Labor and the Environmental Movement: The Quest for Common Ground* (2004), also examines some of the factors that contribute to labor–environmental cooperation. In particular, he focuses on how organizational learning can increase the ability of unions and environmentalists to work together. He also examines the important role played by "coalition brokers," individuals with vested interests in both movements, in bringing labor and environmental activists together into coalitions.[2] Thomas Estabrook, Charles Levenstein, and John Wooding's *Labor–Environmental Coalitions: Lessons from a Louisiana Petrochemical Region* (2018) traces the development of the Louisiana Labor–Neighbor Project, which grew out of a campaign by OCAW to win back the jobs of its members locked out by the BASF Corporation in the 1980s. Estabrook and his coauthors contend that for labor–community coalitions like the Louisiana Project to thrive, they must broaden their agenda, strengthen their leadership and coalition-building skills, and develop access to multiscale resources.

Conservation Efforts

In addition to organizing early antipollution efforts to protect the health and safety of workers, the AFL-CIO also recognized the need to conserve land for recreation use by workers who lived and toiled in industrial cities that lacked wildlands. In testimony in support of the bill to create the National Wilderness Preservation System in 1958, AFL-CIO legislative representative George D. Riley stated, "We [also] favor the preservation of wilderness areas for reasons other than recreation. Wilderness has practical values. Even though they cannot be measured in dollars," he continued, "the scientific value of wilderness should be stressed" (U.S. Senate Committee on Interior and Insular Affairs 1958).

The AFL-CIO launched a national Union Sportsmen's Alliance in 2007 to work for wildlife habitat protections while guaranteeing access for hunters and anglers—measures that created a benefit for all workers (Harden 2007). The eighteen charter member unions include many building trades and manufacturing unions, such as the Boilermakers and the International Association of Machinists and Aerospace Workers (IAM), to name two. The vision statement of the alliance explains that the organization's goal is to "volunteer time and unique trade skills to expand and improve public access to the outdoors, conserve and maintain critical wildlife habitats, restore our nation's parks, and provide mentoring programs that introduce youth to the outdoors" (Union Sportsmen's Alliance 2018).

As historian Scott Dewey notes in his 1998 history of early labor–environmentalism, the labor movement was one of the first organizations to combine the concern for wilderness protection and pollution reduction into one organizational structure. Through the mid-1960s, most Americans viewed conservationism and antipollutionism as separate and unrelated issues. Unions were in the unusual position of showing interest in reducing pollution before most conservation organizations did so and in simultaneously expressing concern for nature conservation before most public health advocates did. These different concerns gradually fused into the modern environmental movement in the late 1960s and early 1970s.

Environmental Justice

According to historian Josiah Rector (2014, 2018), the concept of "environmental justice" was first popularized by activists during the 1970s in the context of growing environmental degradation, racialized urban poverty, and working-class fears of plant closure. To address these problems, leaders in the UAW and other unions formed coalitions with civil rights and environmental groups to advocate for federal policies that would simultaneously reduce pollution and unemployment. Activists such as William Ratliff of the Urban League in South Carolina not only challenged disproportionate pollution exposures but also advocated government planning for full employment, including large-scale job creation in renewable energy, recycling, weatherization, and environmental cleanup programs, all prioritizing the most polluted, impoverished, and segregated communities. By reducing workers' fear of unemployment, these activists argued, unions and civil rights groups would be able to collaborate more with environmentalists.

Unfortunately, by the mid-1980s, all three components of the labor–civil rights–environmental coalition found themselves on the defensive, halted by plant closures, urban disinvestment, and the Reagan administration's attacks on unions and on environmental and civil rights laws. Environmental organizations shifted toward fundraising for legal battles to defend existing environmental protections, and unions shifted toward concessionary bargaining to save jobs, leading both toward narrower political agendas, including an embrace by some unions of the Jobs vs. the Environment master frame. The environmental justice movement continued to spread in the 1990s and 2000s, despite the erosion of institutions that once facilitated its emergence. In sum, Rector's account reveals how the defeat of social democratic politics in the 1970s transformed the terms of national debates about jobs, racial justice, and the environment and paved the way for the types of Jobs vs. the Environment clashes that characterized labor–environmental relations from the 1980s onward.

However, some organizations, such as the Just Transition Alliance (JTA) and more recently the CJA, have continued to attempt to connect labor with environmental justice struggles. And the LCM is, through its calls for a Green New Deal, reasserting many of the same social democratic demands that were abandoned in the previous era. But, as we shall see, the contest over the inclusion of climate justice demands within the various just transition frameworks put forth by the LCM (described in Chapter 5) is a critical intersection for the labor–climate and climate justice movements. Building the broad, cross-movement base of support that is needed for efforts such as a Green New Deal to succeed will require the two movements to expand their issue ranges to incorporate demands for both labor and climate justice.

Opposing Trade Agreements

In 1999, the labor movement and many (though not all) environmental organizations jointly demanded protection of workers and the environment in any international trade agreement and joined in Seattle to protest the founding meeting of the World Trade Organization (WTO). When young environmentalists, some wearing turtle costumes to represent threatened species, arrived at the mass rallies and demonstrations of over forty thousand people, a slogan rapidly spread: "Turtles and Teamsters, together at last!" The ensuing "Battle of Seattle" shut down the global summit called to establish the WTO (Brecher, Costello, and Smith 2000).

Governmental negotiations of international trade agreements such as NAFTA and the Trans-Pacific Partnership have often brought together labor and environmental activists in shared purpose against corporate capitalist globalization. Organizations like the WTO represent a direct threat to both labor and environmental protections because they undermine national sovereignty by allowing corporations to challenge national regulations in the name of promoting "free" trade. Hard-won protections for workers and the environment are put at risk as manufacturing and production from less-regulated areas of the world drive a "race to the bottom" among countries trying to create the best business climate for transnational corporations, which play countries off of one another in their endless quest for lax regulations to maximize profits.

Promoting Green Growth

In the aftermath of the Battle of Seattle, labor and environmental groups organized a major meeting to launch further cooperation. The meeting was scheduled for September 11, 2001, but it was canceled because of the terrorist attacks and never rescheduled. Two new labor–environmental alliances sprang up to continue the collaboration. The Apollo Alliance, which brought together labor, environmental, and some business groups to promote massive investment in a clean energy economy, was founded in 2003. The BlueGreen Alliance was founded in 2006 by the Sierra Club and the USW to fight for "green jobs"; it has subsequently been joined by a number of other unions and environmental groups. In 2012, Apollo merged into the BlueGreen Alliance— and the goal remains the pursuit of green growth.

In the wake of the Great Recession of 2008, many unions got behind newly elected president Barack Obama's economic stimulus plan, including its heavy investments in green jobs, energy efficiency upgrades in the construction sector, electric vehicle batteries and fuel cells in the manufacturing sector, and wind and solar power installations in the energy sector. In Rhode Island, the building trades council was the largest supporter of the nation's first offshore wind farm off the coast of Block Island. Connecticut, Massachusetts, New Jersey, and New York quickly followed suit, with construction unions such as the UBC, IBEW, and International Union of Operating Engineers (IUOE) throwing their political weight behind the projects. For example, the Climate Jobs New York plan, which was developed by more than a dozen labor unions and won the support of the governor, promises to create more than ten thousand jobs constructing offshore wind farms as well as installing solar panels, improving and expanding mass transit, and renovating buildings to make them more energy efficient. In 2022, most U.S. unions and the AFL-CIO supported the Infrastructure Investment and Jobs Act and the IRA, both of which provided funding and tax incentives for investments in renewable energy and green infrastructure.

Interestingly, these green growth programs represent an extension of labor's general support for economic growth, which as we have seen in the previous section of this chapter also prompts some unions to oppose environmental protections. The support of any and all growth leads many unions to have seemingly contradictory stances, supporting renewable energy expansion but also oil pipeline expansion. The common denominator is jobs. Whether simply layering more renewable energy infrastructure on top of the existing system, as the blue–greens advocate for, actually equates to reduced emissions is another question altogether—it could just mean more total energy consumption if either regulations or market forces do not drive down fossil fuel use.

Sustainable Development

Outside of the United States, "sustainable development" emerged as a watchword in the 1990s—unifying social, economic, and environmental concerns and leading many unions to develop their own vision for sustainable development that integrated the needs of the environment and working people. In his retracing of the evolution of trade unionists' thinking about nature and their relationship to the environment, Victor Silverman (2004) uncovers a remarkable spate of intellectual and political activism by labor leaders—mostly from European countries—in United Nations' environmental policy making from the 1950s through the 1980s. He also finds that many international trade union organizations, such as the International Confederation of Free Trade Unions, international trade secretariats, and the European Trade Union Confederation, participated in various international conferences and institutions, including the 1972 Conference on the Environment in Stockholm, the 1992 Conference on Environment and Development in Rio de Janeiro, and the 2002 World Summit on Sustainable Development in Johannesburg. As the 1992 World Congress of the International Confederation of Trade Unions, then the dominant global union federation, put it, "In a world of finite resources, there must be a reconciliation between growth and environmental protection" (quoted in Silverman 2004, 131). They went on to say that "[sustainable development] demanded the creation and maintenance of socially useful, individually fulfilling and environmentally sound employment." This concern went beyond economics and environment to "broader social issues" such as "the struggle for human rights, equity, and social justice" (quoted in Silverman 2004, 131). Although not reviewed here, a good amount has been written about unions in the United Kingdom, Europe, and Australia engaging with issues of sustainability in the workplace (for example, see Farnhill 2014, 2016; Hampton 2015; Räthzel and Uzzell 2013; Snell and Fairbrother 2010). Unfortunately, in recent decades, the AFL-CIO in the United States has too often served as an impediment to rather than a promoter of sustainable development with regard to its stance on climate change.

When Structure Meets Agency: Why Some Unions May Be More Likely to See Environmental Protection as a Labor Issue

Erik Loomis's *Empire of Timber* (2016) demonstrates how changing economic conditions at the macro level can affect labor–environmental politics at the local level. Increased automation, global trade, and technological developments led to decreasing employment in the timber industry through the 1980s. Broader trends in the U.S. labor movement, including a steady decline in membership and political strength, the fear of job loss, a dearth of good job alternatives, and lack of an adequate safety net, made it increasingly difficult for unions to advocate for conservation. However, Loomis also notes how the organizational dynamics of particular unions shaped their responses to these changing conditions. For example, the International Woodworkers of America, which embraced more radical politics, remained an advocate for conservation but was largely overshadowed by the vocal opposition of other unions, such as the UBC. Loomis attributes these divergent responses to the different cultures and leadership styles of the two organizations.

Other scholarship on labor–environmental relations has also pointed to a qualitative distinction between unions that are more or less likely to engage with broader social problems beyond the usual bread-and-butter issues of wages and benefits—such as environmental protection or climate change (see, for example, Obach 2004). Sometimes the difference is as stark as supporting versus opposing particular solutions to social problems, but more often it is a question of whether unions even choose to engage with an issue if it is not directly related to wages, hours, and working conditions on the shop floor. The distinction between unions that are more or less likely to engage with broader social issues is often couched in academic discussions about two ideal typical and opposing forms of unionism: "pure and simple" business unionism versus "social movement unionism," or what the late Stanley Aronowitz (1984) called "instrumental" and "heroic" unionism.[3]

From the instrumental perspective, the labor movement is a loose collection of worker organizations tasked with improving wages and working conditions for their members—mostly through collective bargaining but occasionally through political action and legislation. For instrumental theorists, the labor movement comprises dues-paying members fighting for their shared economic interests and is not concerned with broader working-class interests unless they directly align with the particular instrumental interests of members. This approach aligns closely with pure and simple business unionism.

Conversely, the heroic perspective sees unions as vehicles for ending exploitation, abolishing hierarchy, and establishing a more equal social order. From this perspective, the labor movement is defined as being much more than just unions struggling for employment-based issues—it is the unified working class concerned with the historical task of social transformation. This transformation can come in the form of reform or revolution. For reformists, unions represent a vehicle for progressive change within the capitalist system to create a more just industrial democracy (Larson and Nissen 1987; Webb and Webb 1897). Reformism relies on incremental changes to slowly improve the condition of the working class. For revolutionists, the labor movement is a historical agent for radical social change, including the elimination of capitalism in pursuit of socialism, anarchism, or some other alternative political–economic arrangement (Kimeldorf 1999; Kornbluh 1964; Larson and Nissen 1987). Social movement unionism aligns with the heroic vision of unionism and can manifest anywhere along the spectrum between reform and revolution, depending on the organizational dynamics of a particular union. Unionism in the United States has almost exclusively been reformist since the Red Scare, McCarthyism, and the purging of radical leaders during the Cold War (Kimeldorf 1999).

This heroic-versus-instrumental dichotomy is, of course, an oversimplification of the dynamic nature of the labor movement across space and time, but it does offer some insight by providing two ideal types for the major competing theories about the origin and goals of the labor movement: instrumentality versus social change. Readers with a background in labor will likely be familiar with these terms (and have mixed opinions on their utility). For readers from a climate or environmental background, it would be useful at this point to provide a brief review of these basic theories of the labor movement to help us understand why some unions support efforts to reduce GHG emissions to protect the climate while others, who may support green growth initiatives, oppose GHG reductions. Perhaps most important, why are so many unions remaining silent on the issue altogether?

Pure and Simple Business Unionism

The most conservative theory of labor is that of pure and simple business unionism (Buhle 1999; Commons 1918; Gitelman 1965; Perlman 1949). From this perspective, unions are not inherently antagonistic toward the capitalist order but rather are just one of countless interest groups acting within a pluralistic society. There is no class consciousness or class-based political goal, merely aggregates of working people who, when confronted with incidents of scarcity, develop "job consciousness" and band together for the purpose of protecting their jobs and apportioning available opportunities on an equal basis (Perlman 1949). This does not mean that business unionism is not militant. Business unions take action to get results for their members, but strikes and direct actions are generally used only to exert and maintain their bargaining position. However, business unions also tend to be more cooperative with management because they identify the interests of workers as being aligned with the success of employers.

Structurally, business unions are long-standing, formal, bureaucratic organizations that typically display the entrenched leadership and conservative goals associated with Robert Michels's "iron law of oligarchy" (Voss and Sherman 2000). That thesis, as explained by Michels and elaborated by J. Craig Jenkins, states that over time, organizations tend to develop oligarchical leadership, despite formal democratic practices (Jenkins 1977; Michels 1915 [1962]). This is evidenced by the heavy reliance of business unions on professional staff, which creates distance between leaders and members. Perhaps uncoincidentally, union representatives are often given the title of "business agent" in many unions espousing these business union characteristics.

Major theorists in the school of pure and simple business unionism, such as John Commons and Selig Perlman, believe that unions are actually mechanisms for gaining entry into, rather than opposing, the capitalist system (Commons 1918; Perlman 1949). This belief appeals to and instills a conservative, small-government, pro-growth ideology among many business union leaders and members. It also helps to explain why the various structural factors explored in this chapter have such a strong influence on the decisions of many unions, particularly those that seek entry into, rather than transformation of, the existing order. The business union theory was developed in the United

States as a means of explaining the different form of unionization that took hold there compared with mainland Europe.[4] In relation to the current study, many unions that stand opposed to the LCM are operating as a pillar of support for the fossil fuel industry and therefore display the key characteristics of pure and simple business unionism.

Social Movement Unionism

Perhaps in part owing to the passage of the anti-union Taft–Hartley Act in 1947, which limited the power of unions and led to the purging of radical and leftist leaders during the McCarthy era, the U.S. labor movement entered a period of steady decline in membership beginning in the late 1950s, with precipitous drops in the 1970s and 1980s, when employers embraced a more hostile stance toward labor, taking full advantage of the labor law changes from Taft–Hartley. The rise of neoliberalism, signaled by the elections of Margaret Thatcher in the United Kingdom in 1979 and Ronald Reagan in the United States in 1980, marked the start of a new era of capitalism in which the postwar labor relations system of union organizing and collective bargaining became a target of employers and conservative politicians who sought to free capital from the constraints imposed by union contracts (Vachon, Wallace, and Hyde 2016).[5] Despite this growing capitalist assault on labor, a few unions managed to increase their membership and enjoy some organizing successes during that period (Clawson 2003). The achievements of these unions were due not only to their focus on new organizing efforts but also to their use of innovative strategies and tactics at the local level (Bronfenbrenner and Juravich 1998; Martin 2008; Voss and Sherman 2000; Wallace, Fullerton, and Gurbuz 2009).

Seeing this qualitatively different approach to unionism, many labor theorists began to refer to this new model as "social movement unionism" (or "social justice unionism" or "social unionism").[6] As the name suggests, the social movement union perspective envisions the labor movement as a working-class social movement rather than an oligarchic and instrumentalist organization (Clawson 2003; Fletcher and Gapasin 2008; Johnston 1994; Moody 1997; Robinson 2000; Waterman 1991). The common features among unions that have been referred to as social movements are the use of grassroots mobilization, rank-and-file leadership, face-to-face interaction, and a strong social justice orientation that explicitly rejects the traditional business union model (Lopez 2004). Many of these unions have bypassed the standard union recognition election when organizing new unions, ignoring perceived structural constraints and instead using their agency to deploy creative pressure strategies including direct action, the formation of community alliances, and various forms of political intervention (Martin 2008).

The term "social movement unionism" derives from writings on the industrializing nations of Brazil, the Philippines, South Africa, and South Korea (see, for example, von Holdt 2002). Contemporary analysts describe the unions in these countries as not being exclusively interested in the narrow economic interests of workers but rather pursuing the democratic transformation of societies by building networks and political alliances, being dedicated to democratic practices internally, and being committed to building democratic institutions in the wider society (Lambert 1990; Lambert and Webster 1988; Scipes 1992). Owing to the broad spectrum of demands espoused by these unions—reaching beyond the economic interests of members—and their creative organizing tactics, many scholars felt inclined to designate them as a new type of unionism. These unions seemed to be more akin to the "new social movements" described by European social movement theorists than to the traditional "class-struggle" unions of most Western literature (Melucci 1996; Touraine 1981).

While there is not one authoritative definition of "social movement unionism," nor any real consensus on the use of the term, a review of the literature reveals a number of common features that illustrate ideal typical characteristics of what social movement unionism looks like in the North American sense.[7] First, social movement unionism is based on rank-and-file democracy, with a high degree of member participation in decision-making (as opposed to the oligarchic leadership structures typically associated with business unionism). Similar to McAlevey's "organizing model" in *No Shortcuts* (2018a), workers are the primary agents of change in the social movement form of unionism. This has also been referred to at various points in time as "rank-and-file unionism" or "the CIO model," referencing the way that the early unions of the Congress of Industrial Organizations (CIO) organized workers in the 1930s and 1940s. The idea is that workers do not win demands merely by campaigning, lobbying, or engaging in dialogue; they win by organizing, building power, and mobilizing for social change. Second, social movement unionism involves struggling for more than just wage increases for more than just members (Aronowitz 1984; Obach 2004). This is similar to what has come to be known as bargaining for the common good (BCG) in recent years, or what McAlevey calls the "whole worker" approach (McAlevey 2018a; McCartin 2016; Sneiderman and Fascione 2018). By making broad demands of employers, social movement unionism entails fighting for the whole working class by directly challenging the owners of capital who are the drivers of exploitation and injustice. Third, social movement unionism involves working regularly in conjunction with other community-based groups and social movements on equal footing (environmentalists, women's rights groups, faith groups, peace groups, etc.)—also a central tenet of the BCG approach as well as "community unionism." Fourth, social movement unionism is rooted in a strong commitment to organizing, both internally, as noted in point one above, and also externally for new members, regardless of race, ethnicity, gender, sexual orientation, or country of origin. In fact, this form of unionism often focuses first and foremost on organizing and empowering those who are the least well-off—including racial minorities and immigrants (Finc and Tichenor 2009). And finally, social movement unionism uses innovative strategies and noninstitutional tactics to achieve organizing goals (Bronfenbrenner and Juravich 1998).

A recent example of social movement unionism in the United States was the wave of teacher strikes in southern and western states, including Arizona, Oklahoma, and West Virginia. In February and March 2018, public schools in all fifty-five counties of West Virginia closed for nearly two weeks as teachers joined picket lines. The protest was in response to low pay and underfunding of public education; the state's average teacher salary ranked forty-eighth in the nation. Recognizing that improving their situation required far more than a pay raise and better health insurance, the teachers called for structural changes that would benefit not just teachers but students and the community. As Wendy Peters, the president of the Raleigh affiliate of the West Virginia Education Association, noted, "Wages and health benefits were almost a distraction" (McAlevey 2018b). They argued that the only solution was a more just and equitable distribution of the state's resources, so they called for an increase in the severance tax on the state's profitable natural gas industry to pay for their raises and opposed any cuts to Medicaid or other services to fund schools. The unions also used social media to coordinate with the state's food pantries, churches, and community centers to deliver food to children who relied on their schools for daily nutrition to ensure they did not go hungry during the strike. Further, the strike was largely coordinated and executed by rank-and-file members—as was the continuation of the strike after rejection of an agreement initially bargained for by union leaders and the government. Like the West Virginia teachers, the Oklahoma teachers also argued for structural reform, including the restoration of the millions of dollars in education funding that had been cut from the budget, which led many school districts to shutter schools, increase class sizes, and operate four-day school weeks.

In regard to the current research, the emerging LCM examined in this study encompasses unions that display many characteristics of the ideal of social movement unionism. The unions involved in the movement are taking on the issues of climate change and environmental justice, both of which extend beyond the mere bread-and-butter interests of their members. In many instances, rank-and-file LCM activists are working to transform their unions from within to move away from the business union approach and toward a more social movement approach by producing counterframes that challenge existing structures that promote a conservative stance on the issue of climate change. This approach is similar to that taken by previous movements within labor, such as U.S. Labor against the War and the Labor for Single Payer efforts, both of which were manifestations of rank-and-file union activism moving the position of labor as a whole by challenging existing master frames and reframing the situation.

In a study of unions outside the United States, Nora Räthzel and David Uzzell (2013) find that the unions engaging with climate change are creating identities and organizing campaigns as social movements. But totally apart from issues of climate justice, these unions in the United States are also engaging heavily in labor–community partnerships and alliances with other non-labor social movements to address wider societal issues, such as racial justice, gender equality, access to healthcare, and affordable housing. These social justice values and the use of innovative tactics obviously appeal to individuals with a progressive ideology and in turn help foster such an ideology among members of these organizations. Perhaps not surprising to many readers, these unions also have greater diversity in their memberships and typically operate in sectors of the economy where unions were formed more recently.

From Understanding the Past to Decoding the Present

When several national construction unions expressed their enthusiastic support for the Keystone XL and later the Dakota Access oil pipeline projects because of the jobs they would create, a small but growing number of unions began to publicly decry these projects as potentially huge contributors to deadly climate change, a problem that posed a direct threat to the livelihoods and well-being of all workers, including union members.[8] This emerging fissure between the pro– and anti–climate protection unions underscores a theme present throughout labor's storied history with environmental issues: that the goal of protecting jobs can sometimes come into conflict with the goal of protecting workers in general, a reflection of the recurring distinction between what Perlman (1949) called "job consciousness" and what Marx called "class consciousness," which is at the heart of the climate debate within labor (Marx and Engels 2009).

The growing movement of LCM activists within unions who are pursuing broad working-class interests has begun to push for climate protection measures in their cities and states and at the federal level. They have also pushed within their own unions and the labor movement more broadly to build a working-class environmentalism that sees climate change as a union issue and demands that labor have a voice in solving the problem to ensure that working-class interests are incorporated into the solutions. The stance of the AFL-CIO on environmental issues is of central importance in this struggle. The federation is the bell cow of the U.S. labor movement with regard to climate change; it sets the limits for the movement of labor as a whole toward a more progressive environmental future. The current research is centered on this nascent movement and its efforts to bring the labor movement into the struggle for a Green New Deal–style solution.

From the transportation workers who suffered during Superstorm Sandy to the nurses who confront increasing climate-related health issues every day to the workers who build and operate fossil fuel power plants, the LCM comprises a small but diverse and growing chorus of voices within the U.S. labor movement challenging the Jobs vs. the Environment master frame and promoting the emerging Clean Air and Good Jobs counterframe as a more equitable, just, sustainable alternative. As history has revealed, the role of labor in struggles about the environment has been mixed, and outcomes are largely determined by the decisions of unions to fight for jobs or to fight for workers. The more that labor fights for workers as opposed to just jobs, the greater the challenge it poses to the powerful neoliberal ideology underpinning the Jobs vs. the Environment master frame that is preventing real solutions to the climate crisis.

3

Industry, Interests, and Ideology

Understanding the Labor–Climate Spectrum

E xploring the history of labor–environmental relations in the United States reveals many structural features of the American capitalist economy that have influenced the decisions of particular unions to either support or oppose various environmental protections. From fear of job loss to support for economic growth, unions have often found themselves in struggles over Jobs vs. the Environment. On other issues, such as worker and community health and safety, unions and environmentalists have forged strong alliances to win clean air and water protections. However, the distinctive contribution of this book is a detailed examination of labor on the issues of climate change and climate justice, issues that have much in common with previous labor–environmental questions but also have their own unique structural considerations.

In particular, the industries in which unions operate can have a significant influence on their stance toward climate protection measures, whether they be opposed to climate protection, supportive of green growth, or proponents of more comprehensive Green New Deal–style programs. Unsurprisingly, unions with members directly employed in fossil fuels are most likely to resist strong climate protection measures. However, the unique cultures and ideologies of unions in different industries also shape their understanding of climate change. Often less explored is how and why unions in nonfossil fuel industries either engage with or remain silent on the issue of climate change. Further, as we have seen, the impacts of climate change tend to disproportionately harm those who are already most vulnerable, which has led to the rise of the climate justice movement, which centers issues of equity and justice. Climate impacts are felt unevenly across different unions as well and are often associated with the geography and demographics of their membership—characteristics that are closely tied to their industry of employment. For example, many of the unions poised to lose jobs because of decarbonization are some of the least diverse along the lines of race and gender, while other unions in services or the public sector that are not threatened by decarbonization have more diverse memberships and are feeling the uneven impacts of climate change in their jobs and their communities.

In addition to the material interests associated with particular industries, the prevailing ideology of particular leaders or unions can also shape their approach to the issues of climate change and justice. Ideology, in simple terms, is a system of ideas that aspires both to explain the world and to either preserve it or change it. Unions that embrace pure and simple business unionism accept the dominant capitalist ideology and work within the bounds of that worldview to improve the material interests of their members. Alternatively, unions that have a social movement orientation embrace class consciousness over job consciousness and seek not only to improve the well-being of individual union members but also to challenge social structures that produce and perpetuate inequality and injustice. Thus, for ideological reasons, some unions will be more likely than others to see climate change as a union issue.

To provide an overview of the current state of labor and climate that considers all of these factors, I create an illustration of what I will refer to throughout the book as the "labor–climate spectrum." The spectrum will situate unions by industry in relation to one another on the basis of their tendency to support either the Jobs vs. the Environment frame or the emerging Clean Air and Good Jobs counterframe. Why does the labor movement as a whole, through the AFL-CIO, espouse the views of the most conservative unions on the issue of climate change, shunning calls to meet scientifically informed targets for GHG emissions? Which unions are taking a more progressive stance and why? And how might the LCM shift the position of labor as a whole to shun the dominant Jobs vs. the Environment narrative and instead embrace the emerging counterframe of Clean Air and Good Jobs? These questions are explored in this chapter through the creation of the labor–climate spectrum.

The Labor-Climate Spectrum

Figure 3.1 presents the labor–climate spectrum.[1] To create the labor–climate spectrum, I classified the unions that participated in the three SMOs examined in this study into eight categories based on industries, and then I added an additional category representing union confederations.[2] Union confedera-

Progressiveness of Unions on Climate Change Issues, by Industry

Extraction / Building Trades / Confederations / Manufacturing / Public Sector / Education / Service Sector / Transportation / Healthcare

Jobs vs. Environment   •   *Clean Air and Good Jobs*

Figure 3.1 The Labor-Climate Spectrum

tions are umbrella labor organizations not rooted in any particular industry of employment but instead comprising workers and unions from each of the other categories; thus, they represent the dominant, "shared" position of the member unions. The nine categories, in alphabetical order, are building trades unions, education unions, extraction unions (mining and drilling), healthcare unions, manufacturing unions, public employee unions, service sector unions, transportation unions, and union confederations.

The placement of unions, by industry, along the axis in Figure 3.1 is based on a variety of sources, including public statements by union leaders, union resolutions, congressional testimonies, demands made at rallies, and other primary sources, such as union publications and emails to members. I also draw from my own personal experiences in the field as well as the history of labor and environmentalism presented in the previous chapter to inform the placement of each union category on the spectrum. Have these union categories mostly embraced the Jobs vs. the Environment master frame or the emerging counterframe of Clean Air and Good Jobs?

Perhaps not surprising to most readers, the extraction unions, which represent mining and drilling workers, are on the most conservative end of the spectrum, generally opposing efforts to reduce or limit GHG emissions. At the opposite extreme are the unions in the healthcare industry, which have taken a very progressive stance on climate issues in recent years, calling for strong emission-reduction targets and solutions that promote environmental and climate justice. The remaining unions fall along the spectrum between these two poles, with many supporting green growth but remaining silent on emission reductions.

The positions of the various union categories on the labor–climate spectrum are shaped in part by a variety of structural factors, including (1) the types of workers and the nature of work performed by union members in each industry, (2) the unique features of unions or unionization in each industry, and (3) each industry's relation to climate change and the effects of climate change on workers in the industry. The culture and ideology of various unions also play an important role, with a major distinction between the primarily business-oriented unions and those that espouse a more social movement union style. Let us look more closely at each in turn.

Extraction Unions

To begin with the most conservative unions on climate change, extraction unions represent blue-collar workers engaged directly in the mining of and drilling for fossil fuels such as coal and oil. The largest and most well-known unions in the extraction industries are the UMWA and the OCAW, which is now part of USW. Mining and oil worker unions began to form in the late 1800s in the United States, mostly in small towns and rural areas. Mining unions peaked at about five hundred thousand members in the 1930s but have been shrinking ever since, owing in part to the introduction of labor-saving technologies and the rise of cheaper energy sources such as natural gas, which have led to declining overall employment in the industry. Although union density in the mining industry stood at 12.5 percent in 2017, that represented just about six thousand unionized coal-mining jobs in the United States.[3] However, nearly one hundred thousand retired members of the UMWA rely on their union pensions to support their families and local economies. In the oil and gas extraction industry, union density was only 3.2 percent in 2017, with under three thousand workers unionized. In the growing offshore oil-drilling industry in the Gulf of Mexico and off the coast of California, the majority of oil rigs are operated by nonunion companies, many of which are foreign owned (Corgey 2010). Together, mining and oil union members, who are overwhelmingly white (85 percent) and male (88 percent), represent just a tiny percentage of the more than fourteen million American workers who belonged to unions in 2017.[4] Despite their relative size, extraction unions occupy a historically powerful position within labor and thus can wield disproportionate influence over the stance of labor as a whole on the issue of climate change.

In terms of climate change, it is difficult to imagine an industry that contributes more to GHG emissions than extraction does. Fossil fuels are the primary driver of global warming, and extraction workers are employed to uncover and dig up or drill for more fossil fuels to be used in the global economy. Greater fossil fuel use equates to economic prosperity for the industry and its workers but climate disaster for everyone—including the very workers employed in the industry. Despite the economic gains that greater extraction generates for mine and oil workers, they are not immune to the threats of climate change. Increased frequency and intensity of storms and greater incidence of extreme summer heat, floods, and wildfires make the already dangerous work of extraction even more dangerous and represent a clear example of what Jeremy Brecher (2017) has called climate alienation.

Even so, extraction unions have generally taken an anti–climate protection stance. For example, in response to the stricter GHG emission standards being proposed by the Obama administration in 2014, UMWA members rallied in opposition outside the EPA. "We are fighting for our livelihood," James Gibbs, an at-large vice president at UMWA, told the crowd. "We have to let the president know, we need to let both parties know that we will support candidates that support us" (Sheppard 2014). Many of them stayed true to their promise by helping to swing many Appalachian voting districts in 2016 in favor of Donald Trump, who had suggested that climate change was a hoax and promised to relax regulations and bring coal jobs back. In other words, the Jobs vs. the Environment master frame resonated deeply among extraction workers and their unions.

Given that many miners and former mine workers have blamed strict environmental regulations for the loss of jobs in the industry, it is not surprising that their unions oppose further environmental protections or only reluctantly support them when the alternative seems worse. For example, the 1990 Amendment to the Clean Air Act required reductions in acid rain, which causes sulfur emissions. Coal workers realized they needed coal plants to install scrubbers in their smokestacks or would risk being closed and replaced by plants that used alternative fuel sources. In this case, the unions supported legislation requiring the installation of scrubbers as a means of protecting jobs.

They were unsuccessful in their efforts and witnessed the loss of more than thirty thousand coal-mining jobs, which decimated dozens of mining communities across the economically depressed Appalachian and rural midwestern regions. Many workers blamed the environmental protection law for their job loss and continue to oppose environmental protection measures, seeing them as an attack on workers by "tree huggers." Industry executives fanned the flames of worker discontent by deriding "big government" interference in the market, a tactic that served their own deregulatory interests by further discouraging pro-environmental attitudes, values, and behaviors among workers.

Similarly, in response to the GHG emission-reduction targets embedded in various pieces of climate change legislation, such as the Clean Energy Jobs and American Power Act of 2009, coal-mining unions have supported the development of carbon capture and storage (CCS) technologies as a means of reducing carbon emissions while continuing to burn the most carbon-intensive fossil fuel, coal. Unfortunately, CCS technology is many years away from being a reality, its effectiveness is uncertain, and the projected costs make it an unlikely alternative to simply replacing existing coal plants with newer plants that use cheaper, less carbon-intensive fuel sources (Pires et al. 2011). For this reason, the pursuit of CCS as an answer to the climate change problem has largely been viewed by environmentalists and LCM activists as just a roadblock to pursuing real solutions to the problem and a means to justify carrying on with the status quo. However, the fossil fuel industry's hegemony over the U.S. energy sector has shaped the views of some workers and unions in the extractive industries regarding climate policy. As has been the case with other polluting industries in the past, extraction workers have been confronted with job blackmail and used by the fossil fuel industry and conservative politicians as the public face of opposition to environmental regulations.

Another feature of the extraction industry that makes workers particularly sensitive to job security issues is the rural, often remote location of the work. Because of their economic isolation, unemployed mine workers typically lack other good economic opportunities in their communities, which makes them fierce defenders of the mining jobs that do exist. However, because of this well-known structural problem, the difficulties faced by extraction workers and their unions are a major focus of LCM activists who want to protect the climate but also ensure that their fellow workers are taken care of economically. Even so, unsurprisingly, there was very little participation by extraction union members in the three SMOs examined in this study.

Owing to their relationship to fossil fuels and conservative stance on climate change, extraction unions are placed on the Jobs vs. the Environment side of the labor–climate spectrum in Figure 3.1. It is not surprising that mine workers and oil refinery employees are opposed to measures to reduce fossil fuel use. However, as was noted earlier, union policy is not mechanistically determined by capitalist dynamics or narrowly defined self-interest—one need only to look at OCAW policy in the Tony Mazzocchi era to find a shining exception to economic determinism (see Mazzocchi 1993). But nonetheless, on average, this category represents the most conservative pole on the labor–climate spectrum.

Building Trades Unions

Building trades unions are mostly in the construction industry but also within power plants and other parts of the energy production sector. This category includes unions such as IBEW; IUOE; LIUNA; International Association of Sheet Metal, Air, Rail and Transportation Workers (SMART); United Association of Plumbers and Pipefitters (UA); UBC; and the Boilermakers. Union density in the construction industry is currently around 14 percent, which is higher than the overall rate of union density in the private sector as a whole—

about 7 percent—but much lower than it was in the 1970s, when over 35 percent of construction workers were union members. The members of building trades unions are overwhelmingly blue-collar, skilled workers, and they are predominantly male (91 percent) and white (89 percent).

Several distinct characteristics of building trades unions distinguish them from most other unions. First, they are typically viewed as the more conservative wing of the American labor movement. The building trades unions are descendants of the craft unions of the nineteenth century, which are historically reminiscent of the old guild system. By design, these types of unions derive worker power by way of exclusion. By restricting the pool of workers eligible to perform certain types of skilled construction labor, members of craft unions build occupational power and increase their standard of living. This model of organizing has created a specific understanding of worker solidarity, which Selig Perlman (1949) refers to as "job consciousness" (as opposed to class consciousness), that typically prioritizes the well-being of their members over the broader working class. In other words, many building trades unions display the key characteristics of pure and simple business unionism, as described in Chapter 2.

A second distinct feature of the building trades unions is the relationship of their members to employers through the "hiring hall" structure. In commercial construction, employment is sporadic and can come in fits and starts, depending on the state of the local economy and level of public or private investment in construction projects. An average construction worker may work for two or three different employers in a given year and dozens over the course of their career. They may also spend several months of the year unemployed, waiting for a construction project to begin. Unlike other sectors of the labor movement, building trades unions serve as an employment service, connecting members looking for jobs with unionized construction companies looking to hire large numbers of skilled workers on short notice for temporary jobs. The workers in return are guaranteed the same union pay rate and benefits regardless of the employer and can carry their benefits with them seamlessly throughout their career from one employer to another. Unlike typical factory workers, who become union members by way of employment at a particular workplace and only maintain membership so long as they are employed by that company, construction workers are union members first and employees of a particular company second. In other words, they are connected to the labor market via the union hiring hall.[5]

The sporadic nature of construction work combined with the hiring hall structure creates an incentive for building trades unions to offer political support for any and all construction projects to secure adequate employment opportunities for their members—another example of job consciousness over class consciousness (Perlman 1949). If thousands of members are unemployed for long periods of time, they begin to question the usefulness of paying dues to the union. This leads building trades unions to have an all-of-the-above approach when it comes to supporting construction projects that will create jobs for their members. While other types of unions are obviously concerned with protecting their members' jobs and typically support efforts to increase investments in their industry, the endless quest to create new jobs for a rotating pool of unemployed members is central only to building trades unions.

This all-of-the-above approach often leads building trades unions to support projects that might otherwise be harmful to their members' communities—such as waste incinerators, casinos, and coal-fired power plants. Worse yet, these projects often tend to be situated in low-income, predominantly Black and brown communities, creating further friction between labor and environmental justice activists. Needless to say, the optics of predominantly white unions supporting the construction of polluting plants in communities of color in the name of jobs for their white members, who do not live in the community, have not helped other labor activists build relationships with their would-be allies in these communities.

The problem is further amplified when companies in polluting industries actively seek labor support for their unpopular projects by signing PLAs. A PLA, also referred to as a community workforce agreement, is a prehire collective bargaining agreement between construction companies and labor organizations that establishes the terms and conditions of employment for a specific construction project before it begins. For construction companies, it creates a broad base of support for their projects; for unions, it offers assurance that the jobs will be unionized once the project is approved.

As the threat of climate mitigation increasingly looms over the fossil fuel industry, oil and gas infrastructure companies have become increasingly supportive of signing PLAs with building trades unions to garner their powerful political support for projects that would face another form of organized political opposition: the environmental movement. While PLAs themselves are not inherently a bad thing—they certainly help ensure that labor gets a fair share of the pie—their increased weaponization by employers to effectively hire unions as an antienvironmental political army has led to several Jobs vs. the Environment clashes, such as those associated with various pipeline projects in recent years. If renewable energy companies were to sign PLAs with building trades unions as often as fossil fuel companies do, a powerful pro-green political alliance could be built to turn the tide of labor support away from fossil fuel projects.

The economic influence of large employers has led many building trades unions to become junior partners to capital as they drum up political support for their construction projects—such as fossil fuel pipelines. Large corporations often promote the narrative that blue-collar workers are the real beneficiaries of their projects. Using workers in public testimony and advertisements certainly makes for a better public relations campaign than persuading people of wealthy investors' need to earn profits, especially when a given project may be unpopular for reasons such as pollution. Coincidentally, building trades unions (along with mine worker unions) are perhaps the most common image of organized labor that is used by the mainstream media when they cover labor issues. As we will see, that image is rather outdated because the majority of the labor movement comprises workers in other industries, such as education, healthcare, and various parts of the public sector.

In terms of climate change, construction unions have often espoused blue–green tendencies by supporting environmentally friendly projects that create jobs, but they also support projects that build and maintain all aspects of the fossil fuel energy system, which also creates jobs. Aside from the economic benefits, building trades union members also face several immediate and long-term threats from climate change. In addition to the general risks of extreme weather (particularly heat), property damage, and health-related problems that all workers face, the industry itself faces a unique set of challenges, including a decline in new construction projects in regions prone to extreme weather, such as coastal states, and the likely relocation of construction projects to regions where climate threats are perceived to be less severe. These relocations tend to be away from the highly unionized coastal states to the less unionized southern and inland states, a prospect that some coastal unions are beginning to acknowledge (Fatton 2017).

Despite these threats to their members, building trades unions have predominantly taken a Jobs vs. the Environment stance when it comes to climate change, generally opposing GHG emission-reduction targets and promoting fossil fuel expansion. For example, they have strongly supported projects that expand oil extraction and consumption, such as the Keystone XL and Dakota Access pipelines. They also support the expansion of natural gas pipelines and the construction of natural gas power plants—which have been shown to be even larger contributors to climate change than previously thought, owing to the added contribution of methane gas to global warming. However, as a result of their all-of-the-above pro-growth agenda, building trades unions have also supported large renewable energy projects in some regions. One good example of this is the construction of the Block Island Wind Farm—America's first offshore wind farm. In that project, the Rhode Island building trades unions worked closely with environmentalists and renewable energy activists to win legislative approval in the face of opposition from some coastal property owners.

It is important to note that despite the opposition to climate protection at the national level, particular locals of some building trades unions have taken more pro-climate stances in pursuit of green growth opportunities that would create jobs for members. For example, UBC and IBEW locals in states such as Connecticut, Massachusetts, New Jersey, and New York are currently following the lead of Block Island by pursuing similar and larger offshore wind projects in their states, including mandates for a certain percentage of all electricity to be generated by renewables in the case of Connecticut. However, these efforts are largely instrumental in nature and thus have been geographically limited to areas where opportunities to create jobs in the renewable energy sector are more politically viable.

Other locals have taken steps that appear to go beyond mere instrumentality. For example, IBEW Local 3 in New York City dedicated its summer education program in 2016 to the topic of "A Cry for the Climate," and over 2,400 members and retirees attended. Several IBEW locals in California, including Local 11, have taken bold steps such as opening a state-of-the-art clean energy technology training center for workers and supporting the expansion of community-choice aggregation, which allows cities to come together to procure their own electricity and determine their own renewable portfolio mix. Climate Jobs New York—a coalition of labor unions representing 2.6 million workers—has begun to press not only for strong labor standards in the renewable industry and new investments in green infrastructure but also for transition protections to assist displaced fossil fuel workers and for targeted investments in historically marginalized communities. Together, these actions in the Northeast and on the West Coast stand in stark contrast to the stance of other building trades locals in parts of the country where members are largely employed in the operation and maintenance of coal-fired and natural gas power plants.

Because of their generally conservative stance on climate change, building trades unions are placed on the Jobs vs. the Environment side of the labor–climate spectrum in Figure 3.1. As the descendants of the original craft unions, the building trades typify the ideal type of pure and simple business unionism. As a result of the history of gender and racial exclusion in America, the trades generally lack diversity in their ranks and have typically espoused a conservative political action plan relative to many other unions—especially on the issue of climate protection. Along with extraction unions, the building trades wield disproportionate influence over the position of labor as a whole regarding climate change—although I note that some efforts, such as Climate Jobs

New York and the Climate Jobs National Resource Center, suggest a fissure emerging in this traditionally strong pillar of support for fossil fuels. While some legislative wins have been made in Illinois and New York, it remains unclear whether the industrial category of the building trades is shifting closer to the Clean Air and Good Jobs side of the spectrum.

Manufacturing Unions

Manufacturing unions represent workers in large and small factories producing products as diverse as automobiles, crayons, jet engines, toothpaste, brake pads, vacuum cleaners, fuel cells, and various products for the defense industry, including nuclear submarines, fighter jets, aircraft carriers, and helicopters. The current unionization rate in manufacturing is just under 9 percent, down from 38 percent in the 1970s. This decline is due largely to decades of deindustrialization that have shifted many nondefense manufacturing jobs overseas, where companies can take advantage of low wages and lax labor and environmental laws. The increase in automation and robots in many industries has also taken its toll on manufacturing employment. Still, over one million manufacturing workers belong to unions in the United States. The major manufacturing unions in the United States are IAM; UAW; United Electrical, Radio and Machine Workers of America (UE); USW; and some others. Manufacturing workers are overwhelmingly male (70 percent) and white (80 percent), but a growing percentage of manufacturing workers are Hispanic (17 percent).

Manufacturing unions were one of the great advocates for and beneficiaries of the National Labor Relations Act of 1935, the centerpiece of twentieth-century U.S. private sector labor law. The industrial model of unionism that took hold in the manufacturing industry was markedly different from the old craft and skilled trades unions. Industrial unions sought to organize all workers within a given workplace or plant, regardless of their skill level. Worker power was not derived from exclusion or a monopoly on much-needed skills but rather on solidarity in threatening to withhold work and stop production. This model of organizing is the hallmark of almost all categories of unions described in this chapter except for the building trades, who, as noted above, descended from the craft union tradition that became the basis for pure and simple business unionism. Industrial unions were also organized at particular workplaces rather than through the hiring hall model that encompassed multiple employers.

For workers in the manufacturing industry, climate change poses several distinct threats, including increased heat in already-hot factories, shortages of some raw materials that can drive up production costs and reduce consumer demand, and further outsourcing of jobs to lower-risk localities. As rising sea levels and extreme weather threaten existing plants, one ill-timed superstorm can be the final straw that pushes employers to close up shop and relocate. General relocations of plants from storm-ravaged areas, even if to other areas within the United States, are typically accompanied by deunionization, which further limits labor's voice in addressing climate change. The U.S. export industry also counts on trade partners to purchase goods that are made in America, but many countries that are net importers of U.S. goods are also threatened with climate change, which could undermine existing trade patterns. On the other hand, climate mitigation efforts represent opportunities for the manufacturing of new green technologies in the United States, thus increasing the workforce size and bargaining power of manufacturing workers.

As for addressing climate change, manufacturing unions can be either for or against climate change policy for various reasons. On the one hand, many manufacturing unions fear that increased energy costs resulting from climate change mitigation policies will hurt the competitive position of their industries. For instance, manufacturing unions in the Midwest—a region that depends heavily on coal-fired power plants for cheap energy and coal-fired blast furnaces to produce steel—worry that restrictions on coal use will force more jobs overseas. Unions representing workers producing components used in conventional power generation or by the extraction industry or oil pipeline industry have been more reluctant to support climate protection measures. In the auto industry, workers who manufacture trucks have been opposed to stricter vehicle emission standards because they see trucks as one of the only auto product categories where consumers overwhelmingly purchase American-made brands, although electric trucks are beginning to appear in consumer markets. Further, a large variety of manufactured goods are plastic products whose prime ingredient is derived from oil. For these unions, efforts to move away from fossil fuels are seen as a direct threat to their jobs, and thus they have been reluctant to support climate protection measures.

On the other hand, manufacturing unions also represent many of the workers who build wind turbines, solar panels, batteries and energy storage components, and fuel cells used to combat climate change, making them strong supporters of green growth investments. Others employed in export industries are aware of the stricter environmental standards in other countries that necessitate greener manufacturing in order to compete in these foreign markets. For example, the UAW, while at first resistant to higher fuel-efficiency standards, eventually came around to supporting corporate average fuel economy standards so U.S. companies could remain competitive with imported brands and compete in overseas markets where fuel-efficiency standards are even more stringent. Some manufacturing unions are actively promoting government green growth programs to create jobs producing new products for the green economy, and many have taken a concrete stance on the issue of climate change. For example, in 1990, the USW recognized global warming as "the most important environmental issue of our lifetime," and it has cooperated extensively with the Sierra Club ever since, cofounding the BlueGreen Alliance—a coalition of labor and environmental groups advocating for green jobs—in 2006. After the United States withdrew from the Paris Climate Accord, USW president Leo Gerard (2017) said, "The USW supports job creation. But the union believes clean air pays; clear water provides work. Engineers design smokestack scrubbers, skilled mechanics construct them, and still other workers install them. Additional workers install insulation and solar panels. Untold thousands labor to make the steel and other parts for wind turbine blades, towers and nacelles, fabricate the structures, and erect them." As described by Gerard, green investments are often seen as a means of bolstering domestic manufacturing jobs.

Overall, manufacturing unions have had a mixed message on climate change, in part because of the diverse nature of products made by unionized workers, which often creates competing interests within the major manufacturing unions. Owing to their history, level of diversity, and divided stance on climate change, manufacturing unions are placed squarely in the center of the labor–climate spectrum in Figure 3.1.[6]

Public Employee Unions

This category includes all public sector unions not in the education or transportation fields, which are examined separately. The public employee unions in this category represent government employees at the municipal, county, state, and federal levels. These union members perform various types of work and range from blue-collar maintenance workers in city park departments to white-collar professionals and scientists at the EPA, letter carriers employed by the U.S. Postal Service, and professional firefighters in cities across the United States.[7] Some of the major public sector unions are American Federation of Government Employees (AFGE); AFSCME; American Postal Workers Union (APWU); and Communication Workers of America (CWA). Service Employees International Union (SEIU) also has many public sector union locals in addition to their healthcare and service sector unions. Public sector union members work for sanitation departments, social service agencies, local post offices, state highway departments, public school districts, and more. Public sector workers have a union membership rate of 35 percent, which is significantly higher than the 6 percent unionization rate in the private sector (Hirsch and Macpherson 2017). More than one million federal government workers, two million state government workers, and four million local government workers are represented by unions. Public employees are roughly evenly divided along gender lines and are relatively diverse, with about 17 percent of public workers identifying as Black and 12 percent Hispanic (U.S. BLS 2018a).

The precursors to modern public sector unions began to form in the late 1800s and early 1900s, but the majority of public sector unions were not allowed to bargain contracts in the United States until the 1960s. Wisconsin became the first state to pass legislation allowing collective bargaining for state and municipal workers in 1959. Federal employees, who were excluded from the National Labor Relations Act of 1935, were first granted the right to collective bargaining by an executive order issued by President Kennedy in 1962. This executive order spurred the passage of more favorable collective bargaining laws at the state level throughout the country and fueled the growth of unionization for state, county, and municipal workers. For this reason, the majority of existing public sector unions were formed in the 1970s. However, many states have never authorized public sector bargaining, or they restrict the right to only certain categories of workers, such as teachers or police officers.

In relation to climate change, many public sector jobs are directly related to protecting the environment. From state and federal environmental protection agencies to park rangers and natural resource managers, many public employees have a strong interest in addressing the problem of climate change. Some public workers at the EPA under the Bush and Trump administrations have faced gag orders and punishment for trying to inform the American public about the science of climate change. Public sector workers also experience many direct consequences of climate change. For example, postal workers and firefighters are facing increased incidence of heatstroke on the job because their workplaces are vulnerable to heat waves and other extreme weather (Irons 2013; Miller 2015).

Further, the public costs of dealing with increased forest fires, coastal flooding, heat waves, hurricanes, and drinking-water shortages will increase budget pressures at all levels of the government. Reduced tax revenues from closed resorts and parks, reduced real estate values, and increased insurance rates will further strain budgets. The impact of these budget pressures on workers in the public sector is likely to include extensive layoffs, permanent downsizing, further pressure on wages and benefits, work speedups, and deteriorating working conditions. Budget shortfalls also reduce the bargaining power of public sector unions by reducing the funds available to governments to allocate for labor contracts.

For these reasons and others, many public sector unions have supported climate protection measures and begun to take political action on climate change. For example, in 2008 AFSCME passed a resolution on global warming and green jobs that called for "federal legislation to reduce national GHG emissions to levels consistent with the recommendations from the IPCC." These recommendations urge "60 to 90 percent reductions of GHG emissions from 1990 levels by the year 2050 in order to avoid the worst and most costly impacts of climate change" (AFSCME 2008). In their climate action plan, the union resolved to support "state and local government agencies to accelerate and expand their commitment to GHG emission-reduction programs and encourage them to include specifications for public contracts to include equitable opportunities for green jobs among historically disadvantaged communities, fair wages and benefits for workers, and preference for unionized, local firms" (AFSCME 2010). The union acted on this resolution by joining with the California Wind Energy Association, the Sierra Club, and the American Lung Association to support the passage of SBX1-2, a law that required 33 percent of the state's energy to come from renewable sources by 2020. The CWA endorsed and turned out a large number of members for the People's Climate March in Washington, DC, in April 2017, and other public sector unions, such as AFGE, helped organize the national March for Science later that same month.

Because of their relatively progressive-leaning stance on climate change, public employee unions are placed on the Clean Air and Good Jobs side of the labor–climate spectrum in Figure 3.1. Public sector unions took hold in the 1970s and have represented a relatively diverse membership. They have also been relatively supportive of measures to promote the common good, such as addressing climate change, but in the face of aggressive attacks on their bargaining rights by Republican governors and legislatures in recent years, much of their attention has been diverted from issues such as climate change to the more pressing matter of protecting their right to exist. Nonetheless, public sector unions have been among those most likely to espouse the features of social movement unionism in the United States.

Education Unions

A broad number of workers are unionized in the public sector; however, the size of education unions and the coherent nature of their industry prompted me to consider them apart from other public employee unions, which are discussed as a separate category. Education unions represent workers in primary, secondary, and postsecondary education. Examples of education unions include American Association of University Professors (AAUP); AFT; and National Education Association (NEA). The two largest national unions, NEA (3 million workers) and AFT (1.7 million workers) together represent more than 4.5 million workers. Around 38 percent of primary and secondary school teachers are unionized, and about 14 percent of postsecondary educators belong to unions. Taken together, education workers represent one of the largest groups of organized workers in the country.

The earliest education unions formed around the turn of the twentieth century, but these precursors to the modern teachers' unions were not granted the right to bargain collectively until some state and local governments passed public sector labor laws in the 1960s and 1970s.[8] Prior to collective bargaining, teacher associations worked largely through the political process to effect change in their industry. However, once granted the right to bargain, teachers unionized rapidly. The majority of teachers' union locals, which typically operate at the school district level or university level, were formed in the 1970s. As part of the education field, these unions represent a highly skilled, highly educated, white-collar segment of the labor force and have a larger than average representation of female workers (75 percent in primary and secondary and 54 percent in postsecondary).

When it comes to climate change, the work of educators is not directly tied to fossil fuel extraction or consumption and thus contributes little to climate change beyond the GHGs released from commuting to work and using electricity while there. For this reason, teachers, along with healthcare workers and service workers, are often seen as playing an important part in the future low-carbon economy that is needed to avert the worst of climate change. Also, many who teach social sciences, arts, and humanities are already favorably inclined toward addressing climate change. In addition, of course, educators at a minimum have a bachelor's degree and often a master's degree, which predisposes them to have favorable views toward environmental policies. Further, many education union members are scientists or science teachers and are well informed about climate change, including its causes, effects, and possible solutions. In fact, many teachers are responsible for teaching students about climate science as part of their jobs.

The direct effect of climate change on education workers includes the deterioration of healthy and comfortable teaching environments resulting from increasing temperatures, rising water levels, mold in buildings, and increased incidence of disease and illness. For example, the prevalence of asthma and other breathing conditions among students has skyrocketed in recent years, particularly in older, deteriorating schools, which are often in poor urban or rural school districts. The pressures of climate change on local budgets also challenge the ability of teachers' unions to bargain for collective gains and potentially exacerbate the already-existing problems of crumbling school infrastructure and increasing class sizes.

Overall, education unions have communicated a pro-climate stance, but they have just begun to take action on the issue. At the national level, AFT adopted a strong resolution on climate change, and NEA adopted a resolution on teaching climate justice in classrooms (AFT 2012; Bigelow 2016). In 2020, AFT became the fourth national union, after SEIU, the Association of Flight Attendants-CWA, and National Nurses United (NNU), to endorse the Green New Deal. And in 2022, the AFT further resolved to divest pensions and retirement funds from fossil fuels and reinvest them in workers and communities. NEA and AFT both participate in the Coalition for Green Schools, which also includes the Parent Teacher Association and the U.S. Green Building Council. The goal of the initiative is to secure investment in new school infrastructure, which will provide a healthy environment conducive to learning, reduce energy costs, and reduce pollution, including GHG emissions. The green schools initiative is also a vehicle for job creation. NEA has pointed out that "an initial $50 billion school renovation program would employ 500,000 workers—a third of the 1.5 million construction workers that are currently unemployed" (NEA, n.d.). However, beyond stating an opinion or joining a group effort, the majority of tangible efforts by education unions to address climate change have occurred at the local level in particular geographic regions, such as the West Coast and the Northeast. State and local education unions have supported the adoption of state- and municipal-level legislation to reduce GHG emissions and have also led efforts for school districts to purchase scientifically accurate textbooks that adequately consider the breadth and depth of the problem of climate change.

Beyond climate change, education unions more generally have been at the forefront of BCG campaigns in recent years, espousing social movement union characteristics by partnering with community organizations and fighting for broad social demands such as divestment from private prisons, diversity in hiring, healthy food and green spaces for students, noncooperation with Immigration and Customs Enforcement, community jobs programs, community gardens, reduced standardized testing for kids, free public transportation for students, and affordable housing in overpriced housing markets. The successful strike by the Chicago Teachers Union in 2012 inspired a strike wave of teachers throughout the country making broad demands to protect public education. The recent strike by members of the United Teachers of Los Angeles in January 2019 provides a great example of what common good bargaining looks like in action. The union partnered with parents, students, and allied community organizations such as the Association of Californians for Community Empowerment to tackle issues at the heart of public education and central to the working-class communities the school district serves. The teachers won commitments from the school district to reduce class sizes, increase investment in the schools, hire school nurses and full-time librarians, reduce standardized testing and random searches of students, provide more green spaces for students, and launch a dedicated hotline for immigrant families who need legal assistance. In 2022, the union and community partners introduced an entire article into bargaining elaborating the elements of healthy green schools, including electric bus fleets, renewable energy, and free public transportation.

Owing to their low-carbon intensity, relatively high levels of diversity, and progressive-leaning stance on climate change, education unions are placed on the Clean Air and Good Jobs side of the labor–climate spectrum in Figure 3.1. Teachers' unions are increasingly diverse and are largely composed of women. They also represent highly educated workers who have shown great support for climate protection measures relative to many other unions. The category is placed about halfway between the center and the right border of the spectrum, indicating that the union has voiced support for climate protection, but it has just begun to take action and appears to be moving further toward the Clean Air and Good Jobs side of the spectrum.

Service Sector Unions

The service sector has been the fastest-growing area of the U.S. economy for decades, currently comprising about twenty-three million workers. Much of the service sector consists of typically low-paying jobs such as clerks; custodians; hotel and food service workers; call center workers; taxi drivers; fast-food workers; entertainment, travel, and leisure industry workers; and big box store employees, but the sector does include many higher-end service jobs such as flight attendants, estate managers, financial service agents, and private chefs. The growth of low-paying service sector work in the shadow of declining manufacturing jobs sparked a massive expansion of service sector unions throughout the 1990s. Some of the major service sector unions in the United States are SEIU; United Food and Commercial Workers (UFCW); and Union of Needletrades, Industrial, and Textile Employees–Hotel Employees and Restaurant Employees (UNITE-HERE). CWA and the Teamsters unions have also increased their share of service sector union members in recent years. Currently, service sector workers consist of roughly 50 percent women, over 12 percent Black, and over 20 percent Hispanic.

Many jobs in this industry have proven difficult to organize for a variety of reasons, including aggressive anti-unionism by large employers such as Walmart. Another impediment to unionization in this sector, particularly in the fast-food industry, is the joint employer nature of employment. Most fast-food chain restaurants are locally owned by franchisees but are required to follow strict guidelines, including those concerning employment issues, that are laid out by the corporate office. The National Labor Relations Board has been modifying its rules on this issue for several years—in particular, determining who should be deemed "the employer" for the sake of bargaining. Many other elements of the service sector have been moved from the traditional employment relationship into the gig economy, where companies such as Uber hire drivers as independent contractors. Altogether, about 2.7 million workers in the service sector are unionized, but this constitutes only about 4 percent of workers in the industry, and unionization is uneven across different service industries. For example, about 15 percent of grocery store employees belong to unions, but only 1.5 percent of restaurant workers are unionized. Although the recent wave of new union organizing by service workers at employers such as Starbucks, Chipotle, and Trader Joes is challenging this status quo.

Most service industries are not major direct contributors to climate change, at least not as clearly as the building trades or extraction industries. However, some services, such as air travel, vehicle rentals, and some forms of tourism rely heavily on fossil fuel consumption and as such contribute to GHG emissions. Many other services, such as retail sales, play a more indirect role in the climate problem because most of the carbon footprint for merchandise is created long before the store clerk scans it at the point of sale. Other service industries, such as weatherization, energy efficiency, resource conservation, and retail sale of sustainable technologies like solar panels and electric cars are actually directly involved in combating climate change.

As for the impact of climate change on service workers, it is already having a negative effect on some segments of the service sector, including tourism, food service, and commodity sales. Extreme weather has led to the destruction of many resort and vacation facilities. Receding beachfronts mean less coastal tourism. Climatic shifts that lead to deforestation, wildlife migration, and expanded mating seasons for mosquitos, ticks, and other insects that carry vector-borne viruses have affected wilderness tourism. The effects of droughts on agriculture are harmful for food service workers because the price of basic ingredients increases, pressing employers to squeeze their already low-paid workforce even further. Off the job, many low-paid service sector workers live in areas that have already been subject to a history of environmental injustice and are likely to experience the worst consequences of climate change as well.

As a result, some service sector unions have begun to engage with the issue of climate justice. For example, when SEIU's property services Local 32BJ in New York learned that 40 percent of carbon emissions in the city come from buildings—much of it from commercial real estate operated, maintained, and cleaned by their members—the union responded by pioneering programs in green building management. Their 1,000 Green Supers program helps "ensure the gains made through retrofits are fully realized by a well-trained property services workforce" (quoted in Brecher 2017, 41). California Local 1000 proposed the creation of a Joint Labor–Management Committee on Greenhouse Gas Emissions Reduction during bargaining in 2008. Other service sector unions such as the CWA District 1 and Teamsters Joint Council 16 also played a central role in helping to organize and coordinate labor's participation in the historic People's Climate March in New York City in September 2014. SEIU was the first national union to endorse the Green New Deal, taking a stance directly opposed to that of the extraction and building trades unions.

More recently, on February 27, 2020, more than four thousand unionized janitors working at high-rise towers in Minneapolis—members of SEIU Local 26—went on strike demanding not only that wages and working conditions improve but also that their employers take action on climate change. Working with partners from Minnesota Youth Climate Strike, Environment Minnesota, the 100% Campaign, MN350, the North Star Chapter of the Sierra Club, and the Minnesota Black, Indigenous, and People of Color Climate and Environmental Justice Table, the union presented a set of climate justice demands to the commercial building owners they worked for. The demands included creation of an Owner and Community Green Table; closure of the Hennepin Energy Recovery Center incinerator, a major source of both GHGs and air pollution that harms nearby communities of color; and adoption of the union's proposed Green Cleaning Training program.

Because of their progressive-leaning stance on climate change, service sector unions are placed on the Clean Air and Good Jobs side of the labor–climate spectrum in Figure 3.1. Along with education and healthcare unions, service sector unions represent the growing low-carbon, reproductive workforce that will be needed for "caring and repairing" in a zero-emissions society. They are also newer unions with many women and nonwhite members—including many who have experienced environmental injustice. Through various public statements, including the SEIU endorsement of the Green New Deal, workplace initiatives such as the 1,000 Green Supers program, and participation in rallies and marches such as the People's Climate March, service sector unions have clearly displayed a Clean Air and Good Jobs frame and represent challengers to the dominant Jobs vs. the Environment narrative. While many elements of the service sector union movement have embraced climate justice and are working to achieve it (and none have opposed it), many unions have not yet engaged with the issue in a meaningful way, but along with the education unions, they appear to be moving closer to the Clean Air and Good Jobs side of the spectrum.

Transportation Unions

Transportation unions represent workers who drive buses, operate trains, pilot commercial airplanes, work in subway systems, and drive delivery trucks. Some of the major transportation unions are the Teamsters, ATU, TWU, and United Transportation Union (UTU). The earliest unionization efforts by transport workers date back to the 1800s, when commodities were transported by horse-drawn wagons—hence the name Teamsters. Various railway unions, such as American Railroad Union (ARU), organized by Eugene Debs, were formed in the late nineteenth century. The oldest continuously operating transportation union, the Teamsters, was formed in 1903. Overall union density in the transportation industry is much higher than in the economy as a whole. Almost 25 percent of all transport workers are unionized. To look more closely, 74 percent of railroad workers, 50 percent of airline workers, and 20 percent of local truck drivers are unionized. Some sectors, however, such as long-haul trucking, are virtually nonunion at this point in history.[9] Overall, transportation workers are predominantly men (75 percent) but diverse racially, with 20 percent identifying as Black and 18 percent Hispanic.

Transportation unions are generally organized at the workplace or employer level, with all of the workers employed by a particular transportation company or its local operation, constituting a bargaining unit. In some companies, such as the United Parcel Service, all drivers throughout the United States are part of a union and are covered by one master contract nationally, whereas for others, such as Coca-Cola Bottling, the drivers at some local distribution centers have unions and those at other centers do not. Unions in the railroad and airline industry are governed by their own national labor law, called the Railway Labor Act, which is separate from the National Labor Relations Act and attempts to avoid strikes in these industries by settling labor disputes through bargaining, mediation, and arbitration. Some transportation workers are public employees of public transit systems, and others are employed by quasi-public corporations like Amtrak, but most are employed in the private sector.

In terms of climate change, transportation is the second-biggest contributor to GHG emissions, after electricity generation. Transportation in the United States produces more GHGs than any other country's total emissions from all sectors, except China. Globally, transportation makes up about 29 percent of all GHG emissions annually; of that amount, the United States is wholly responsible for one-third. About half of all transportation emissions in the United States come from commercial transportation—trucks, planes, ships, rail, and buses. The other half comes from private automobiles, which reflects the huge underinvestment in affordable public transportation in the United States (Wright and Rogers 2015). Serious efforts to combat climate change must include changes in the transportation and logistics industries and will have major impacts—both positive and negative—on employment in key industries. Unions representing transportation workers in trucking, rail, ports, buses, mass transit, and airlines will have to confront these changes. The 2008 spike in fuel prices provided an indication of the type of changes that could occur: airlines and trucking companies cut back, while rail traffic and mass transit ridership increased.

Some transportation unions such as TWU and ATU have taken a firm stand on climate change, issuing a joint statement in 2011 saying, "We need jobs, but not ones based on increasing our reliance on tar sands oil." The statement called for major New Deal–type public investments in infrastructure modernization and repair, energy conservation, and climate protection as a means of "putting people to work and laying the foundations of a green and sustainable economic future for the United States" (Brown 2011). This stance put them squarely at odds with the leadership of some building trades unions who were at that time lobbying for approval of the Keystone XL pipeline project to carry tar sands oil from Alberta, Canada, to refineries on the U.S. Gulf Coast. In a resolution adopted at the 58th national convention in 2016, ATU stated:

> Transit can reduce greenhouse gas emissions by providing a low emissions alternative to driving, facilitating compact development, and minimizing the carbon footprint of its operations. As urban populations spike, members of the millennial generation are discovering that they prefer to get around a city by public transportation. As the largest labor union representing transit workers in North America, ATU can play a huge role in advocating for more sustainable transit—saving our jobs and our planet at the same time. (ATU 2016)

It is also worth noting that the late president of ATU, Larry Hanley, made the issue of climate change a key part of his vision for the organization. The rise of activist leaders such as Hanley can often lead unions to shift away from business unionism and move toward social movement unionism (Voss and Sherman 2000).

At the start of 2018, ATU also spearheaded Transit Equity Day, on the birthday of Rosa Parks, as a national day of action to demand equal access to public transportation as a civil rights and climate justice issue. After years of supporting the opening of Alaska's National Wildlife Refuge to oil drilling, the Teamsters changed direction to oppose it and then joined the BlueGreen Alliance, stating that "global warming is for real" and that "we let the big corporations pollute and the jobs went overseas anyway. We didn't enforce environmental regulations and the economy still went in the toilet. . . . ENOUGH IS ENOUGH! No more false divides. The future, if we are to prosper as a nation, will lie in a green economy" (Pope 2008). Because of their progressive-leaning stance on climate change, transportation unions are placed on the Clean Air and Good Jobs side of the labor–climate spectrum in Figure 3.1.

Healthcare Unions

I move now to the most progressive unions on climate change. Healthcare unions represent workers employed in the healthcare industry, such as nurses, health technicians, and doctors. Currently, 18 percent of registered nurses are union members, and around 8 percent of physicians are unionized (Hirsch and Macpherson 2017). Together, over one million healthcare workers are organized, and the major unions they belong to include SEIU District 1199, NYSNA, and California Nurses Association (CNA; now known as National Nurses United, or NNU). AFT also has many healthcare locals in addition to their education unions. Early healthcare unions date back to the early twentieth century, but unionization in the industry really took off in the 1960s and 1970s, in conjunction with the growth of employer-based health insurance plans and greater consumer demand for healthcare. Unlike the building trades and extraction unions, healthcare workers are overwhelmingly women (78 percent) and are a diverse group, with 17 percent identifying as Black and 13 percent Hispanic (U.S. BLS 2018a). All have at least an associate's degree, and many have a bachelor's or more advanced degree, making them a highly educated segment of the workforce.

Healthcare unions operate in both the private and public sectors and so are governed by a myriad of labor laws. Some states do not allow public sector healthcare workers to engage in collective bargaining, while others only allow some categories of workers to bargain and classify some workers—such as doctors—as managers. This leads to tremendous geographic diversity in organizing patterns, with strong healthcare unions in California, New York, and parts of New England but practically none in the South. Unions are typically organized at the facility or network level, with all workers of a certain job classification or occupation, such as nurses, within a particular hospital or hospital system organized in local unions.

As for climate change, these workers, who are largely employed in hospitals, community health centers, and clinics, confront the impact of climate change through the hastening spread of infectious disease, waterborne and foodborne pathogens, and health conditions related to air pollution. They are also responsible for caring for and treating patients affected by environmentally related health conditions, such as asthma, allergies, cardiovascular diseases, heatstroke, and other adverse conditions brought on by climate change and related pollutants. Members of healthcare unions also contend with the aftermath and injuries from traumatic events related to the increased frequency and intensity of extreme weather events and natural disasters.

For these reasons, healthcare unions have been proactive on the issues of climate change and climate justice. This should not be surprising because these unions are also among the most progressive in the labor movement, pushing for single-payer healthcare, supporting the Occupy Wall Street movement, and some endorsing Senator Bernie Sanders of Vermont for president early in the 2016 Democratic Party primary election. NNU, for example, has supported legislation to ban hydraulic fracturing—or fracking—for fossil fuels, stating that "drilling and fracking for oil and gas comes with inherent risks to public health and must be banned to safeguard public health, especially that of children, who are most vulnerable" (*Akron Beacon Journal* 2012). The nurses have also promoted a Robin Hood tax as a means to generate government funding for a transition to a green economy. "The Robin Hood tax can fund the transition to a nonfossil fuel–based economy. Wall Street reaps billions from oil companies; it's time for them to pay us back—to address the effects of climate change and support a sustainable economy. Green manufacturing, clean energy, and mass transit, funded by a tax on Wall Street transactions, would make the development of the tar sands and the Keystone XL pipelines unnecessary" (DeMoro 2015). Unsurprisingly, healthcare union leaders and members were involved with the SMOs in this study at all levels—locally, nationally, and internationally.

Interestingly, the adverse effects of climate change can actually lead to a greater demand for the services provided by healthcare workers. In other words, climate change could actually create more healthcare jobs, yet the nurses' unions instead see that their mission is to protect the health of the public—not increase their share of employment. However, as others have noted, healthcare, along with education and services, also represents a relatively low-carbon component of the U.S. economy, and employment in this industry could be expanded as part of a "caring and repairing" economy to supplant the existing extractive economy that consumes finite resources and causes ecological crises, such as climate change. With the aging of the baby boomer generation, the demand for health services is sure to increase. However, owing to the history of patriarchy and the overrepresentation of female workers in this industry, healthcare labor is typically undervalued and suffers a disparity of bargaining power compared with the more blue-collar, male-dominated industries. Further unionization remains the single best vehicle for increased wages and benefits for the healthcare industry.

Because of their low-carbon intensity, high level of diversity, and progressive stance on climate change, healthcare unions are placed on the Clean Air and Good Jobs side of the labor–climate spectrum in Figure 3.1. Despite the "craft" nature of most nurses' unions, they represent the most progressive pole on the spectrum of union categories considered in this chapter, making them the strongest challengers to the dominant frame within the labor–climate spectrum. This category also provides a clear example of the distinction between the ideal type of business unionism versus that of social unionism: if healthcare workers were exclusively self-interested, they might embrace climate change and environmental disasters on the grounds that they would increase the demand for their labor.

Union Confederations

Finally, union confederations are umbrella organizations with which unions in a geographically defined area may choose to affiliate in order to build cross-sector solidarity and increase worker power for collective actions and legislative efforts. For most intents and purposes, they are viewed as representatives of the will of labor as a whole within a defined geographic boundary. Examples of union confederations include central labor councils, which typically operate at the metropolitan or county level and are composed of union locals; state federations ("state feds"), which operate at the state level and typically include local-, state-, or regional-level unions; and the AFL-CIO, which is a confederation of national-level unions. Union confederations often take stances on political and economic issues based on the interests of their member unions. However, since these confederations rely on voluntary membership dues to operate, they are often at the mercy of any one union or group of unions either promoting or vetoing a stance on a particular issue by threatening to exit and become unaffiliated. The importance of this structural feature of union confederations will become apparent as we examine the efforts of climate activists within the U.S. labor movement.

In the United States today, the largest national union confederation is the AFL-CIO, which comprises fifty-five national unions and represents some 12.5 million workers in almost all industries. Most major unions mentioned above are affiliated with the AFL-CIO, with a handful of notable exceptions. Aside from many small or local-level unions that are independent of the AFL-CIO, the following influential national unions are not affiliated with the confederation: International Longshore and Warehouse Union (ILWU), SEIU, the Teamsters, and UBC. Several large unions, such as LIUNA, SEIU, UBC, and UFCW, broke away from the AFL-CIO in 2005 to form a separate confederation called Change to Win, but that confederation has since eroded, and most unions, aside from those listed previously, have returned to the AFL-CIO. The building trades unions have their own national-level confederation in the United States, North America's Building Trades Unions (NABTU), which, as a block, has significant influence within the AFL-CIO.

Union confederations date back to the earliest days of unionism in America. The AFL was formed in 1886 and operated as an independent labor confederation until 1955, when it merged with the CIO. The early AFL consisted overwhelmingly of skilled white male workers from the dominant craft unions of the era. Unskilled workers, African Americans, and women were generally excluded from the AFL, which saw them as a threat to jobs because they were typically paid lower wages.[10] As a result, the early AFL provided little to no support for unionization efforts by women or African Americans. The CIO was formed as a committee within the AFL in 1935 to encourage the AFL to organize workers in mass-production industries along industrial union lines. Having failed to change AFL policy from within, the CIO broke from the AFL and formed a rival union confederation in 1938. Unlike the AFL, the CIO was more open to African Americans and women and in some cases actively built strong multiracial unions.

After World War II ended, the postwar economy provided new challenges for organized labor, and the AFL and the CIO merged to form one large union confederation in 1955. The merger brought together the often-conflicting interests of the craft unions and the industrial unions under one umbrella for the benefits of greater political power and union strength that were afforded by having one large and unified labor confederation. During negotiations, CIO leaders set out a number of conditions for the merger with the AFL, such as constitutional provisions supporting industrial unionism, guarantees against racial discrimination, and internal procedures to clean up corrupt unions, but the CIO, being the smaller of the two confederations, was forced to compromise on many of these demands. At the time of the merger in 1955, union membership in the United States reached a historic high of 35 percent of all private sector wage and salary workers. Union density has steadily declined since then, with just 11 percent of workers belonging to unions today.

As for climate change, union confederations in the United States have a long history of supporting coal and other fossil fuels because they include unions whose members work for mining, drilling, transportation, and power-generation companies that produce and burn those fuels. In recent years, various U.S. union confederations, including the national AFL-CIO, have taken a cautious, conservative approach to climate policy and voiced support for CCS as a means to address climate change without quitting coal. Unlike the International Trade Union Confederation (ITUC) and national confederations in other countries, the AFL-CIO has never supported the Kyoto Protocol or other science-based emission-reduction targets. Historically, the AFL-CIO's climate and energy policy has been shaped predominantly by a small number of unions in extraction and construction, and the rest of the labor movement—representing the vast majority of union members—has mostly steered clear of what is, or could be, a divisive issue within the confederation. Most recently, the powerful Energy Committee of the AFL-CIO issued an open letter in opposition to the Green New Deal resolution promoted by Representative Ocasio-Cortez and Senator Markey (U.S. Congress 2019). However, several lower-level confederations, such as the Maine and Vermont state AFL-CIOs and the Los Angeles Labor Council have resolved to endorse the Green New Deal, reflecting a fissure opening in this pillar of support for the fossil fuel industry.

With their history and rather conservative stance on climate change, union confederations are placed on the Jobs vs. the Environment side of the labor–climate spectrum in Figure 3.1. The AFL-CIO represents workers from all industries, but the confederation dates back to the early craft union days of the AFL, and particular unions—such as the building trades unions, which occupy an incumbent role in the labor movement—have had oversized influence on the confederation's stance on the issue of climate change.[11] Many other unions that are concerned with protecting the climate, reflecting the more progressive industrial unionism of the old CIO, have refrained from bringing the issue up for fear of sowing division within the confederation. However, considering the nature of confederations, those other unions are a space for contention within labor on the issue of climate change. The LCM is challenging the position of incumbent power holders who have largely shaped the AFL position on climate and is seeking to bring labor as a whole to support a Green

New Deal–style solution to the climate crisis. With the passing of Richard Trumka and the rise of Liz Shuler as the first woman president of the confederation, there is a mix of uncertainty and hope, but the direction of the confederation on climate change remains in question, and the actions of the LCM will likely play a key role if the AFL-CIO is to move closer to the Clean Air and Good Jobs side of the spectrum.

The Big Picture

The labor–climate spectrum presented in Figure 3.1 provides a picture of the relationships among the union categories regarding climate change. It is important to note that the placement of each category on the spectrum is based on aggregated data and cannot capture the types of local variation within union categories that were alluded to in the descriptions above. However, from this illustration, it becomes clear that there is a pattern based on the industry of unions and the progressiveness of their stance on the issue of climate change. The unions on the Jobs vs. the Environment side of the spectrum are often directly involved in the fossil fuel industry and are most likely to display the characteristics of the business union model as described in Chapter 2, a model that emphasizes job consciousness over class consciousness. Moving across the spectrum, we find that the newer unions are more likely to support climate protection measures. These unions are more likely to display the characteristics of social movement unionism, including greater diversity, participation in coalition work, and an expanded goal orientation that includes issues that benefit the working class beyond just the union's membership ranks.

The transportation union category is an outlier in this illustration, as a result of their historically unique character—as an older, traditional union, but one that is increasingly moving toward technologies that support renewable energy—and the role that a key part of its industry can play in addressing climate change. For public transportation workers, increased use of rail and buses helps both the environment and their job prospects and bargaining power. In the case of the ATU, the influence of an activist president who took the issue of climate change to heart helped to move the union in the direction of progressive social movement unionism. The transportation union case may be an ideal example of a union in transition and a harbinger of the future, moving from pure and simple business unionism to a more social movement orientation, and could serve as a model for other traditional unions.

Looking at the location of the union confederation category relative to others, we get a sense of the power relations and underlying tensions that govern the interests and actions of different unions regarding climate change. Although the majority of unions occupy the second half of the spectrum, union confederations remain on the Jobs vs. the Environment side with the building trades and extraction unions. While the AFL-CIO is made up of unions from all categories, their stance on climate protection remains decidedly conservative compared with the majority of unions. Also, some progressive unions that might otherwise be strong advocates for renewable energy are often tempered in their stance by their membership in the AFL-CIO. Figure 3.1 does not capture the variation among state union confederations, many of which (such as Connecticut, Maine, Vermont, and Washington) have taken a more proactive stance on climate than have similar coalitions in other states. However, the position of the national union confederation in relation to its constituent elements suggests a disproportionate influence by more conservative unions within the AFL-CIO when it comes to the issue of climate change and an overall adherence to the business union model that accepts the current political–economic structure rather than challenging it. It also illustrates the hegemony of the fossil fuel industry in shaping the discussion about jobs and economic growth in the United States.

For the LCM, union confederations are spaces of contention where challengers can oppose the Jobs vs. the Environment frame and promote alternatives that confront this major pillar of support for the fossil fuel regime. Incidents of climate catastrophe, such as Hurricanes Katrina, Sandy, and Maria or the perennially larger wildfires in California and floods in the Midwest, create opportunities for challengers to take action. One of the major ways this action is carried out is through collective action framing struggles, as we shall see in Chapters 4 and 5 (Benford and Snow 2000; Goffman 1974; Snow et al. 1986). During these periods of contention, challengers such as the LCM propose and seek to mobilize consensus around a different definition of the situation, one in which collective agency can overcome perceived structural limitations. Incumbent power holders such as the building trades unions seek to operate within and maintain the old order, but through sustained mobilization, the insurgent movement may be able to slowly institutionalize a new frame—Clean Air and Good Jobs—that espouses a broader class consciousness (DiMaggio 1991 [2012]; McAdam, Tarrow, and Tilly 2003).

4

"Climate Change Is Unequivocally a Labor Issue"

Defining the Problem and Identifying Targets

On September 21, 2014, over three hundred thousand demonstrators took to the streets of New York City to join the single largest protest on climate change in history at that time, the People's Climate March (Munguia 2014). Organized by community organizations, environmental groups, and labor groups from across the country, the People's Climate March was set to coincide with a September 23 global summit on climate change called by United Nations Secretary-General Ban Ki-moon, who had himself expressed frustration at the slow pace of progress on climate change mitigation. With companion demonstrations in other cities around the world, from Paris to Papua New Guinea, it was estimated that more than six hundred thousand demonstrators joined the event worldwide.

Described by organizers as "an invitation to change everything," referencing Naomi Klein's 2014 best-selling book about climate change, titled *This Changes Everything*, the invitation to the march read:

> With our future on the line and the whole world watching, we'll take a stand to bend the course of history. We'll take to the streets to demand the world we know is within our reach: a world with an economy that works for people and the planet; a world safe from the ravages of climate change; a world with good jobs, clean air and water, and healthy communities. To change everything, we need everyone on board.

On the day of the march, it appeared that everyone was indeed on board—the turnout broke records and included a diverse cross section of society. Environmental activists, students, and climate justice activists brought colorful signs and urgent demands. Labor union members were an unmistakable presence—by many accounts the largest single contingent in the march (Hertsgaard 2014). At a rally stop along the route of the march, standing beneath a banner reading "Healthy Planet and Good Jobs," IBEW Local 3 business manager Chris Erikson exclaimed: "Today we make history. This is your Woodstock. This is the day our children will remember us for."

Several thousand members of service sector unions, transportation unions, healthcare unions, education unions, public sector unions, some manufacturing unions, and a few local building trades unions came from numerous states to join the thousands of New York City labor activists participating in the march. Many came on charter buses organized by activists affiliated with Unions for a Sustainable Economy—the national-level organization in this study. Others came via expanded and discounted public transportation negotiated by labor, religious, and climate activists from the State Partnership for Employment and Climate—the state-level organization in this study. At a press conference announcing this expanded public transportation service and reduced fares for riders attending the march, the president of the state AFL-CIO said, "We stand here today to expose the false framing of 'Jobs vs. the Environment' and to tell a different story." She went on: "The [state] AFL-CIO is proud to play a leading role in [SPEC]. And in New York City, our union members will march side by side with their neighbors, friends, and family members for a future of good jobs, clean air, and healthy communities for all."

The various labor participants I spoke with at the march explained that climate change must be considered a labor issue because the problem is driven by capitalism and causes suffering for workers. Many mentioned how Superstorm Sandy, which hit the Northeast in October 2012, made climate change very real for them as they experienced firsthand the devastating impacts of extreme weather. Several also noted that, as with Hurricane Katrina in New Orleans and other extreme weather events, the most vulnerable members of society were the ones who were hit the hardest. Sandy destroyed communities and also laid bare and exacerbated the inequities that existed before the storm. Working people, the poor, the young, the old, women, immigrants, and people of color were all suffering disproportionately. As some noted, these communities gained the least from the patterns of fossil fuel investment and suffered the most from the environmental neglect that helped create the climate crisis, leading climate justice activists at the march to demand a clean, sustainable, and democratically controlled energy system that addresses the needs of current workers and the many who are under- or unemployed.

Labor supporters of the People's Climate March maintained that the climate crisis could be addressed by creating well-paying union jobs that reduce GHGs and transition the economy to a sustainable, equitable model with energy efficient buildings, improved and expanded public transit systems, renewables-based power, and sustainable waste systems. A statement by USE (the national-level organization in this study) in the lead-up to the People's Climate March read in part: "Addressing the climate crisis is an opportunity to reduce unemployment, grow our unions, improve our community's health, and restore balance to our environment." In sum, the message of LCM activists was that the two crises of the climate and the economy have one solution: put people to work making a climate-safe economy.

However, not all unions supported and participated in the People's Climate March that day. To refer back to the labor–climate spectrum developed in Chapter 3, the relative position of the various unions on the spectrum regarding the issue of climate change maps well with their representation in the march. The unions with the more traditional organizational forms, often adhering to the business union approach to unionism and situated on the Jobs vs. the Environment side of the labor–climate spectrum in Figure 3.1, were not present at the march. On the other hand, most of the newer unions, which display some characteristics of social movement unionism and are situated on the Clean Air and Good Jobs side of the spectrum, constituted the labor contingent at the march.

Enter the Labor–Climate Movement

Within those unions that participated in the People's Climate March, there is a movement of activists seeking to address the climate crisis from the perspective of the working class; they are the LCM. Consisting of climate-conscious union leaders and rank-and-file union members, the LCM seeks to create better jobs for workers now and a better environment for their communities' and for the planet's future. It was the activism of these LCM activists that helped to bring their particular unions to participate in the People's Climate March and demand immediate action to address the dual crises of climate change and inequality. The LCM is the organized voice within the labor movement pushing for ecological sustainability and protections for workers and communities hurt by the effects of climate change as well as the changes that must be made in order to transition away from fossil fuels to transition to renewable energy.

Social movements like the LCM emerge only when there is a transformation of consciousness and behavior among potential movement participants (Piven and Cloward 1979). In terms of consciousness, the key issue is the perception that the existing social order has lost its legitimacy and that current social arrangements are unjust and wrong. With regard to behavior, movement participation is most likely when people come to believe that change is possible and that their participation will make a difference—that is, movements emerge only when people recognize and identify a particular injustice and believe they have the ability to do something about it. For movements to grow and thrive, leaders must educate others to achieve these dual changes in consciousness and behavior. This is done predominantly through the process of collective action framing.

As we have seen in the previous chapters, many structural features of the American capitalist system, both historically and in the present, complicate these efforts. A political–economic structure underpins the positions of many unions on the issues of climate change and justice. Nonetheless, LCM activists are choosing to confront rather than work within the existing structural framework. Through the act of framing, these social actors are using their agency to attempt to redefine the situation, shift the ideological perspective of unions, and build a movement to create an alternative path forward. It is in the contestation over the definition of the problem and its possible solutions that alternative paths are being shaped. The results of such contests ultimately influence the ability of LCM activists to achieve their goal of shifting labor as a whole to support climate protection measures.

Collective Action Framing and Frame Alignment Processes

Collective action frames are "action-oriented sets of beliefs and meanings that inspire and legitimate the activities and campaigns of a social movement organization" (Benford and Snow 2000, 614). These frames have many dimensions and functions that are actively negotiated as movement actors generate a shared understanding of the social problem and its potential solutions. The first framing task, "diagnostic framing," identifies the social problem, characterizes its nature, and attributes blame or responsibility. A key component of the diagnosis is distinguishing the target or targets of the movement. The second task, "prognostic framing," identifies possible solutions and corresponding strategies. The third task, "motivational framing," provides the rationale and motivation for collective action, which is then translated into specific actions (Benford and Snow 2000). This chapter will focus on the diagnostic framing processes of the LCM, from defining the problem to identifying the targets and aligning their frame with other movements, organizations, and individuals to generate broad participation.

From a bird's-eye view, a person's or group's general understanding of the world can be conceived of as a series of interconnected collective action frames that are broad in scope, functioning as master algorithms that both influence and constrain the actions of social actors (Benford and Snow 2000). These existing master frames underpin the existing capitalist hegemony—the ensemble of discourses, identities, and practices that organize consent to existing political arrangements in society (Gramsci 1971). Collective action framing involves defining a situation in such a way as to challenge the legitimacy of certain aspects of the dominant ideology in society and to create an alternative worldview that is both more just and also achievable through collective action. In other words, movements develop counterframes to challenge the existing master frames in society. In this way, emerging counterframes are acts of counterhegemony (Carroll and Ratner 1996). Importantly, frames (both master and counter) have the ability to foster support and mobilization across disparate groups in society if they are sufficiently broad in interpretive scope, inclusive, flexible, and culturally resonant.

With regard to labor and climate change in the United States, the master frame associated with the dominant free market ideology is Jobs vs. the Environment. For decades, this has been the mantra of the mainstream media when it comes to unionized workers and environmental issues. High-profile cases like the historic struggle between timber workers and defenders of the spotted owl in the Pacific Northwest have served as great news stories for media outlets concerned with ratings and advertising revenue (Brecher 2014; Foster 1993). When the Endangered Species Act was applied to protect the owls, loggers were fearful of losing their jobs in the region, and many conflicts sprang up between workers and environmentalists—some violent. The logging companies helped to stoke the fire by holding meetings on paid work time to create a climate of fear among workers and to train them to oppose the regulations (Bari 1994).

More recently, support for the Keystone XL and Dakota Access oil pipelines pitted unionized construction workers against environmentalists, farmers, and Indigenous peoples concerned with water quality, pollution, and climate-changing GHGs. The pipelines, which were being constructed to carry especially carbon-intense crude oil from Alberta, Canada, to the U.S. Gulf Coast for refining and export, cross through multiple U.S. states, threatening the water supplies of countless communities and farms as well as the sacred lands of the Standing Rock Sioux in North Dakota. Seeing these projects as a quick way to put thousands of unemployed construction workers back on the job after the Great Recession, many building trades unions sided with the fossil fuel industry and pipeline company, TransCanada, to push for congressional and presidential approval of the projects. Before the project was approved, the company signed project labor agreements with the unions that guaranteed high prevailing wages and union hiring for the construction jobs to garner their political support for the project. President Barack Obama, after much deliberation and pressure from environmentalists, opted to block the pipeline. Within two months of being inaugurated in 2017, President Donald Trump reversed President Obama's decision. Lauding the jobs it would create, Trump approved the construction of the Keystone XL pipeline, reactivating the powerful Jobs vs. the Environment master frame. President Joe Biden ultimately blocked the project after taking office in 2021.

The Jobs vs. the Environment master frame is rooted in the neoliberal ideology of free market fundamentalism. It assumes that in a capitalist economy either there can be jobs or there can be protections for the environment that hurt the profits of corporations and thus eliminate jobs. This false choice is indicative of the existing capitalist hegemony and its constraints on democracy (Wright and Rogers 2015). From this perspective, economic growth and capitalist profitability are seen as the driving force of the economy and set the boundaries for legitimate discussion of policy alternatives for all issues on the public agenda. Economic growth is portrayed by the dominant culture as creating a social good for all members of society, and all political demands must begin from the starting point that they will be good for, or at worst do no harm to, the accumulation of profits. This core tenet of capitalist ideology is powerfully captured in the iconic aphorism often attributed to Charles Wilson, president of General Motors during the 1940s: "What's good for General Motors is good for America."[1] In terms of labor and the environment, the demand constraints of capitalist democracy prevent citizens from seeing, let alone demanding, actions by the government that would both protect the environment and ensure the financial well-being of workers should certain polluting facilities or industries need to be phased out for the common good of society.

The emerging counterframe put forth by the LCM—and the title of this volume—is Clean Air and Good Jobs. As briefly explained in Chapter 1, this frame rebukes the false choice that capitalists offer to workers: that they must choose to have either a job or a healthy environment in which to live. The simple rhetorical shift from "versus" to "and" in this expression challenges the legitimacy of the existing social arrangements and strikes at the heart of the dominant free market ideology by suggesting that nonmarket mechanisms are not only acceptable but likely necessary to construct a more legitimate social order.

The intentional placement of "clean air" before "good jobs" in the counter-frame also signals a sharp departure from the dominant frame. The primacy of protecting the climate is even more explicitly captured in another movement slogan that was occasionally used by LCM participants: "There are no jobs on a dead planet."[2]

In challenging the dominant free market ideology of U.S. society, the Clean Air and Good Jobs frame seeks to push back against the constraints of capitalism on democracy by expanding the scope of issues that are on the table for discussion (Wright and Rogers 2015). A robust democracy does not stop at the sphere of conventional politics but involves an active, engaged, and informed citizenry participating in decisions about the economy as well as other arenas of social life. By pushing for democratic voice and public intervention into economic decision-making, the Clean Air and Good Jobs counterframe puts the common good ahead of the profitability interests of capitalists. This frame is deeply embedded in calls for a Green New Deal, both before and after the introduction of the resolution to Congress.

Figure 4.1 presents several variations of the emerging counterframe that have been used by LCM activists at protest events. In the top left photo, union workers from USE and other organizations carry a banner reading "Union Workers for a Clean and Just Economy" at the front of the labor contingent of the People's Climate March on Washington, DC, on April 29, 2017. In the top right photo, UAW members carry a banner at the head of the New York City Labor Day Parade on September 6, 2014, that reads "Climate Justice Is Labor Justice: People's Climate March! 11:30am Sept. 21st @Columbus Circle." The bottom photo shows LCM activists from the People's Climate March in New York City carrying a banner that reads "Healthy Planet and Good Jobs" at the front of the labor contingent of this historic march.

The emerging counterframe depicted in these photos, which demands two social goods that few people would be opposed to—Clean Air and Good Jobs—appears to be sufficiently broad and flexible to appeal to a wide range of disparate groups, encompassing environmentalists, labor groups, and ordinary citizens. One complicating factor is the simultaneous support for green growth and opposition to emission reductions by many U.S. unions. LCM activists hope the frame can help move some unions from the Jobs vs. the Environment side of the labor–climate spectrum discussed in Chapter 3 over to the Clean Air and Good Jobs side of the spectrum or, at the least, inspire unions already on the Clean Air and Good Jobs side of the spectrum to take more deliberate action. But, as we have seen in Chapter 2, owing to many structural factors, including capitalist constraints on democracy, labor has a checkered history of fighting for clean air alongside its continuous struggles for

Figure 4.1
Banners Displaying Labor–Climate Movement Frames.

Top: People's Climate March in Washington, DC (April 29, 2017).

Middle: New York City Labor Day Parade (September 6, 2014).

Bottom: People's Climate March in New York City (September 21, 2014).

Photo credits: author (*top*), Michael Belt (*middle*), Brooke Anderson (*bottom*).

good jobs (Dewey 1998; Silverman 2004, 2006; Vachon and Brecher 2016). In particular, unions that espouse the characteristics of pure and simple business unionism are inclined to work within the existing system to fight for material gains rather than challenge the system to pursue broader worker-class interests.

One of the main ways that challengers to the dominant master frame garner support for their counterframe is through what is called the frame alignment process. Four major frame alignment processes connect SMOs with potential supporters or spur cross-movement mobilization: frame amplification, frame bridging, frame extension, and frame transformation. While each functions differently, the end result of these four processes is the same: the generation of a shared understanding of an issue by way of linking the interpretative framework of an SMO with congruent or complementary beliefs held by individuals or groups.

One of the key factors affecting whether a frame resonates with potential constituents is the extent to which it taps into existing beliefs, cultural values, and narratives. *Frame amplification* involves "the idealization, embellishment, clarification, or invigoration of these existing values or beliefs" (Benford and Snow 2000, 624).[3] *Frame bridging* involves the linking of two or more ideologically consistent but structurally unconnected frames regarding a particular issue. Bridging can occur across social movements or between a movement and individuals, through the connection of an SMO with an unmobilized pool of people who have shared sentiments. In sum, "frame bridging" refers to efforts by movements to increase their appeal to disparate groups by drawing parallels between the group they represent and the sentiments or beliefs of the groups or individuals they are courting.[4]

Frame extension entails extending a social movement's interests and frame beyond its primary interests, or outside of its normal organizational range, to incorporate issues and concerns presumed to be of importance to potential adherents (Benford and Snow 2000). The organizational range of a movement, or the scope of the issues with which the movement engages, can be broad or narrow. In the case of the labor movement, for example, unions espousing social movement characteristics tend to have a broader organizational range than business unions.[5] *Frame transformation* refers to the changing of old understandings and meanings or the generation of new ones. Some suggest that the term "ideological transformation" would more accurately describe this process, which involves either the transmission of an ideology to a new believer or the reconstruction of an existing ideology (see, for example, Oliver and Johnston 2000).[6]

Each of these frame alignment processes relates to the LCM at some point in its evolution. For example, the construction of the climate and inequality crises as two interconnected elements of one common injustice represents an instance of frame amplification that inspires action by potential participants who strongly value social justice. The tying of workplace health and safety issues to broader environmental issues is an instance of frame bridging to develop an overlap in framing with mainstream environmental organizations in order to foster cooperation. Efforts by LCM activists within their own unions to build support for labor action on the issue of climate change represents a clear example of frame extension. The quest to move "more traditional" unions from the Jobs vs. the Environment frame to the Clean Air and Good Jobs frame is an effort to transform the frames of those workers and unions. In this way, participants in the LCM seek to move "labor as a whole"—that is, both traditional and more progressive unions—into the Clean Air and Good Jobs domain of the labor–climate spectrum.

Defining the Problem: Diagnostic Framing in the Labor–Climate Movement

LCM activists, like other environmentalists, see climate change as an eminent threat to humanity and all life on the planet. For example, Dylan, a leader in a national service sector union, said, "It has been known for a long time that the nature of our economy, particularly the burning of fossil fuels, is causing real dramatic, serious climate change. I think it's existential. . . . If we continue along with business as usual, this will not be a world where people will enjoy living." Or as was stated in a resolution passed by the Plumbers and Fitters Local 393 on the West Coast, "The future is clearly coming much faster than science predicted. Global warming is no longer just a threat. It is increasingly a reality and a menace to our children, our loved ones, and civilization as a whole" (Plumbers and Fitters Local 393, 2016).

However, unlike the mainstream environmental movement, the LCM approaches the issue of climate change from a labor-centered or working-class perspective. As a resolution adopted by a local manufacturing union involved with SPEC, the state-level organization in this study, stated, "Climate change is unequivocally a labor issue, as working people will undoubtedly bear the brunt and consequences of climate change." To further illustrate, John, a national leader of a manufacturing union, said, "Climate change disproportionately affects the poor, working class, communities of color, and Indigenous people." He added, "The destruction of jobs and pollution have a common cause: corporate desire to privatize profits and socialize costs." A resolution adopted by his union at the national level affirmed this sentiment: "The energy profiteers want a world where both labor and environmental standards are in a race to the bottom. If they get their way, we get poverty and a poisoned planet."

Participants in the LCM commonly use the term "frontline communities" to describe the social groups who are hit first and hardest by the climate crisis. Importantly, the term is used to describe several different groups of people. In the first use, "frontline community" refers to the most vulnerable—the poor and predominantly nonwhite communities, including Tribal communities, who, as a result of existing inequalities in society, live in areas that already are and will continue to be hardest hit and least prepared to confront the climate crisis. Images of poor and working-class Black residents in New Orleans after Hurricane Katrina or the residents of inland Puerto Rico after Hurricane Maria capture the essence of this group of climate victims.[7] The second use of the term refers to deindustrialized communities, depopulated rural communities, and communities where jobs are at stake when the government takes measures to curb carbon emissions by cutting fossil fuel use. Images of the predominantly white workers who have lost their jobs as coal miners or in coal-fired power plants are the quintessential example of this group. The combination of these two groups of vulnerable people under the common title of "frontline communities" further accentuates the idea of shared interests among all working people that LCM activists continually convey. However, not all members of frontline communities agree that the plights of the two groups can be equated. Environmental justice community members often remind labor activists that the white workers who face unemployment as a result of decarbonization have at least had the opportunity to benefit economically for generations from the fossil fuel jobs that nonwhites have been systematically excluded from and disproportionately affected by in the form of negative health consequences as a result of pollution. Addressing this particular issue and aligning the frames of the labor–climate and climate justice movements will be an important task for LCM activists in order to build the broad base of support needed to address the dual crises of climate and inequality.

Even in light of this area for potential conflict, the LCM's focus on the working class and frontline communities separates them from the mainstream environmental movement in one important way. These activists see unmitigated climate change as a threat, but they also express deep skepticism about many of the solutions proposed by environmentalists and liberal politicians. Current proposals that seek to mitigate climate change are often geared toward helping the most affluent in society at the expense of others, they simply ignore the situation of the poor and working classes, or, worse yet, they directly threaten the livelihoods and well-being of working people.

At the very least, the LCM activists in my study contend that many climate mitigation plans focus exclusively on protecting the affluent and most politically influential elements of society. As with so many NIMBY movements, many local environmental groups seek solutions that benefit themselves at the expense of less influential social groups. For example, it has long been established that working-class communities, particularly communities of color, are more likely to be adjacent to toxic facilities and exposed to the associated health risks (Bullard 1993). When it comes to climate change, remedies such as flood protection measures, solar installations, and air-conditioned schools begin in affluent neighborhoods and often never trickle down to the poor and working-class communities. Environmental justice activists within the LCM raise issues about access to green jobs for all community members, particularly people of color, who may not have been afforded the opportunity to land an energy sector job previously.

A more direct threat to workers and their communities is the elimination of their jobs in a transition away from fossil fuels to renewable sources of energy. The reduction of coal mining in recent decades has had a devastating effect on many working-class communities in Appalachia (Hochschild 2016). To be sure, many of the job losses were in fact caused by automation and market forces, such as the rise of natural gas as a cheaper alternative fuel for power generation; nonetheless, many workers blame stricter environmental regulations for their job losses. This has led many workers and politicians to despise government efforts to protect the environment and spurred a surge in support for the coal industry by workers and politicians in coal-rich states. For example, the states of Kentucky and West Virginia offer specialty "Friends of Coal" license plates for automobiles, which read "Coal Keeps the Lights On." Many workers in these traditionally Democratic-leaning districts switched their allegiance to support the 2016 presidential campaign of Donald Trump, who promised to "bring coal back" and held large campaign rallies throughout the Appalachian region under the banner of "Trump Digs Coal" (Davenport 2016).

The depth and breadth of support for coal in places like Kentucky, West Virginia, and western Pennsylvania goes beyond the fear of further job losses and erosion of the local tax base. Coal has been woven into the fabric of Appalachian life for more than a century. Mining is not just a job—it is a cultural identity. It has a rich oral, musical, and cultural legacy. Songs such as "Dark as a Dungeon," written by Merle Travis in 1946 and later performed by the likes of Johnny Cash, Willie Nelson, and John Mellencamp, to name a few, reveal the love/hate relationship the working class has had with coal over the years in Appalachia. Like so many others, this song has been used not only during struggles by miners decrying deadly working conditions in the mines but also in celebration of the dignity involved in doing an honest, albeit deadly, day's work to support one's family and power the nation's economy. For many in Appalachia, the emotional response to what has been dubbed by the industry as a "war on coal" is part anger at job loss but also part sorrow for what is slipping away—a culture deeply rooted in a place—and part fear at what the future may bring for that place.

Beyond the coalfields, the inequality crisis in recent years has become particularly urgent in areas downstream from the actual mining of coal—in particular, communities that are home to coal-fired power plants. These utility plants get less media attention than the mines, but they are more widespread geographically and are experiencing a much more immediate decline. Coal mines have been shedding jobs for decades, but coal-fired plants are experiencing their biggest declines right now, squeezed by competition from cheaper natural gas as well as government regulations on their copious carbon emissions.

For example, Dayton Power and Light in Adams County, Ohio, notified the state and its workers in 2016 that it intended to close its two coal-fired plants in the county in June 2018. The plants had been in operation since the 1970s and were by far the largest employer and taxpayer in that county, which has a population of twenty-eight thousand and by one measure of median family income is the poorest of Ohio's eighty-eight counties (MacGillis 2018). The announcement left the county with barely a year to figure out how it was going to make do without the plants. The reduction in purchasing power of workers as well as the reduction in tax revenues to fund public education, infrastructure, and social programs caused the pain to ripple out from the frontline workers to the community as a whole. In addition to the ones in Adams County, at least twelve other coal-fired plants were scheduled to close throughout the United States in that same year alone, many in remote areas where they are the major, if not the only, employer as well as the largest contributor to the local tax base that funds local schools and social services. Unlike some unions who take a more reactionary approach and revert to the Jobs vs. the Environment perspective in these instances, LCM activists see the two problems of climate change and economic security as intertwined and in need of a solution that addresses both.

Finally, the LCM activists in this study are dismayed that the U.S. labor movement has done little to develop and promote a solution to the climate crisis that incorporates working-class interests. The tepid support thus far for the Green New Deal is emblematic of the problem. From the perspective of these activists, if the labor movement is not fighting for the interests of the working class, then nobody is. Many leaders repeated the phrase "If you are not at the table, then you are probably on the menu." The point is that climate change is real, and it will have to be dealt with eventually. The question is whether workers will have any say in the solution or whether they will be absent from the discussion and just bear the brunt of the cost of the solution.

In sum, the LCM constructs the problem as follows:

- Unmitigated climate change poses a serious threat to all people but particularly workers and frontline communities who are most likely to experience the worst effects of climate change and who have the least resources to prepare for or recover from climate disaster.
- Most mitigation strategies currently under consideration harm frontline communities and current fossil fuel workers by either ignoring them altogether or posing a direct threat to them by eliminating their livelihoods and reducing much-needed tax revenues for their communities.
- The mainstream environmental movement is not considering working-class interests in their efforts to address climate change and are often pushing for mitigation strategies that exacerbate Jobs vs. the Environment conflicts that harm workers.
- To the peril of the labor movement, large segments of it are not actively fighting for solutions to climate change that incorporate broader working-class interests; instead, they serve as a major pillar of support for continued fossil fuel use.

Attributing Blame: Identifying Targets of the LCM

Integrally related to defining the problem is attributing blame (McAdam 1982). The identification of responsible parties, or "production of targets," is bound up with previous patterns, or repertoires of contention and configurations of power (Bartley and Child 2014; McAdam 1982; Tilly 2008). Repertoires of contention are historically specific, routinized sets of targets, tactics, and understandings of social change that provide loose scripts that social movements enact. For the labor movement, these scripts include employers as targets and fairness and dignity as demands. For environmentalists, the target is typically the state, but often it is polluting corporations as well. Configurations of power involve complex sets of actors embedded in networks that have the capacity to "organize and control people, materials, and territories" over time (Mann 1988, 2; see also Downey 2015).

For the LCM, I have identified three direct targets:

- The state for its inaction regarding, or at best tepid response to, the urgent crisis of climate change, which has typically placed the burden of mitigation on workers
- The middle-class culture of the mainstream environmental movement that promotes solutions to climate change that ignore the concerns of workers, further exacerbate Jobs vs. the Environment conflicts, and in the end do not create a truly sustainable economy because they fail to address the underlying structural inequalities embedded in a neoliberal capitalist system
- The culture of business unionism in much of the labor movement, which creates a structural constraint on the consciousness of workers, leading them to serve as a pillar of support for continued fossil fuel use, through either complacence or direct material and political support for the forces against climate protection

Target 1: The State

The LCM identifies the state, at all levels, as one of its key targets. A traditional understanding of social movements is that they are based on "a set of opinions and beliefs in a population which represents preferences for changing some elements of the social structure and/or reward distribution of a society" (McCarthy and Zald 1977, 1217). From this perspective, targeting the state is fundamental, and movements are expected to select strategies most likely to generate policy changes that result in instrumental gains for movement participants (J. Jenkins 1983). Importantly, LCM activists acknowledge that profit-maximizing corporations in the capitalist system are also to blame but cannot be expected to change unless forced to do so by governments. In other words, the targeting of individual corporations would be like the fabled efforts of Hans Brinker, the little Dutch boy who saved Holland by plugging a leak in the dike with his finger (Dodge 1918). Plugging one hole does not address the underlying problem, which is the reduced structural integrity of the dike. For the LCM, targeting an individual corporation is similarly futile if the environment in which corporations operate is not fundamentally altered.[8] However, the rise of neoliberalism as the dominant governing ideology in the United States (and most other capitalist democracies) has meant a decline in government regulations that interfere with markets.

USE issued its first-ever public statement shortly after its founding in 2009, following the failure of the U.S. Congress to pass a climate change bill and the failure of world leaders to come to an agreement at international climate talks in Copenhagen. The statement read in part:

> As the torturous Copenhagen negotiations and the already-inadequate US climate protection legislation falter, the earth is being imperiled by a failure of its political systems. We know what needs to be done to halt global warming; we have the technology and resources to halt it; we know the consequences of not doing what we know must be done. If the "world's top leaders" recognize that global warming is a problem and do nothing about it, they are part of the problem, not part of the solution.

After criticizing the inadequate responses of national and international governing bodies to the problem of climate change, the statement went on to say, "The failure of current climate protection strategies tells us that the current strategy of lobbying governments to fix global warming will not work" and that what is required is a new "climate protection movement" that is "a convergence of those in the environmental, labor, food, globalization, anti-poverty, peace, student, and other movements who grasp the urgency and believe radical action is the only way forward."

LCM activists understand that the free market alone has proven incapable of addressing the pending climate crisis in a timely manner, but they also see ineffectual action by a feckless state as perpetuating rather than resolving the problem. For these reasons, the movement targets the government to press for immediate and effective climate protection measures. To successfully avoid the worst consequences of climate change, the government needs to be a proactive agent of change to counter the collective action failure of markets to deliver an essential public good: a livable climate. Whether it be a carbon tax, a cap-and-trade system, stricter emission regulations, massive investments in renewables, a government-run green infrastructure plan, new forms of public ownership of power plants and utilities, or some combination of these and other proposals, the state is needed to intervene in the market to ensure the provision of this public good. However, considering the relationship between capital and increasingly neoliberal governments, it is unlikely that governments will do it on their own without being pressured.

In a policy paper from 2017, LUPE—the international-level organization in this study—elaborated on the failures of the market and private investments to adequately address the climate problem:

> We believe that an honest review of the data and the policy history leave no doubt that the dominant policy paradigm—justified (and perhaps blinded) by a constant insistence on the need to "mobilize private sector investment"—has failed, even on its own terms, either to generate the kind of momentum needed to drive a full-on energy transition or to seriously impede the rise in fossil fuel use. We believe such a review also shows that the prospects for the dominant policy paradigm to produce results consistent with any serious effort to reduce emissions—let alone meet the Paris targets—are extremely poor.

The paper went on to conclude that "unions and their allies are well positioned to challenge the myth that a transition to renewable energy can only be accomplished by catering to the interests of big companies and private investors. The . . . labor movement . . . should demand and fight for a viable transition . . . that is anchored in public financing, social ownership, and democratic control."

If one were to consider the United States to be a pluralist society, as many do, then various interest groups such as the LCM would be expected to compete in a zero-sum fashion against other interest groups for state policies that favor their perspective (Lijphart 2020). However, the state can generally be expected to side with capital in the perpetual quest for economic growth, green or not (Schnaiberg 1980). Further, capitalist elites can be expected to utilize their unequal access to powerful institutions and networks to prevent non-elite challenges to the dominant free market ideology that opposes state intrusions into the market (Downey 2015). The powerful fossil fuel industry in particular has tremendous influence in the American political arena, especially among elected officials from states where extracting, refining, and importing or exporting fossil fuels make up a sizable portion of the economy (as well as a sizable proportion of their campaign contributions).

In the wake of the 2016 elections, the federal government witnessed a meteoric rise of fossil fuel boosters, primarily within the Republican Party, into top leadership positions at major government agencies, such as the EPA, Department of Energy (DOE), and Bureau of Land Management (BLM), and within the White House itself. For example, before becoming EPA director, Scott Pruitt sued the agency at least fourteen times on behalf of fossil fuel companies trying to block environmental rules. The Sabin Center at Columbia Law School did an analysis of Trump appointees to environmental, energy, and natural resource agencies and found that 28 percent had close ties to the fossil fuel industry (Wentz 2017). According to a May 2017 report in the *New York Times*, Trump reversed course on twenty-three environmental rules and regulations during the first hundred days of his administration, many with potentially serious repercussions, such as approving the completion of the Dakota Access pipeline and revoking a rule that prevented coal-mining companies from dumping toxic debris into local streams (Popovich and Schlossberg 2017). The Republican Party's control of the executive branch and Congress and their majority on the Supreme Court meant that the passage of progressive climate policies at the federal level was less likely. Since the election of Joe Biden, many in the labor and climate movements and the LCM see a historic opportunity to pressure a federal government that should in theory be more susceptible to such pressures.

Beyond the federal government, the LCM operates at multiple levels, and as the opportunity structure closes at one level, it can simultaneously open at other levels. For example, various Democratic state governments, such as California, Oregon, and Washington on the West Coast and New Jersey, New York, and the New England states on the East Coast have proven fruitful targets for labor and environmental activists. Large municipalities, such as New York City and San Francisco, as well as small enclave cities such as Burlington, Vermont, have also proven to be viable targets for enacting climate protection measures. As an illustration of the more favorable opportunity structures at these subnational levels, when Trump announced he would withdraw the United States from the Paris Climate Accord, former New York City mayor Michael Bloomberg proposed that the hundred-plus mayors who had pledged to implement the accord would seek to join it in place of the U.S. government, and when Trump proposed to eliminate NASA climate research, California Governor Jerry Brown replied, "If Trump turns off the satellites, California will launch its own damn satellite" (Bloomberg 2016; Schlossberg 2016).

James, a state-level leader of a manufacturing union and a member of SPEC—the state-level organization in this study—stated the following about opportunity structures and targeting decisions in an editorial:

> While global cooperation is required to address global warming, national governments are so far failing to adopt the necessary agreements and policies. Therefore, local communities and governments must take the lead and start protecting the climate by reducing GHG emissions locally and regionally. [Our state's] history of bipartisanship and broad public support for climate action provide an opportunity—and a moral obligation—to provide national leadership.

Following the inauguration of Donald Trump in January 2017, USE issued a statement about the role of the LCM in the Trump era, which said in part,

"For the climate protection movement, the Trump ascendancy means that . . . lobbying and [the] 'inside game' . . . can no longer be effective, at least at the federal level . . . [but] progress is still possible at a state and local level." In other words, the LCM will continue to target the state at all levels, but it recognizes that existing political opportunity structures can make success more likely at the state and local levels than at the national level. As this shift illustrates, the identification of targets and the nature of the opportunity structure are both flexible and interrelated.

Target 2: The Mainstream Environmental Movement

Some critics have argued that most major social movement theories have wrongly assumed that domination is organized by and around only one source of power (the state), that political and economic structures of society are primary and determining, and that cultural factors are separate from structure and secondary in importance. Alternatively, a more comprehensive approach views domination as organized around multiple sources of power, each of which is simultaneously material and symbolic.[9] In the case of the LCM, I identify two additional targets of the movement that are separate from the state: the mainstream environmental movement and the labor movement itself.

When it comes to the issue of climate change, there are three major segments within the environmental movement: the mainstream environmental movement, the environmental justice and climate justice movements, and the LCM. By "mainstream," I refer to the big green organizations as well as local organizations that seek to protect nature and the environment, typically from a middle-class and predominantly white perspective. This represents the largest and most recognizable element of the American environmental movement but does not include the environmental justice or climate justice movements, which are rooted predominantly in poor and working-class communities of color seeking to address issues of environmental racism and injustice—sometimes the result of efforts by mainstream environmentalists to push ecological problems out of their own communities.

The mainstream environmental movement has been the dominant voice in the environmental movement for over fifty years and has made many gains in terms of federal and state regulations protecting the environment. However, many of these gains have disproportionately served the interests of the predominantly affluent members of the movement. It is this feature that has led some social movement scholars to consider the environmental movement to be a nonmaterialist movement rooted in lifestyle issues. It is also the reason for the rise of the environmental justice movement, which has challenged the mainstream movement to draw attention to the particular plights of frontline and Indigenous communities that are typically ignored by mainstream environmentalists. Environmental justice activists struggle for a "more just sustainability" than is demanded by mainstream environmentalists by mobilizing disadvantaged and unorganized people to demand a new society that addresses social and environmental concerns together (Agyeman and Evans 2004; Rudel, Roberts, and Carmin 2011). Similarly, the climate justice movement offers a parallel critique of mainstream environmental solutions to the climate crisis.

From the perspective of LCM activists, the mainstream environmental movement has also ignored the interests of workers. Local environmental crusaders have often showed up outside of power plants or mills demanding they be shut down without ever reaching out to the workers inside the plant. This failed strategy has led to countless Jobs vs. the Environment confrontations, which, through colorful portrayals by the mainstream media, have helped to solidify this master frame that leads environmentalists and unions to be suspicious of each other.

Looking more closely at these intramovement dynamics, I find that the labor–climate and climate justice movements have in some instances been aligned in seeking solutions to climate change that not only protect frontline communities and workers but also increase overall equity by undoing past injustices (Bullard 1993). Together, these two segments represent a growing working-class pole within the U.S. environmental movement. However, the relationship between some more conservative unions—particularly in the fossil fuel sector and on the "jobs vs. the environment" half of the labor–climate spectrum in Figure 3.1—and the climate justice movement has not always been one of cooperation. In other instances, such as the People's Climate March, all three segments of the climate movement came together to demand action on climate change. But, as can be seen in the variety of frames put forth on banners and protest signs, the demands of the working-class segments of the environmental movement tend to be more radical than those of the mainstream movement. The call for more radical solutions seeks to address the existing inequalities that they see as an integral feature of the climate crisis and that stem from the shared root cause of human and environmental exploitation—capitalism.

The goal of the LCM with regard to mainstream environmentalists is cultural. LCM activists seek to educate and help expand the framing of the mainstream environmental movement to include working-class interests, such as protections for displaced workers and affected communities. From the LCM perspective, the middle-class culture of the mainstream environmental movement prevents it from seeing the class-based and racial nature of the climate crisis. To better understand and adopt the demand of these communities, the mainstream environmental movement needs to listen to and incorporate the voices of workers and frontline communities in discussions about policy formation and advocacy.

Target 3: The Labor Movement

The third target of the LCM—the culture of the labor movement—differs from the previous two targets in one important way: the state and the environmental movement are external targets of the labor movement, while the LCM is situated squarely within the labor movement itself. Drawing on lessons from previous movements within U.S. labor, such as U.S. Labor against the War—a movement of labor activists within labor pressing the national AFL-CIO to take a stance in opposition to the Iraq War—LCM activists typically espouse social movement union tendencies, such as fighting for broad working-class issues that go beyond the workplace and the immediate economic interests of members. They consider the leadership of many unions and of the national union confederation—the AFL-CIO—to be guided by pure and simple business unionism, which favors job consciousness over class consciousness. For the labor movement writ large to confront the climate crisis, LCM activists believe the culture of the labor movement will have to move away from business unionism and toward social movement unionism. For this reason, the LCM has emerged as a "movement within a movement" seeking to alter the cultural meaning systems within unions and to win the hearts and minds of fellow union members and leaders and shift them to the Clean Air and Good Jobs side of the labor–climate spectrum (see Figure 3.1). In other words, the culture of the broader labor movement becomes a target for collective action by the LCM.

To put these two competing visions of unionism into perspective and to help explain the current divide between unions on the issue of climate change, Jake, a leader in USE and former high-level leader in a national union confederation, draws on the historical differences between the AFL's craft union model of unionism and the industrial model espoused by the CIO unions during the 1930s and 1940s:

> It's easy to blame the building trades. They are a sizable block within the federation [AFL-CIO]. They do, you know, carry the AFL vision of unionism—that's their mantle and they fight for that, which is a fiercely worksite-only vision of trade unionism. Whereas the CIO vision, which I come out of—you know, my folks were both CIO organizers and they always referred to CIO which we know stands for Con-

gress of Industrial Organizations—they referred to it as Community in Operation, and they had buttons that said "Community in Operation," so they had this broader vision. I think that's worth fighting for.

The phrase "Community in Operation," used by Jake, underscores some of the key features of social movement unionism, particularly the connection of labor to the community and broader movements for the common good—a historical division between traditional AFL and CIO unionism in the middle of the twentieth century. In other words, Jake believes the labor movement should be a movement that is guided by class consciousness and not just job consciousness. From this perspective, climate change is a working-class issue and thus requires solutions from working-class organizations. He went on to say, "I think the future of the labor movement is more secure when we find a way to become a central player in the movement to build a sustainable future for the planet and its people. And that historically is more of a CIO vision." For Jake, the current division between business unions and social movement unions on the issue of climate change is a contemporary manifestation of an age-old tension within the American labor movement.

Addressing this tension requires bringing unions from all industries that have traditionally espoused business union characteristics from the Jobs vs. the Environment frame on the first half of the labor–climate spectrum over to the Clean Air and Good Jobs frame on the second half in order to build a powerful and unified political force. For example, Josh, a local leader of a large public sector union, discusses the political importance of having a variety of unions be a part of the movement to protect the climate. He also identifies a variety of structural reasons that some elements of labor are either uninvolved or opposed to climate protection, and why these elements are an important target for the LCM:

> If we could get the union leadership on board, or at least a significant amount of union leadership on board on this issue, we could have tremendous political power. It's just that, you know, either we've got leadership that is overwhelmed by other issues, leadership that is not all that aware of the issue of climate change, and of course, we also have some leadership that is very fearful and is worried that their members are gonna lose jobs.

Josh went on to explain that the LCM needs to reach out to all elements of labor to build the movement. That includes unions that currently oppose climate protection measures, those in support of fossil fuel expansion, or even those blue–greens who support green growth but not emission-reduction targets. Importantly, this outreach must also include unions who have no members in fossil fuels and have just not spoken up or taken action on the pressing problem of climate change that is already affecting their members and communities. Some unions, he said, are in favor of climate protection but fearful of putting their necks out on the issue and drawing the ire of the building trades and extraction unions.

Another problem lies in the reluctance of some union leaders to embrace social movement unionism. Dylan, a leader in a service sector union, described what he saw as a disconnect between rank-and-file members and union leadership on the issue: "I think that a lot of workers understand climate change, and, in my experience, a lot are way ahead of leaders on this stuff. They are feeling it. They see it. Many are already involved with local environmental organizations." However, he said, the leaders are not making the connection that this is a working-class issue that unions must engage with. He went on to say, "I think it's about rethinking the labor movement. Who is the union? What is the union for? Fighting for jobs is different than fighting for workers. Fighting for coal jobs. Those are dead jobs walking. They're going to be gone. Why do you fight for them? Fight for the workers." Again, the change that is sought is cultural, a shift from the constraining business union model to the more broadly working-class social movement union model.

Jacob, a leader of SPEC, elaborated further on why labor must be a key target. He said that a broad goal of the LCM is "to be one part of the effort to break down the Jobs vs. the Environment frame." To do this, he said, requires "recognizing that labor is one of the key constituencies nationally, and therefore internationally, that has to come around on this issue [of climate protection] if we're going to really be able to do what has to be done to save the planet." Elaborating further, he said, "Corporations and all the folks that would normally be the enemies of labor are able to use this particular issue to say 'Well, look, we're trying to protect your jobs!' And exploiting that false [Jobs vs. the Environment] narrative in very effective ways, so that US labor has been a cornerstone of the resistance, internationally, to comprehensive climate policy." Jacob makes clear that labor is a key pillar of support for continued fossil fuel use, and insofar as it continues to consider its primary function to be fighting for particular jobs as opposed to the interests of the broader working-class, it must be a primary target of the LCM.

Tying together the targeting of the labor movement and the mainstream environmental movement on cultural grounds, Jake, a leader in USE, shared the following anecdote about a presentation he often makes to union workers about climate change:

A sure way to ingratiate yourself with a union crowd is to say something derogatory about environmentalists. You get cheers, and everybody's like "Yeah, right on!" So, I start with my Achilles' heel of the
environmental movement. And their Achilles' heel, I say, is that they
have never found a way to understand and appreciate the primacy of
work in people's lives. It's that basic. They don't get it, and because of
that their messaging exudes a tone deafness to the needs of working
people. And so that gives me big cheers from these [union] guys, as I
knew it would. And then I say, "But we have an Achilles' heel too,"
and now everybody gets uncomfortable 'cause no one wants to own
up to their own Achilles' heel or their own frailties. And I say, "Our
Achilles' heel is we have never found a way to adjust to changes in the
economy. The economy grows and moves in different directions, and
we circle the wagons and protect a shrinking base and we have to find
a way to get past that."

The first Achilles' heel described by Jake rationalizes the decision of the
LCM to target environmentalists. It is imperative for them to understand
the primacy of work in people's lives and to adjust their framing accordingly.
The predominantly middle-class culture of this quintessential "new" social
movement lacks a class-based lens through which to view the climate problem
(Inglehart 1977; Melucci 1985). The second Achilles' heel relates to the debate
about job consciousness versus class consciousness (or business union versus
social movement union) within the labor movement. If environmentalists are
concerned only with stopping fossil fuel use, they will face stiff opposition
from organized workers who feel threatened. If unions are concerned only with
protecting the existing jobs of current members, they will become increasingly
irrelevant as those jobs all fall by the wayside in the face of economic shifts,
including the transition away from fossil fuels to save the planet from devastating climate change.

These excerpts from movement participants reveal a unique insight into
the LCM's production of this key target. The business union culture in much
of the labor movement has made it reluctant to take on broader working-class
issues such as climate change. Or in the case of the blue–greens, some unions
have come to embrace green growth, but they oppose measures to reduce GHG
emissions. This culture that opposes challenging the logic of capitalism has
led the labor movement to succumb too often to the false choice of Jobs vs. the
Environment. However, despite the myriad of structural and cultural constraints, the LCM represents a "movement within the movement" seeking to
win the hearts and minds of labor writ large and to extend its frame to include

broader working-class issues that go beyond the worksite (Tarrow 1992). They seek to expand labor's organizational range to include a safe climate for workers to live and work in. In this sense, LCM activists are not merely "bridge builders" promoting coalition work with environmentalists but also "change makers" within labor (Polletta 1998; Sink 1991)—that is, unlike the protagonists in previous labor–environmental research, participants in the LCM are working within their unions and the broader labor movement to develop a social movement union culture that espouses a new working-class environmentalism (see, for example, Mayer 2009; Obach 2004; Vachon and Brecher 2016). As Steve, a leader in LUPE and member of an education union, said, "We can't just leave environmentalism to the environmentalists."

Indirect Targets

It is important to consider that social movements have at times targeted particular institutions as a means of indirectly targeting the state or some other target (Walker, Martin, and McCarthy 2008). In the case of the LCM, the second two targets described above—the mainstream environmental movement and the labor movement—could be considered indirect targets through which the movement is hoping to effect change at the ultimate target, which is the state. Additionally, while there are few examples of labor directly targeting capital to reduce GHG emissions, the targeting of the state is ultimately intended to change the behavior of capital through regulations that alter their incentive structure in such a way as to reduce GHG emissions.[10] LCM activists understand that capital operates on a decision-making model rooted in profit maximization—and thus the only way to elicit change within the capitalist logic is to alter the cost benefit matrix, which can be done primarily in two ways: altering consumer behaviors (affecting the demand side) or changing the regulatory landscape in which businesses operate (affecting the supply side). The LCM participants in this study overwhelmingly believed that targeting consumer habits was inadequate to address the problem and saw it as a tactic from the playbook of market-based solutions that are often embraced by the mainstream environmental movement. They instead opted to indirectly target the production side of the business calculus by targeting the state to enact regulations on industry. Many LCM activists promoted yet a third alternative, energy democracy, or the decommodification of energy by making companies publicly or community owned and thus not for profit—a change that would likely also involve government action. Figure 4.2 presents a complete map of the targets of the LCM, including both direct (black arrows) and indirect (gray arrows) target paths.[11]

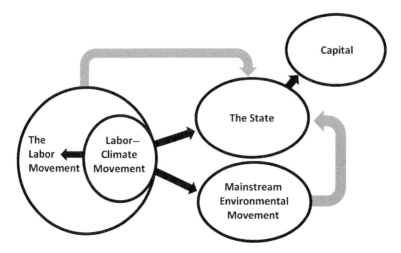

Figure 4.2 Direct and Indirect Targets
of the Labor-Climate Movement

As the figure shows, the purpose, at least in part, of the LCM's targeting of the culture of labor is to undermine a key pillar of support for fossil fuels and to build a worker-friendly climate protection movement to pressure the state to take action on the issue of climate change. And in targeting the environmental movement, the broader goal is to transform that movement's messaging to include working-class interests in its own demands on the government.[12] Ultimately, the goal of directly and indirectly targeting the state is to alter the behavior of capital that exploits both labor and the environment to maximize returns.

Building the Base: Frame Alignment Processes in the Labor-Climate Movement

As we have seen, framing is an interpretive scheme that renders social movement issues and goals meaningful to individuals and groups (Snow et al. 1986). The mobilization of individuals for collective action in the social movement depends on the alignment of actual and potential movement adherents with the social movement frame. In this case, union leaders and members see workplace issues as reasonable goals but may not see climate protection as an appropriate goal for unions. Frame extension occurs when an SMO extends "the boundaries of its primary framework so as to encompass interests or points of view that are incidental to its primary objectives but of considerable salience to potential adherents. In effect, the movement is attempting to enlarge its adherent pool by portraying its objectives or activities as attending to or being congruent with the values and interests of potential adherents" (Snow et al. 1986, 472). Or, to paraphrase Machiavelli's advice to the prince: introduce change by dressing it up in the clothes of the population's existing beliefs.

The term "organizational range" refers to the scope of goals sought by various movement organizations. The more the goals of various organizations overlap, the more likely they are to find common ground and thus work together in a collaborative way. Unions espousing social movement characteristics overlap with business unions in their goals to address workplace issues, they overlap with environmentalists in their concerns about climate change, and they also overlap with climate justice organizations in their goals to address racial equality and other forms of social justice in society. Unfortunately, the goals of most business unions do not overlap with the goals of climate justice organizations and only occasionally do so with mainstream environmental organizations.

By targeting the culture of the labor movement, the LCM is attempting to extend labor's frame to include climate protection as a legitimate goal of the movement. Doing so is going to require getting unions that support green growth, but not decarbonization, to start supporting emission-reduction targets. It is going to take getting unions that support emission-reduction targets in writing to take real action to make them a reality. For some of the more conservative business unions, it will require a wholesale frame transformation to shift from the Jobs vs. the Environment master frame to the Clean Air and Good Jobs counterframe. This requires convincing them that pursuing climate protection will provide jobs for their members, support expansion of their apprenticeship programs, and provide other benefits to their members.

In targeting the mainstream environmental movement, the LCM is also hoping to inspire frame expansion within that movement that would lead them to incorporate workers' interests into their demands for environmental protection. Most importantly, LCM activists want environmentalists to speak with and listen to labor and communities about their concerns and interests, rather than paternalistically advocating for what they feel is best for those communities. When the frames of these two movements are sufficiently expanded to overlap, the process of frame bridging can occur, as has happened on occasions such as the People's Climate March. In sum, the primary goal with regard to these two targets is to expand the movements' frames, increase their organizational ranges, and ultimately increase the informal alignment between the two movements.

The special positions of the labor–climate and climate justice movements warrant additional consideration as these two movements are well situated to serve as primary bridge builders between labor as a whole and the mainstream environmental movement. Each movement represents the most progressive tip of their respective larger movement, and each is targeting their broader movement, pushing it to extend its range. The LCM is pressing the labor movement to embrace scientifically informed GHG emission-reduction targets and the environmental movement to fight for worker protections. The climate justice movement is pressing both the mainstream environmental movement and the labor movement to embrace climate justice demands, including addressing historic inequities, promoting Indigenous rights, and redistributing resources and power to local communities. The more the LCM and the climate justice movement can embrace each other's demands and align their frames, the stronger the unified movement for labor and climate justice will be.

Redefinition

Confronting the dual crises of climate and inequality, the LCM has, through the process of collective action framing, redefined the situation as follows. Unmitigated climate change is a serious threat to all people but particularly to workers as well as people from marginalized communities, including communities of color, Tribal communities, and the poor. And most mitigation strategies currently under consideration (and supported by the mainstream environmental movement) pose a threat to the livelihoods and well-being of many workers and their communities, further fueling Jobs vs. the Environment conflicts. Further, the lack of active engagement by the labor movement to fight for solutions to climate change that incorporate working-class interests makes them a major pillar of support for continued fossil fuel use.

From this diagnosis, the LCM identified three distinct targets: the state, the middle-class culture of the environmental movement, and the business union culture of the labor movement. These targets capture both the structural dimensions of power, which are rooted in large-scale patterns of resource exchange, and the cultural dimensions of power, which are based on symbolically potent images and discourses (Polletta 2008). The state represents the one target that can deliver instrumental gains to movement participants by changing some elements of the social structure or reward distribution of society. However, the middle-class culture of the environmental movement and the business union culture of the labor movement represent constraining forces preventing the LCM from achieving its instrumental goal of climate solutions that protect workers and vulnerable communities.

These two dimensions, the structural and cultural, can often intersect and be mutually constitutive, which leads the LCM to strategically exploit opportunities in both dimensions within these multiple targets (Gamson 1989). Further, while the LCM directly targets the state as well as the environmental and labor movements, it is also indirectly targeting the state through potential changes made in the culture of either of the two movements it is targeting. This form of proximate targeting creates more opportunities for action because the LCM can shift targets in response to changing opportunity structures and rising or waning vulnerabilities.

In targeting the culture of the labor and environmental movements, the LCM seeks to expand the frames of these two movements and thus increase their organizational ranges. To the chagrin of LCM activists, the labor movement has largely espoused a business union culture with a restricted organizational range that focuses narrowly on material workplace issues—and if it does talk about climate, it does so only in the context of creating green jobs, not reducing emissions. Various structural factors elaborated in Chapters 2 and 3 have contributed to the unique positions of various unions on the issue of climate change, but the goal of the LCM is to overcome perceived structural constraints by redefining the situation. Reframing climate protection as a labor issue challenges business union culture by seeking to expand the organizational range of labor to include broader working-class issues that align more with a culture of social movement unionism. The ultimate goal of the LCM is to shift all unions further to the progressive half of the labor–climate spectrum, where they reject the Jobs vs. the Environment master frame and embrace the Clean Air and Good Jobs counterframe. Similarly, the LCM believes the middle-class culture of the mainstream environmental movement prevents the latter from understanding the class-based and racial nature of the climate crisis and thus leads them to pursue solutions that hurt workers and marginalized communities or, when they do include some forms of labor and community rights, to do so in a paternalistic manner that does not include local unions or community voices.

Like the LCM, the climate justice movement also represents an emerging challenge to the broader climate movement. Seeking to reframe climate discourse, the climate justice movement contends that the people who are most affected by pollution should be in the leadership of crafting policy solutions. The relationship between the LCM and the climate justice movement is likely to play a significant role in determining the effectiveness of either of these two movements to push a justice-focused agenda that centers the voices of workers as well as frontline and vulnerable communities. The ability of these two movements to align their frames, I contend, represents a crucial juncture and will determine whether the broad-based movement needed to promote just solutions to the climate crisis will arise to win a Green New Deal–like solution that centers workers and communities.

5

Union Workers for a Clean
and Just Economy

The Prognostic Frames of a Just Transition

Climate change and the many mainstream proposals for reducing carbon emissions pose a real threat to the livelihoods and well-being of working people and many communities. Lack of action from the federal government, little understanding of workers' issues within the mainstream environmental movement, and a culture of business unionism in much of the labor movement have only served to exacerbate these problems. So what is the solution? Or to ask the age-old question: "What is to be done?"

Prognostic framing involves the articulation of a proposed solution, or at the very least a plan of attack for confronting a problem as identified by a social movement. During my time participating in and studying the LCM, I repeatedly encountered a concept articulated by movement participants as a prognosis for addressing the interrelated problems of climate change and inequality: *just transition*. While the prognosis was regularly conveyed by participants from all three organizations—SPEC, USE, and LUPE—the exact meaning of "just transition" varied from one context to another. As time passed, I became increasingly aware that the term was in fact contested as I identified multiple distinct uses. When it comes to collective action framing, this type of "meaning work," or politics of signification, often involves a struggle over the production of key mobilizing ideas (Hall and Woollacott 1982; Snow and Benford 1988)—that is, social movement participants are not merely carriers of ideas and meanings that grow automatically out of existing structural arrangements but rather are social agents actively engaged in the production and maintenance of meaning for their constituents, antagonists, and bystanders.

Despite the variation in usage of this key mobilizing idea within the LCM, all the definitions of "just transition" have one common feature, the principal demand that defines the outer boundary for membership in the LCM, which is decarbonization of the economy. In other words, although the term has many competing meanings, they all share the underlying demand that GHG emissions must be reduced to address climate change, an assertion that is at odds with many unions and blue–green coalitions that support green growth. Another important point of contention is the extent to which just transition demands made by the LCM will align with demands for social and racial justice raised by allies in the climate justice movement.

Apart from these misalignments with external movements such as the blue–greens and at times the climate justice movement itself, the varied use of the term "just transition" within the LCM was generally tolerated—a fact that appears to stem from the unique strategic benefit each frame has in relation to the three distinct targets of the movement (the state, environmentalists, and labor). The differentiated but interconnected frames are also deployed strategically at different levels of mobilization—state, national, and international. However, before exploring the variation in usage of the term "just transition" and when and how it was deployed by the LCM, it will be helpful to briefly explore the origins of the concept as it relates to labor and climate justice.

Just Transitions: A Brief History of the Concept

The genesis of the concept of "just transition" is commonly attributed to the work and ideas of the late American labor and environmental leader Tony Mazzocchi of OCAW and a network of activists, including Michael Merrill, Les Leopold, Brian Kohler, and others in the 1990s. The term is believed to have been first publicly used in 1995, by Leopold and Kohler during a presentation to the International Joint Commission on Great Lakes Water Quality (Dimitris, Krause, and Morena 2019; Hampton 2015). As a concept, just transition merges the often-conflicting projects of economic transition and the pursuit of social justice into one endeavor. For Mazzocchi, it was very much about countering the right-wing narrative that pitted workers against environmentalists and communities. In academic writing, the transition side of the equation first appears in studies of sociotechnical transitions, including energy transitions, that require long-term and complex reconfigurations of policy, technology, infrastructure, and social and cultural practices (Geels and Schot 2007; Newell and Mulvaney 2013; Scrase and Smith 2009). Discussing transitions provides a convenient political and policy framework for approaching the societal movement toward sustainability (Meadowcroft 2011). Talking about transition enables aspirations for sustainability to be channeled into efforts to achieve long-term goals such as a zero-emissions economy.

On the "just" side of the just transition equation, we find social movement actors raising the crucial political and economic questions of who wins, who loses, how, and why, as they relate to the existing energy system and any proposed transition to an alternative system. The determination of whether a transition will be "just" raises the following questions: Who suffers currently or has suffered historically from the effects of fossil fuel extraction, production, and energy generation? Who benefits from it? Who will bear the social and economic costs, and who will reap the greatest benefits of decarbonizing our economy? For any transition to be just, there must be an analysis of the distributional outcomes and a corresponding plan to mitigate the ill effects, particularly for the most vulnerable elements of society, including marginalized communities and workers.

As should be clear by now, just transition is by necessity a political project. An economic transition toward renewable energy and sustainability, even without pursuing social justice, is immediately political because our current economic institutions do not naturally put us on a course of sustainable development—that is, the market system alone will not produce a carbon-free energy system, at least not in time to avoid climate catastrophe. This means that some form of state intervention is inevitably required to initiate a transition. A transition to a sustainable economy will almost certainly require changes to law and regulations, such as the imposition of a carbon tax, the creation of a GHG emissions cap-and-trade system, or perhaps the outright nationalization of the energy sector itself. It will likely also require a significant expenditure of public revenue to accelerate the development and deployment of new technologies and to ease societal adjustment to new patterns of production and consumption. Such changes can only be orchestrated through political processes and enforced through institutions of the state.

Beyond the economics of transition, incorporating demands for social justice further politicizes the process. In a purportedly pluralist society such as the United States, with countless competing interest groups, the government is perpetually engaged in negotiating distributional impacts from various attempts to address social or environmental injustices. The state must contend with the consequences of rising or declining industries, as well as economic impacts on regions, workers, community members, business owners, and so on that result from any transition efforts. Unsurprisingly, the most politically organized and resource-rich elements of society generally win concessions, as has been the case with many NIMBY movements. This unequal access to power and resources has over time created an environmentally racist configuration of the U.S. energy production and waste disposal systems (Bullard 1993). Alleviating these forms of injustice requires a degree of economic and social planning that is anathema to the current neoliberal institutional arrangements embedded in the U.S. state.

Notwithstanding the fundamentally political nature of just transition, many people from across the political spectrum agree that the world is on an unsustainable path and that "business as usual" is not an option (Leiserowitz, Kates, and Parris 2005). However, there still remain many "hard" and "soft" disagreements about the most desirable form of transition (Scoones et al. 2007). The hard disagreements arise from those that are fundamentally opposed to change, such as institutions and businesses whose profits and power are necessarily interlocked with the status quo, making them key pillars of support for the fossil fuel regime. Yet even among those who share a broad "green" consensus, there lies a range of hotly contested visions of sustainability that define the framing of and approach to transition (see Stevis, Krause, and Morena 2019; Stevis and Felli 2015). These soft disagreements are equally important, and they too implicate material questions of economy, material interest, and resource allocation. They also lead to varied conceptions of what just transition means and what it should entail—that is, there arises a set of distinct, contested, but interrelated frames for the concept of just transition.

Just Transition Frames in the Labor-Climate Movement

In my study of the LCM, I distinguish three uniquely identifiable, but not entirely mutually exclusive, frames for the usage of the term "just transition": protective, proactive, and transformative.[1] I also incorporate a fourth category that I call oppositional, which is a counterframe put forth by some workers and some unions, particularly in the fossil fuel industries, who find the phrase "just transition" to be toxic. It is important to note that within the opposition frame resides a contingent of unions, largely in the building trades, that supports green growth initiatives but opposes emission-reduction targets. This relationship between growth agendas, emission-reduction plans, and just transition plans will be examined more closely later in this chapter to explore how they help shape the preferred mode of change promoted by various social actors. However, this section will focus on elaborating each of the just transition frames identified in the LCM—protective, proactive, and transformative.

Protective Just Transition: "A Superfund for Workers"

"Why do we treat dirt better than we treat workers?" asked Tony Mazzocchi in a 1993 article in *Earth Island Journal*. "There is a Superfund for dirt," he stated, so "there ought to be one for workers." Mazzocchi's definition of the Superfund for workers is premised on the basic principle of fairness, in which the burden of policies that are necessary for the good of society—such as protecting the environment or the climate—should not be borne by workers who through no fault of their own would be victims of their side effects.[2] The Superfund for workers is perhaps the best example of what I will refer to as a "protective just transition." In this frame, just transition is focused on protecting workers in vulnerable industries and, where job losses are unavoidable, creating a safety net for those workers and communities that stand to lose out, in part by guaranteeing full wages and benefits to employees who lose their jobs as a result of environmental regulations until a comparable job can be found. In my research, the protective frame was deployed most by LCM activists from the state-level organization and the building trades and manufacturing unions but also from the national organization as part of a larger plan for a managed retreat from fossil fuel use.

Protective just transition would include provisions such as a fund to provide financial support, health benefits, and opportunities for higher education for workers displaced by environmental protection policies. While it is true that, on balance, environmental policies tend to create more jobs than they eliminate, this fact is of little comfort to the workers in industries that use or produce fossil fuel who lose their jobs as a result of climate protection policies, including coal miners, power plant workers, and oil refinery workers (Goodstein 1999). For both moral and pragmatic reasons, these workers should be protected. First, it is simply the right thing to do. The workers who have toiled in dirty and dangerous jobs to power the economy for decades should not be left on the scrap heap. Second, providing support for these workers is also necessary to help build the broad-based support required for implementation of strong climate protection measures. Without a Superfund or safety net in place, displaced workers can rapidly become "Fox News poster children" for the threat posed to workers by climate protection (Brecher 2015). Jake, a top labor leader in USE and a former high-ranking officer in a national union confederation, summed it up this way: "Unless workers and communities are protected against the unintended effects of climate protection, there is likely to be a backlash that threatens the whole effort to save the planet."

There is some historical precedent for protective just transition measures in the United States, particularly for workers who have been adversely affected by government trade policies. For example, the Trade Act of 1974 and subsequent programs, such as trade adjustment assistance after NAFTA, provided compensatory benefits to working people who lost their jobs as a result of trade agreements. Unfortunately, inadequate funding, restrictive eligibility requirements, scant benefits, and poor administration mean that most trade adjustment programs have been insufficient to provide displaced workers with a new start in life and as such have earned a bad reputation among working people who have been displaced by government policies (more on this in the oppositional just transition counterframe below). Proponents of protective just transition argue that a similar, but better, program can be developed for workers affected by energy transition policies. Specifically, people who lose their jobs because of the transition to a climate-safe economy should be eligible for full wages and benefits for a period of time and receive education or training, including free college tuition, or decent pensions with healthcare if they are ready to retire.

The protective just transition frame was adopted by many LCM participants, particularly those from SPEC and various manufacturing unions and building trades unions, including machinists, carpenters, and electrical workers. Jacob, a leader with SPEC and a community organizer, had this to say about just transition:

> I think of the coal miners that I used to work with in West Virginia. It's not their fault that they're stuck in dangerous, back-breaking jobs that are not healthy for them or the planet. But they've been doing this for generations and that's their way of life, and so the changes that we need to make as a society, they shouldn't have to bear the full burden of it. And that we need to create a way to bring them along and to provide sustenance for them and their families. And in some ways it's addressing the structural changes that are gonna be affecting them anyway, regardless of what we do about climate change, even if it's the market that is destroying their way of life.

As this passage indicates, the protective vision of just transition appeals to the value of fairness. One way to make the transition from fossil fuels fairer is to provide a safety net for those who have done the hard work of powering our economy but will lose their jobs by no fault of their own.

Jonah, also a participant in SPEC and a leader in USE, said that a just transition program could resemble the GI Bill of Rights, which "provided education and training, loan guarantees for homes, farms, and businesses, and unemployment pay for veterans returning from war." The GI Bill of Rights has been cited as a fundamental component of the economic boom that followed (Altschuler and Blumin 2009). Jonah argues that a similar program is needed today for those who are displaced from their jobs as we transition to clean energy alternatives. James, a statewide leader from a manufacturing union affiliated with SPEC, said, "We should be able to provide income replacement for people . . . displaced from fossil fuel jobs and we should be able to provide education, healthcare, and those sorts of things. It may seem pie in the sky, but I think you have to fight like hell for the most aggressive platform that you can, and keep pushing it, because if we don't, as representatives of the workers [who] are affected, who's going to, you know?"

Josh, a leader in a large public sector union local affiliated with USE, also emphasized the importance of protecting the communities that are affected by the transition:

> So a just transition, I think, has to address not only the workers themselves, but also the local businesses and those folks that are kinda dependent on those unionized workers who spend their money in the area. So, you know, it's a big lift, and we talk about just transition and that's just great, but the problem is that we're not likely to be building the windmills or the solar panels in the town where the coal mine was closed. You can't just say to somebody, you know, we're closing a coal mine in upstate New York, and we're building windmills now in Connecticut, so why don't you just move your family down to Connecticut. I think the idea that, as we displace workers, we've got to have something in place to either provide really enhanced retirement programs or real effective retraining with a local jobs program so there's a job to go into at the end.

Ron, a leader in a local union confederation, described his own experience with a community that was facing the closing of a local coal plant—the primary employer and source of tax revenue for the town. In collaboration with local unions—including the teachers' union, whose members' schools were facing closures, and a local environmental justice group that wanted to ensure that the closure was done equitably—the labor federation and community groups organized and won a just transition that included short-term income replacement for workers, the passage of a state law that provided tax assistance to communities affected by the closure of fossil fuel plants, and the creation of an economic development plan for the town as the economy transitions to new forms of business. However, cases like this, Ron said, are the exception and not the norm when it comes to displaced workers and their communities, "but that's what labor needs to fight for."[3]

At the core of the protective vision of just transition is a set of protections for workers who are displaced as a result of government policy that is deemed necessary to protect the common good. This would primarily affect workers in the extraction industries but also some building trades workers employed in the energy sector and some in manufacturing. Again, quoting Mazzocchi: "Paying people to make the transition from one kind of economy—from one kind of job—to another is not welfare. Those who work with toxic materials on a daily basis . . . to provide the world with the energy and the materials it needs deserve a helping hand to make a new start in life" (1993, 40).

Promoters of the protective just transition frame also argue that without a clear program to protect working people from the effects of climate protection–related policies such as plant closures and drilling bans, the struggle for clean energy can easily come to be perceived as an environmentalist struggle against American workers—even though climate protection will benefit rather than harm those workers. A protective just transition program could provide a critical element for drawing together workers, unions, and allies around a broader program for protecting jobs by protecting the climate. Making a protective just transition program for workers a central feature of climate change mitigation plans, proponents argue, could make the difference between united support for a sustainable and equitable economy and a never-ending battle over Jobs vs. the Environment.

Proactive Just Transition: "A Green New Deal"

The second just transition frame I identify is the proactive one. While inclusive of many aspects of the protective frame, this second, more expansive frame incorporates two additional key elements: (1) a forward-looking plan, usually involving large-scale public investment and government intervention into markets, to transition the economy to a more sustainable model; and (2) a seat at the table for labor in the development and administration of the transition program.

The first component of this frame aligns closely with the essence of a Green New Deal, both as was introduced in the Green Party platform in 2012 and as was elaborated by Representative Ocasio-Cortez and Senator Markey's 2019 congressional resolution (U.S. Congress 2019). In fact, the exact phrase "Green New Deal" was often used by participants in the LCM to describe their vision of a massive government infrastructure program to replace fossil fuels with renewable sources, increase energy efficiency, and create good union jobs.[4] The second component of the proactive frame corresponds with the following statement by the International Labour Organization (ILO): "The notion of Just Transition is in line with the long-standing philosophy that has inspired the creation and the history of the International Labour Organization: the idea that social concerns have to be part and parcel of economic decision-making, that the costs of economic transition should be socialized as much as possible, and that the economic management of the economy is best achieved when there is genuine social dialogue between social partners" (Cunniah 2010, 122). While the term "social dialogue" has a specific meaning in the European context, the general idea of having a seat at the table in policy formation and implementation resonates with the demands for a proactive just transition. Importantly, the proactive framing goes beyond the creation of a Superfund or safety net to protect workers who are displaced—it envisions a large public program developed with input from labor that seeks to proactively address climate change and minimize the social costs of transition rather than merely reacting to closures and job loss on a case-by-case basis. The proactive frame was deployed most often by LCM activists at the national level and by many public sector unions, education unions, and some state-level union confederations.

The phrase "Green New Deal" is a play on President Roosevelt's New Deal programs, which comprised government spending and economic planning to address the economic hardships of the Great Depression in the 1930s. Seeing climate change as a similarly universal, if not an existential, problem, the supporters of proactive just transition promote massive government investment in renewable energy projects, green infrastructure, reforestation, and energy efficiency upgrades that create good jobs while simultaneously reducing GHG emissions and dependence on fossil fuels. The ideas of social dialogue and industrial planning, as envisioned by the ILO and embraced by the ITUC, provide a road map for what a proactive just transition might look like. Beyond merely protecting workers when disaster strikes, proactive just transition demands labor be at the table to help craft policies that will protect the environment and workers simultaneously.

Proactive just transition also poses a strong challenge to the culture of business unionism within U.S. labor because it envisions unions participating in economic and political planning that extends beyond the workplace. As John, a national leader of a manufacturing union, stated, "Neoliberalism was born when the American labor movement agreed to only focus on issues within the four walls of the workplace and leave everything else up to capital." In other words, the adoption of a business union perspective conceded authority and power to capital, but the proactive vision of just transition challenges that free market ideology and seeks to wrest some power back into the hands of labor to help shape the broader political economy of the nation and the world—a goal more in line with the "heroic" social movement union culture.

Environmental justice scholars who have also defined just transition as a proactive process argue that efforts to steer society toward a lower-carbon future must be underpinned by attention to issues of equity and justice. In other words, just transition away from fossil fuels must not only be protective in its plan to address the concerns of those whose livelihoods are affected by and dependent on a fossil fuel economy but also be proactive in addressing the social injustices faced by those currently without access to reliable energy supplies and living in poverty or those who have been historically excluded from opportunities to work in the energy sector but have disproportionately experienced the consequences of the pollution generated by it (Newell and Mulvany 2013). Many LCM participants who were also involved with environmental justice groups pushed hard to keep this aspect of just transition on the table. Supporters of the proactive frame agreed that just transition needs to address past racial injustices, but many environmental justice activists in the movement complained that the issue was often moved to the back burner when issues affecting current union members arose. In such instances, participants in the LCM often struggled to maintain their relationships with both union leaders and climate justice leaders. Overall, those participants supporting a proactive just transition called for the creation of support structures, such as compensation and retraining for new employment opportunities, for people and sectors that stand to lose out as a result of decarbonizing the economy. They emphasize that new jobs created in low-carbon sectors must be good jobs that pay a living wage, provide decent working conditions, allow access to people with a range of skills—including those from historically marginalized communities—and offer opportunities for career growth.

Support for the proactive just transition frame came from participants in all three LCM SMOs, but it was more often promoted by activists at the national level. Dylan, a leader in a national service sector union and participant in USE and LUPE, lays out his proactive vision of just transition in this way:

> We ought to demand a permanent roundtable where all constituencies are there to figure out how this planning, this just transition, social and economic, will take place. How is money going to be spent? What are the values on which it is spent? What are the projects on which it is spent? We should be making those demands as a labor movement. Protect workers. Protect all workers. Prepare for the dislocation that's going to come. Get used to it. Make sure that we have a healthy soci-

ety going forward. As we go forward—spending money, leveraging money, guaranteeing money for all of the work that needs to be done to transition us to this new sustainable society—workers, people of color, poor people, immigrant folks, everybody has to be at the table in a formal way, and we need to make those demands. That's what just transition is to me.

Dylan refers to a permanent roundtable to plan the transition, a demand that echoes the ILO's call for social dialogue and the inclusion of all stakeholders in society-wide economic decision-making. Labor leaders fear that if workers are not involved in the planning, then worker issues will not be incorporated into the transition—as has so often been the case with many of the policy proposals and demands made by mainstream environmental groups. Like many other participants, Dylan believes the labor movement needs to take the lead in demanding a just transition plan, which he feels it currently is not. Dylan repeated a refrain that I heard often among LCM activists: "The environment is too important to be left to the environmentalists," a sentiment that challenges the assumption of some social movement scholars that the environment is not an issue that traditional, materialist movements like labor are concerned with (Inglehart 1977; Melucci 1985; Touraine 1981).

Manuel, a leader in USE and a labor–community organizer, also takes a proactive view of just transition, but he places more of the onus on labor to begin transforming the jobs in the renewable energy economy into good jobs by organizing those workers now:

I think it really does have to be broad, because it's not going to be a straight up, one-to-one replacement in the energy sector from fossil fuels jobs to renewable energy. There's a lot of work that's got to be done in terms of organizing within the renewable energy sector to make sure those jobs are good-paying jobs when workers are transitioning into them. There's a lot of work in terms of bringing manufacturing of renewables here as well so those are good-paying jobs, but even beyond that, there's just got to be a real good analysis around the transition, a real goal to organize the new jobs and a big program for how we do that.

In addition to organizing to make renewable energy jobs into good jobs, he promotes economic and trade policies that would ensure that the manufacturing of renewable energy components such as wind turbines and solar panels is done in the United States with decent wages and strong labor protections—a long-standing demand of labor. Finally, he refers to the need for a long-term plan, or Green New Deal, which he went on to say needed to be similar in size and scope to the U.S. government preparations in the lead-up to World War II. This form of massive public investment, promoted by several LCM participants and outlined in policy papers by USE, was commonly referred to as a "World War II–style mobilization of the economy."

Public sector unions were also more likely to convey the proactive just transition frame. For example, Josh, a leader in a large public sector union local, acknowledges that a proactive just transition is unlikely to begin in the current U.S. political climate, but he makes the case that plans must constantly be made from a working-class perspective and presented to policy makers so that in a moment of crisis when leaders are scrambling to respond, they will have something they can look at and possibly latch on to. He said:

> I do think we're gonna get to the level where people actually start to freak out a little bit on this and they get truly scared as the intensity of storms increases and roads flood, et cetera. And I'm concerned that we have a piece that's ready to go at that point, that we can say, look, this is what we need to do at the national level and at the state level and even at the city level in terms of trying as quickly as possible to turn this ship around in terms of where we're going on the climate crisis. Because I think if we are not positioned to do that, I fear a kind of typical reaction from the government which could well end up with martial law in places and further concentrations of power and wealth in the hands of the few. We've seen that to some degree already with Katrina and whatnot. And I'd like to think that we would have some kind of program in hand, ready to go.

This strategy is reminiscent of Naomi Klein's "shock doctrine" thesis (2007), in which she argues that neoliberal economists who were once on the fringe in policy circles kept making plans and presenting their case until, when in moments of crisis, policy makers who needed something to grab on to would pick up the first thing they could find that looked like a solution; in those cases, it was privatization and deregulation. The concept of "disaster capitalism" has certainly taken hold in the era of human-caused climate change as large corporations, private equity firms, and other powerful actors find great opportunities for profit in the wake of devastating storms, wildfires, and floods. Supporters of the proactive just transition frame, like Josh, envision the opposite of disaster capitalism—a proactive plan that would "increase the power of workers and communities in the wake of catastrophes rather than stripping them of their rights to further enrich the one percent."

At the state level, Drew, who is involved with SPEC and is a staff organizer with a building trades union, discussed the ways that construction unions could actively promote proactive transition through the types of projects they put their political weight behind:

> As it goes for just transition for my union, a lot of what we're involved with is new construction. We're not dealing with materials extraction or we're not dealing with maintaining a coal fire power plant. We're not the people who are doing the safety monitoring of the pipeline or cleaning it or anything like that. We are building new things. So, the just transition, as it pertains to commercial construction, is a question of which projects we decide to work on and move towards as a union. The whole idea of a transition is you have the old infrastructure and you get rid of it because it's bad, and then you go to the new thing. Our side is more on building the new things that create good jobs and create good energy. So, in my immediate experience, it's being able to have us move towards new industries, new construction, new development that's going to support that.

He said that unfortunately the decisions about which projects his union chooses to promote are often determined by a project's perceived ability to win the political struggle as well as the number of jobs that will be immediately created—both factors that have contributed to support for natural gas power plants and pipelines rather than renewable sources in recent years. He did note that he participated in SPEC in part to form the kind of alliances that might increase the chances of winning the political battles to build renewable energy projects such as offshore wind farms.

Jared, also a leader in a building trades union involved with SPEC, discussed local workforce investment boards as a way to create a pipeline of training and job placement for workers into renewable energy sectors. These boards could target hiring in marginalized communities, and unions could target these jobs for organizing. Jonah, also a participant in SPEC and USE, talked about the need for a federal jobs program, like the Works Progress Administration during the New Deal. "By ensuring jobs for everyone, fixing the climate, and addressing unmet social needs," he said, "we could address the climate problem as well as begin to address a lot of the injustices and environmental racism that we see in our cities and states." One of the weaknesses of the original New Deal was its uneven incorporation and sometimes exclusion of Black Americans and other minority groups from many of the government programs, largely to appease the demands of southern Democrats ("Dixiecrats") who would not vote in favor of broadly egalitarian and integrative programs. Climate justice activists within the LCM fear that without a strong focus on remedying historic racial injustice, a Green New Deal could just recreate most of the existing social inequalities within a greener economy.

In sum, the proactive just transition frame incorporates many elements of the protective just transition frame but adds the components of planning ahead for an economic shift and bringing labor to the table to help craft a large-scale public plan to address the climate crisis. Rather than just having a safety net for certain workers who are adversely affected by specific plant closures—which some adherents of the proactive frame referred to as a "reactive transition"— just transition should be a plan developed with input from all stakeholders in society, but especially labor, to grow the renewable energy sector and also create good jobs. For proponents of this frame, the only reasonable way to ensure that any transition plan serves the interests of workers is to have workers and their organizations at the table to help craft the plan. As various participants told me during this study, "If you're not at the table, you're probably on the menu." Proactive just transition is a vision of labor having a voice in economic planning and engaging with policy makers to address the climate crisis and ensure that workers' concerns are addressed in all transition plans. Possibly connected, but as yet not certain, is the question of how much this frame will make demands for remedying the historical legacies of racial and social injustice a central component of the transition. The answer will depend in part on the degree to which a social movement union perspective is adopted and whether LCM activists embrace struggles for the benefit of workers beyond just current union members.

Transformative Just Transition: "System Change Not Climate Change"

The third and most radical framing of just transition is what I refer to as a transformative just transition. As stated by the ITUC in a workshop at the Durban climate talks:

> Climate is also our issue because addressing it implies recognizing the need for a huge transformation in our societies, in our production and consumption systems, and therefore also on jobs. And recognition alone is not sufficient. Leadership by the labor movement is needed for transforming the system. Unless we fight for making this transformation

work for the people, ensuring a Just Transition towards a truly sustainable model, we will only see superficial changes towards more inequality and environmental degradation. (S. Smith 2017)

Transformative just transition is about more than just protecting workers or planning ahead for sustainability. The central goal of this frame is transitioning to a socioeconomic model that addresses the root causes of environmental degradation, worker exploitation, and social injustices (Bond 2012; Okereke 2010). This frame owes much of its ideological underpinnings to the environmental justice and climate justice movements, as well as the broader socialist movement. Within the context of the LCM, the two key elements of the transformative transition frame I identified in my data are (1) enacting different models of ownership and economic decision-making and (2) eliminating existing social and economic inequalities and injustices. Importantly, while most promoters of the transformative frame embraced both of these elements, some prioritized just one of the two but still called for radical transformative change, in the form of either capital–labor relations or the elimination of the existing racialized and patriarchal social hierarchy. The first of these components of the transformative frame was deployed most vocally by LCM activists from the international organization, as well as those from service sector, transportation, and healthcare unions; the second aspect was deployed largely by activists who participated in both the LCM and the climate justice movement.

Looking more closely at the first component, transformative just transition embodies a radical reorganization of society by envisioning a postcapitalist world order. Where the protective frame makes demands on the state to participate in the economy in the form of taxation and funding of a social safety net and the proactive vision makes a stronger challenge on free market ideology by demanding some limited economic planning and a voice for labor in policy making, the transformative vision encompasses demands ranging from democratic socialism on one end to a complete reorganization of the political economy to eliminate the distinction between the owners of capital and labor on the other end.

In the second component, we see that transformative just transition understands the historical use of racism and colonialism to sow division among the working classes of the world and seeks to directly remedy that history of injustices through its solution to the climate crisis. From this standpoint, just transition is rooted in alliances among the climate justice, environmental justice, Indigenous rights, and labor movements in what some participants have referred to as a process of "de-silofication," or recombination of activists who have been sorted into specific issue-based "silos" that focus exclusively on one issue, such as climate change; labor rights; environmental justice; or economic, racial, or gender equality. Challenging the assumption that new social movements such as environmentalism and social justice are not material in nature, the transformative just transition frame unites activists at the intersection of jobs, justice, and the environment—a natural fit for those in labor who adhere to the social movement vision of unionism and for those from the climate justice movement who embrace labor justice in their demands. Those who embrace both components of this frame see just transition as a means to address the multiple and overlapping concerns of many individual social movements—if they all would come out of their silos and see how their issues interconnect.

In my data, the transformative frame was used most often by participants in LUPE and among LCM activists who were also involved with environmental justice and climate justice groups. For example, Dylan, a leader in a large service sector union and a participant in USE and LUPE, advocates for a progressive labor agenda as a necessary component of a transformative just transition:

> I think that just transition is something that if we approach it correctly is a way to achieve a lot of our social economic goals in a much broader way throughout society. I think that just transition can really be a transformative idea and program. . . . The labor movement needs to define what it means, and it should obviously mean first and foremost a just transition for workers who are displaced. But we need to think bigger. We must argue that our [labor] program of full employment, income maintenance, and healthcare for all are a social necessity if we want to avoid chaos and insurrection as [climate catastrophe] takes place. I think that this crisis will really necessitate a rethinking of what our economic and social demands are.

From this perspective, linking climate protection to the addressing of a myriad of other social problems is both an opportunity and a necessity.

Many participants referred to Klein's book *This Changes Everything* (2014) as making a strong case for linking a variety of social, economic, and environmental struggles into programs designed to address the climate crisis. "The real inconvenient truth," Klein says, referencing the title of Al Gore's film about climate change, is that "it's not about carbon emissions—it's about capitalism" (2014, 8). The convenient truth, she argues, is that citizens can seize on the existential crisis posed by climate change to transform the failed capitalist system and build something radically better. "The real solutions to the climate crisis are also our best hope of building a much more stable and equitable economic system, one that strengthens and transforms the public sphere, generates plentiful, dignified work, and radically reins in corporate greed" (125). This argument corresponds with the framing that supporters of transformative just transition put forward.

To be sure, creating a low-carbon and sustainable economy will bring significant challenges and opposition from a broad array of interest groups, but the challenges are amplified for those espousing the transformative vision that demands relinquishing private ownership and control over the energy sector to local communities or other public entities. This is the primary goal of LUPE, which conceives of energy democracy—or public ownership and control of the energy sector—as the only realistic way to address the problems of climate change and inequality in a timely fashion. As Steve, a leader in LUPE and member of an education union, stated:

> The markets have no answer. The political discourse of the Democratic Party has no answer. We, the labor movement, have to provide the answer. It means we have to do the hard work of developing a policy that not only can solve the problem of GHG emissions and climate change, but do it in a way that there is justice, good jobs with equal opportunities for all, but over and above, we at the end of the day will control the new energy system, democratically. It will be public investment, public ownership, and public management.

Steve and others involved with LUPE make the case that the neoliberal capitalist model of economic decision-making will not adequately address the climate crisis. Carbon markets and other market-based solutions are inadequate and do not address the root cause of the problem. Only when decisions are made on the basis of human need and the public good rather than profit margins can we make the type of rapid and dramatic changes to the energy sector that are needed to avoid catastrophe.

In addition to envisioning a publicly owned and controlled energy sector, many who deploy the transformative frame also advocate for seizing the assets of highly profitable fossil fuel companies as a way to muster the funding to make a rapid shift to a sustainable energy system. For example, James, a leader in a manufacturing union, said:

> I think that working on climate change in the long run calls for evolving social structures and economic structures that are more democratic, less profit driven, and more mindful of the different interests that society has. Fossil fuel companies have made billions of dollars.

We should be grabbing hold of big chunks of that money that is now sitting in the bank of these companies that want to walk away not only from the workers, but also the communities, and leave devastation in their wake. That is money that can be used to build the sustainable economy we need.

So, be it nationalization, the transfer of ownership and control to local communities, or the seizure of assets of polluting companies, the proponents of the transformative just transition frame adopt a decidedly more radical vision for addressing the problems of climate change and inequality than is prescribed by either the protective or proactive frames. As such, the transformative frame provides perhaps the most comprehensive prognostic solution but is also the most difficult to achieve, at least in the context of the contemporary United States. It is also important to note that aside from the tangible demand for public ownership and democratic control of the energy sector, there is generally lack of a clear vision of what a broader postcapitalist society would look like and of a process for realizing it, which raises questions of whether the talk of transformation is largely a symbolic use of language whose function is to indicate a rejection of the status quo.

Beyond making demands for different models of ownership and control, the transformative just transition frame draws from its roots in the environmental and climate justice movements by acknowledging the interconnectedness of existing economic inequality, social injustice, and the climate crisis. None of these problems can be solved without addressing the others. Aaron, an LCM activist from a local labor confederation in a large city, discussed the importance of building solutions to economic and environmental inequality into any transition. By way of example, he described his organization's effort to require rooftop solar panels on public buildings in the city. "The good news," he said, is "the city agreed to put solar panels on public buildings, but unfortunately the battle is not over because the plan adopted by the city would allow private corporations to own the panels, making private profit rather than generating cost savings for public agencies providing vital social services who are facing perpetual budget shortfalls." Further, the units would be installed primarily on public school buildings in the most affluent communities, thus reinforcing or possibly exacerbating existing inequalities. Aaron said, "This is what transition looks like when neoliberals are at the wheel. We in labor must fight to use the transition as a way to flip the whole logic of the system and make it serve the people."

The transformative frame is typically portrayed in the protest chant and slogan "System change, not climate change," which many labor–climate and climate justice activists embraced at the People's Climate Marches in New York City in 2014 and Washington, DC, in 2017. This antisystemic approach has also been referred to as "radical environmentalism," rooted in the belief that the "enduring power structures of sovereignty, capitalism, scientism, patriarchy, and even modernity generate and perpetuate the environmental crisis while consolidating structural inequalities" (Pettenger 2013, 132). Hakim, a participant in LUPE and a leader of a local transportation union, supported this claim when he emphasized how climate change and the current mitigation efforts promoted by mainstream "liberal" environmentalists "disproportionately affect certain frontline and marginalized communities, thus reproducing and exacerbating existing social and economic inequalities."

Because the transformative frame is the most radical just transition frame, many participants in the LCM were unwilling to publicly adopt the frame, but many privately acknowledged their support for it. Apart from those quoted above, many labor leaders I interviewed expressed in confidence that they believed a transformative shift was indeed the only real way to effectively address the problems of both climate change and inequality. They said, however, that they chose not to aggressively advocate for this approach; they believe that conveying too radical a view would undermine their credibility within their unions, labor at large, and American politics in general—and that it is better for them to adopt a less radical frame in order to accomplish some small amount of good than to adopt the transformative frame, which might scare others away and lead to no change at all.

Others have expressed that the 2016 presidential campaign of Senator Bernie Sanders of Vermont opened windows of opportunity for them to lean left a bit more. As the senator who describes himself as a democratic socialist gained traction among union workers, some union leaders felt free to speak more openly about more socialistic solutions to the problems faced by American workers. Senator Sanders also introduced the Clean Energy Worker Just Transition Act, which lays out a proactive plan for providing protection for workers and communities affected by the necessary shift away from fossil fuels—a plan that, as we shall see in the next chapter, most LCM activists support. It is important to note that although they adopt the ideals of transformational change, the major tangible objective put forth by participants in the LCM who support the transformative just transition frame in this study was public ownership and control of the energy sector, which in the current political climate represents a radical shift but in the big picture falls short of creating a new postcapitalist world order. Aside from this tangible demand for energy democracy, the transformative frame appears to function largely as a way to "push the envelope" and promote higher aspirations rather than as an implementable plan—and it seems that it will (and probably should) proceed in continuing tension with more reformist approaches in the Green New Deal era.

Opposition to Just Transition: "A Fancy Funeral"

Most of the data on prognostic framing in this study can be classified into one of the three previously discussed just transition frames, but a counterframe emerged in my research that captured some participants' opposition to, or at least reluctance to use, the term "just transition." The oppositional frame is highly prevalent among the elements of the labor movement who are not involved with the LCM and thus not included in this study—such as many extraction workers. Some participants said that many workers and union leaders see just transition as a code word for job loss and nothing more than false promises that will never materialize to help workers. For example, Beverly, a leader in a state union confederation, said, "If you say 'just transition' to a steelworker in my state, they flip out like 'You're coming after my job, aren't you?!'"

James, a leader from a manufacturing union, said he had spoken with two national leaders in his union, and they said, "That'll never happen. It sounds nice, but you know what'll really happen? These folks are gonna lose their jobs, they are never gonna get as good a job again in their life. And that's that." James said unfortunately that is probably accurate—"at least, the history of it." Even past AFL-CIO president Richard Trumka, whose roots are in the UMWA, famously said of just transition, "It's just an invitation to a fancy funeral."

This oppositional frame appears to be expressed most by workers and leaders from manufacturing unions who have had bad experiences in the past with government promises of retraining and job placement that amounted to the elimination of well-paying union jobs with benefits—only to find low-paying service sector employment at the other end of the process. This frame is also deployed by some labor leaders who are supportive of efforts to address climate change but skeptical of the ability of the state to actually deliver on programs. For this reason, many chose to support green growth initiatives while opposing any emission-reduction measures that would lead to plant closures. Some union leaders from other countries involved with LUPE are less turned off by the concept because, unlike the United States, their countries have a history of actually following through on such plans. Most other affluent capitalist democracies have several pieces of a just transition plan already built into their large social safety nets, in the form of universal healthcare, free or low-cost education, and public pensions.

For these reasons, a small minority in the LCM in the United States believes that the term "just transition" has become too toxic and should be abandoned. For example, Barry, a national-level leader in a transportation union, had this to say:

> The problem is that the word itself has become something that really is not looked on kindly by people in the coal industry or the building sector, because they have seen unjust transition. Every transition that has been made has really left working people in the lurch, and nobody stands up for the people who lose their jobs. People who used to have really, really good jobs suddenly don't anymore, and their self-esteem tanks, and their ability to hold their head up in the community just evaporates, and they start doing all kinds of horrible self-destructive things, like voting for Donald Trump, taking drugs, alcohol, and all sorts of things that are not the answer, but they can't figure out what the answer really is, and so, the whole [term] "just transition" is something that we probably ought to transition away from, because it has such a bad meaning to so many working people, especially in the US.

Despite his criticism of the term, he went on to say that "we have to figure out a new construct" and insisted that "it's all about education and organization." Like others who thought the term needed to be abandoned, Barry still believed in the idea behind it and went on to say that labor needs to demand new jobs that are *better* jobs and don't threaten the environment or climate.

Manuel, a leader in USE and supporter of a proactive just transition, expressed sympathy for those who were opposed to the term: "It's understandable why so many are skeptical about just transition. . . . It's been false promises, or for many years failed promises. . . . It's totally understandable why folks would be like 'This is just bullshit, what are you talking about?'" But he went on to defend the principle behind just transition, even if the phrase needed to be changed: "So all the more reason why the labor movement really needs to be in the lead on this and not leave it up to other folks to define these programs, because otherwise, the interests of the workers are just going to get left out. I don't think it's a plan that we should give up on, but if we've got to use a different word, that's fine."

Aside from the few somewhat dissident voices among the participants I interviewed and spoke with during my observation, the vast majority of participants in the three SMOs examined in this study supported one of the first three frames for just transition. However, understanding the opposition to the term "just transition" is as important as understanding the contested meanings of this key mobilizing concept for the LCM.

Comparing the Frames

When in previous chapters we explored the ways that existing structural arrangements can shape the positions of workers and unions on the issue of climate change, we saw how the constraints on democracy within a capitalist society can limit the demands made by citizens (Wright and Rogers 2015). To recap, the assertion is that because economic growth is believed to create a common good, all decisions in society must be made in such a way as to ensure a good business climate and maximize growth. This "treadmill of production" restricts what is on and off the table for discussion in the democratic system and essentially constrains the ability of workers and others to call for measures that would challenge the underlying motive of profit-maximizing corporations in the energy sector. The presence of this demand constraint is illustrated by some LCM participants' private comments that they believe that the transformative frame is the real solution but would not call for it in public. However, in the face of this demand constraint, each of the first three just transition frames identified in this analysis represents a challenge to the dominant free market ideology that permeates American society. Movement participants espousing these frames are actively engaged in the production of meaning for their constituents, antagonists, and bystanders in order to promote and build support for an alternative social arrangement.

The protective frame calls for some form of government intervention in the market to redistribute resources in a more equitable way than the economy otherwise would. The proactive frame goes one step further by calling for some limited degree of economic planning that gives labor a voice equal to capital in designing a plan to move from the current fossil fuel–driven economy to a more sustainable economy. Finally, the transformative frame seeks to eliminate the underlying class structure of the ownership and control of the energy sector while also calling for some form of postcapitalist, postcolonialist economy that is not clearly defined. While each frame is progressively more radical in its demands, they all share the common theme of challenging the logic of neoliberal capitalism to put the interests of workers ahead of profits.

Table 5.1 provides a side-by-side comparison of the just transition frames adopted by different LCM participants, excluding the oppositional counterframe. Taken together, these frames capture the major components of just transition as a key organizing concept. The protective frame envisions a generous social safety net for displaced workers in the form of income replacement and early retirement, as well as support for affected communities through tax-base replacement and economic development plans. The proactive frame also in-

TABLE 5.1 COMPARING THE THREE JUST TRANSITION FRAMES ADOPTED BY LABOR–CLIMATE MOVEMENT PARTICIPANTS

	Just Transition Frames		
	Protective	Proactive	Transformative
Features of Transition Frames			
Provide income replacement, early retirement, education, and job placement for displaced workers	X	X	X
Provide economic support for affected communities, including tax-base replacement and economic development planning	X	X	X
Develop a long-term economic plan to decarbonize the economy in an orderly manner with built-in protections for workers		X	X
Ensure social dialogue, including a seat at the table for labor in the development of a transition plan		X	X
Prioritize the remediation of existing social and racial injustices as a central component of the transition plan		?	X
Transform the structure of the energy sector from profit-driven to a public-interest model of decision-making by shifting ownership and control from private companies to public entities			X

X—The particular feature is a central part of the transition frame.
?—The feature is still being contested among supporters of the frame.

cludes these first two forms of protection for affected workers and local communities but goes on to call for the development of a long-term economic plan to decarbonize the entire economy and guarantee a seat at the table for the development of such a plan. Whether this frame will center remedies to historical injustices along the lines of race and gender by focusing on the cleanup of "sacrifice zones" and prioritizing the placement of historically marginalized workers in new green union jobs is uncertain, but supporters of this frame who are also involved with climate justice organizations are certainly pushing for it, and only time will tell if they will prevail. Finally, the transformative frame includes the four demands espoused in the proactive frame as well as demands to address past environmental injustices and contends that, to succeed, the transition must involve a marked shift away from capitalism and toward social ownership and control of the energy sector.

Contrary to my expectation that there would be open struggle between the supporters of the three different uses of the term, I instead found that the nested nature of the three frames allowed for strategic deployment of each; that is, the choice of frame used by each of the three SMOs was not always consistent during my period of observation. LCM participants and SMOs would often shift between these frames depending on the context and changing opportunity structures at play during the moment. The ability of participants to shift between frames is due in part to their shared commitments to emission-reductions targets and strong worker protections. However, a number of structural and cultural factors have helped shape the decision of individuals or organizations to support one frame over others.

Explaining Variation in Just Transition Frames among Labor–Climate Movement Activists, Unions, and Social Movement Organizations

Each of the distinct but nested frames of just transition described above involves material questions of economy and resource allocation. Thus, it is important to consider the possible sources of variation in the framing of the concept. How does one's personal and organizational relationship with the issue of climate affect one's choice of framing? Is organizational framing consistent, or does context matter? My data reveal three broad sets of factors that contribute to prognostic frame variation: structural explanations, institutional–cultural explanations, and individual explanations. Each of these is explored briefly below, keeping in mind the three distinct units of analysis considered: individual LCM activists, their unions, and the three SMOs in which they participate.

Structural Explanations for Frame Variation among Individual Labor–Climate Activists

Generally speaking, the stable patterns of interaction among members of a society, institution, or organization constitute its social structure (Allardt 1972). The structural factors that help explain the variation in prognostic framing among individual participants in the LCM include their level of participation in the movement (state, national, international), the industry of their union (construction, transportation, education, etc.), and their position or rank within their organization (rank-and-file member, local leader, national leader, etc.).

As noted in the just transition frames described above, participants from the state-level organization, SPEC, were most often associated with the protective frame, and participants from the national and international organizations, USE and LUPE, were more likely to deploy either the proactive or transformative frames. This is likely driven in part by the goals and perceived possibilities for social change at each of these levels.[5] The more locally focused activists are confronting issues of climate change, jobs, and justice on a case-by-case basis and attempting to forge local coalitions and solutions for specific problems. For example, the pending closure of a nuclear power plant in the home state of SPEC prompted local LCM activists to advocate for measures to protect the workers and the economic viability of the community that depends on those jobs and the tax base the power plant provides.

At the national and international levels, the emphasis on large-scale planning and transformative change is more common because they are the types of demands that can be made of nations and international bodies. A World War II–style mobilization of the economy is by necessity a national, not a state or local, demand. Further, the U.S.-based participants in LUPE were in regular contact with LCM activists from countries outside the United States that have histories of making more radical demands. In fact, Rob, a former leader from a U.S. national union confederation, said, "The labor activists in Europe are more radical on environmental issues than the environmentalists are in the US." Regular conversations and collaboration with more progressive and radical international labor leaders may work to shift the prognosis by U.S. activists to the left as transformative ideas become more normalized.

A second structural factor shaping individual frame variation is the industry of the participant's employment—and thus his or her union or organizational affiliation. For example, participants from building trades unions and some manufacturing unions generally had a more pragmatic and less idealistic outlook than participants from the more progressive unions in education, the service sector, or healthcare industries. Table 5.2 presents the most common frame deployed by individuals from each type of union in my study.[6] Participants from unions in industries in which their members had jobs that would be threatened by climate protection measures were the most likely to express opposition to the term "just transition" and to adopt the more conservative protective frame. Participants in industries in which members confronted the consequences of climate change regularly on the job, such as healthcare and transportation, were more likely to adopt the proactive or transformative frames. Beyond this distinction, the unions with more traditional organizational forms and business union tendencies tended to adopt the more conservative frames, and the newer unions were more likely to be progressive. The culture of organizations in these different industries is also a factor that is discussed further below.

A third structural factor exerting influence on the prognostic framing of participants in the LCM is rank and position within their respective unions

TABLE 5.2 THE MOST COMMON PROGNOSTIC FRAMES OF INDIVIDUALS BY ORGANIZATION	
Organization	Most Common Frame
Extraction union	O/PT
Building trades union	PT
Union confederation	PT
Manufacturing union	PT/PA
Public sector union	PA
Education union	PA
Service sector union	PA/T
Transportation union	PA/T
Healthcare union	T
Prognostic frame: PT = Protective, PA = Proactive, T = Transformative, O = Oppositional.	

and organizations. The majority of participants in this study occupy some form of leadership position within their unions. In some cases, this gives them license to deploy more radical and militant stances, but in most cases, it tempered their framing—as was the case with those who confided in me that they personally believed in the transformative vision of just transition but publicly advocated for the protective or proactive frame. This was largely due to an anticipated negative reaction from rank-and-file members or higher-level leaders. Perhaps contradicting that fear, the rank-and-file union members who participated in the three SMOs were all on the more radical end of the spectrum: three-fourths deployed the transformative frame, and all stated a desire to push their unions to take a stronger stand on the issues of climate change and climate justice. This is not to say that all rank-and-file members are more militant than their union leaders but rather that those who are engaged with this issue clearly appear to be. Further, as I will discuss below, these particular individuals appear to be influenced more by their personal ideology than by their position within the labor movement.

Structural Explanations for Frame Variation among SMOs

The key structural explanations for variation in SMO framing are the level of the organization (state, national, international) and their collective action target (the state, labor, environmentalists). Beginning with the level of the organization, I find that just as with individual participants, SMOs focusing on state and local action were more likely to adopt the protective frame, whereas SMOs operating at higher levels were more likely to adopt the proactive or transformative frames. State organizations are confronted with local issues they typically deal with case by case, building coalitions and developing solutions, often in response to unanticipated, highly localized events. Organizations operating at the national and international levels are better positioned to craft demands that include long-term and global plans for transitioning to a sustainable and equitable economy.

The second key structural factor influencing prognostic frames of SMOs was the stated target of the movement at a particular time: the state, the mainstream environmental movement, or the culture of labor. Table 5.3 identifies the most common prognostic frames adopted by the organizations based on their level and the target at hand. I note that SMO framing is not always consistent across levels and can shift depending on the target. While the SMOs pursued all three targets simultaneously, they would often focus most of their efforts on just one target, depending on the existing political opportunity structure (McCammon et al. 2001). This process of what I refer to as "frame shifting" is explored further in the next chapter in consideration of the action mobilizations of each of the SMOs. Looking at the major patterns of frame deployment in Table 5.3, we see several trends.

First, within the state-level organization, the prognostic frame fluctuated between protective and proactive depending on the target. When activists from SPEC were taking political action directed toward the state, it almost always was proactive. However, when targeting mainstream environmentalists or the labor movement, they would fluctuate between the protective and proactive frames, urging environmentalists and unions alike to ensure protections for workers in some instances and to become more involved in crafting a worker-friendly plan to address climate change in others. Second, the national-level organization deployed all three frames at varying points during my time in the field. The proactive frame was most common and used across all three targets, but the protective frame was sometimes deployed when engaging more

TABLE 5.3 THE MOST COMMON PROGNOSTIC FRAMES OF SMOs BY LEVEL AND TARGET

Level of SMO	Target of SMO		
	The State	Environmentalists	Labor
State (SPEC)	PT/PA	PT/PA	PT/PA
National (USE)	PA	PA/T	PT/PA
International (LUPE)	T	T	T

Prognostic frame: PT = Protective, PA = Proactive, T = Transformative.
Note: The designation "State" as a level includes actions taken at the substate level (local unions, municipalities, etc.).

conservative elements of the labor movement. The transformative frame was used when communicating with more radical movement partners. The issues of social justice would be used in both the proactive and transformative contexts when the organization was working with climate justice movement partners. Finally, the international organization always deployed the transformative frame, regardless of the target.

Institutional–Cultural Explanations for Frame Variation among Labor–Climate Activists' Unions

Institutional culture refers to the socially constructed, historical patterns of symbols and practices, including assumptions, values, and beliefs that individuals and organizations use to provide meaning to their daily activity. It also shapes how organizations organize time and space, use their resources, and reproduce their lives and experiences (Thornton and Ocasio 2008). As we have seen, the labor movement is not a monolithic entity but rather a highly decentralized, loosely connected network of organizations with unique histories and organizational cultures. In my data, I identify two key institutional–cultural factors that contribute to prognostic frame variation among LCM participants and their unions: a culture of local autonomy versus top-down control and a social movement union culture versus pure and simple business unionism and the corresponding ideologies associated with each.

The degree of local autonomy varies greatly among unions and stems from long-standing traditions, organizational forms, and distinctive cultures of internal organizing (Stinchcombe 1965). Some unions allow a great deal of autonomy, with various locals having vastly different stances on the same issue. Other unions exert more centralized control over political positions, not allowing local unions to take positions on issues that the union has not weighed in on at the national level and forbidding locals from taking contradictory stances. Culturally, unions with a history of socialist and anarchist activities before the Red Scare are believed to have developed a stronger culture of local autonomy, whereas traditional craft unions have maintained a more centralized power structure (Stepan-Norris and Zeitlin 2003). A case can be made for the benefits or weaknesses of both approaches in terms of organizational effectiveness, but in terms of my data, some trends can be found in the relationship between autonomy and just transition framing.

There are two major takeaways: (1) in unions that do not have a strong pro-climate stance at the national level, local autonomy increases the likelihood that local unions might adopt more progressive transition frames; and (2) in unions that have progressive national leadership that has already taken a pro-climate stance, centralized control increases the likelihood that local unions might adopt a more progressive transition frame than that of the national organization. In other words, the character of national leadership is important in setting the tone for union activism, but in organizations with greater local autonomy, locals can stand up for issues that rank-and-file members and leadership believe are important in their city, state, or region.

Perhaps the best example of local autonomy helping the cause of the LCM comes from one of the building trades unions, the electrical workers. At the national level, the union does not have a particularly strong pro-climate stance; in fact, they were opposed to President Obama's Clean Power Plan, which would have reduced GHG emissions by phasing out coal-burning power plants. However, at the local level, electrical workers' unions on the East and West Coasts have taken strong positions in support of climate protection, including leading coalitions to negotiate just transitions, as IBEW Local 1245 in San Diego did when the Diablo Canyon nuclear plant was facing closure. Some electrical workers' unions have also supported local and state initiatives to increase the percentage of energy sourced from renewable energy sources. For example, IBEW Local 11 in California, representing thirteen thousand workers, has become deeply involved in expanding community-choice aggregation in the Los Angeles area and in shaping its policies to achieve a full transition from fossil fuels to clean energy and to provide good local jobs. They have also opened the Net Zero Plus Electrical Training Institute, the country's largest Net Zero Plus commercial retrofit, using efficient design and technology to generate more energy than its own annual energy demand of nearly one megawatt. IBEW Local 3 in New York dedicated its summer "critical thinking" institute to training members about the threat of climate change and the ways the union can be a force for climate protection and then organized a large contingent to participate in the People's Climate Marches in 2014 and 2017. As these cases show, local autonomy has allowed local unions who are inclined to do so to adopt protective and proactive just transition frames when the national union was largely opposed to just transition.

For unions with centralized power, the framing is largely dictated by national leadership and thus shaped by the character of those leaders. For example, the national leadership of the transportation union adopted a proactive frame on climate change and just transition. In this instance, they even brought local leaders and stewards, many of whom were skeptical of the union's stance on the issue of climate change, into the national office for training on the importance of combating climate change and the reasons the union must be a part of the struggle for climate justice. On the other hand, one of the large manufacturing unions with a highly centralized power structure has taken a notably tepid stance on addressing climate change at the national level, which left many locals of the union frustrated because they wanted to be more progressive and outspoken on the issue. In fact, several of the rank-and-file participants in the labor–climate SMOs were from unions with centralized power structures that had not taken a strong stance on climate, let alone just transition, at the top levels of leadership. In these cases, the burden is on the rank-and-file membership and local leaders to build a case for supporting climate protection measures and to organize within their own unions to push their national leaders to take a stance. As we see in Chapter 7, this is one of the major actions that activists from USE have been undertaking.

A second, and perhaps the strongest, cultural–institutional factor that affects prognostic framing is a union's culture of political activism. Sociologists and labor historians have long contrasted the difference between AFL and CIO unionism, and contemporary scholars have debated the differences between social movement unionism and business unionism.[7] While these are slightly different concepts, many similarities exist. For the LCM, the most important distinction is the propensity of a union to engage with issues that affect the entire working class rather than just the narrow material interests of their members within the confines of the workplace. The former is a characteristic of the ideology that is historically associated with CIO unionism or, in modern terms, social movement unionism, while the latter is the traditional AFL business union model that still pervades large segments of the contemporary union movement.

Regarding just transition framing, unions with a social movement culture are significantly more likely to engage in efforts to achieve climate justice because they more easily conceive of it as a working-class issue and, as such, one in need of attention by working-class organizations like unions. For unions that have historically maintained a business union culture and adhere to the corresponding ideology, climate change is seen as an issue for environmentalists to address—and when their efforts affect union members' jobs, the unions deal with the issue from a defensive stance to protect their members' material interests in the workplace. This is at the heart of the dominant Jobs vs. the Environment master frame portrayed by the media and exploited by fossil fuel companies to keep workers and their unions as a major pillar of support for the industry.

Individual Explanations for Frame Variation

I identify two individual-level factors that contribute to variation in framing among participants: personal demographic characteristics and personal beliefs or ideology. Regarding demographics, I find on balance that participants from minority racial groups, Indigenous people, and women are more likely to adopt the proactive or transformative frames and especially to promote demands for climate justice. It is important to note that the majority of participants in the three SMOs are white and predominantly male, but the nonwhite and female participants I interviewed were decidedly committed to the more progressive frames that incorporated solutions to existing inequalities. In part because of personal experiences with injustices such as racial or gender discrimination or the intersection of environment and race in the form of environmental injustice, these participants were more sensitized to push for social justice measures as part of the prognosis during meetings and rallies. They also made up a core group of activists within the LCM who were pushing to make social justice a central component of the proactive frame.

The second explanation for individual variation is personal belief systems or ideology. As noted earlier, many of the rank-and-file members who participated in the three SMOs did so because they personally adopted the transformative frame despite the more conservative stance of their unions. These union members have preexisting worldviews that align with the ideals of public ownership of the energy sector, racial and environmental justice, and economic equality. Some are self-identified leftists or socialists and embrace the transformative frame as most closely aligned with their personal beliefs and values. However, these individual factors can be tempered by structural factors such as rank and position in the labor movement. Having the least to lose, rank-and-file members can more easily take militant stances in opposition to their union leadership, whereas low- and midlevel leaders would find themselves in a precarious position if they directly challenged the stance of higher-level leadership, even if their personal ideological beliefs would suggest they should.

From Framing to Action

The LCM activists in this study share a common solution, or prognosis, to the dual crises of climate and inequality: just transition. While the phrase "just transition" is regularly conveyed by participants from all three organizations, several distinct uses of the term exist, ranging from less to more radical in their prognosis, with each challenging free market ideology more than the previous and all aiming, to various degrees, to shift power away from private corporations and wealthy individuals and toward workers and communities.

The first—protective just transition—involves creation of a social safety net in individual cases where workers face unemployment as a result of changes necessary to decarbonize the economy. This involves minimal state intervention in the economy in the form of taxation and redistribution—practices that are not uncommon even in more neoliberal capitalist democracies. The second—proactive just transition—goes beyond the first and envisions direct participation by labor in the creation of a forward-looking plan to shift society to a more sustainable energy system. In this instance, the challenge to capitalism is greater because it envisions some form of economic planning and the inclusion of labor in policy formation. The third and most radical frame—transformative just transition—involves a massive shift in power and ownership from the corporate sector to the public and the reorganization of the economy to put people before profits, including major efforts to eliminate existing social inequalities. In other words, the transformative vision aims to directly challenge the underlying power structures of a capitalist economy by seeking to eliminate the distinction between the owners of the means of production and the labor employed to operate it. However, the vision for a postcapitalist society and the process for achieving it remain underdeveloped; the only tangible plan put forth at the time of this writing has been bringing the energy sector back under public ownership and control—an important and fundamental challenge to neoliberal ideology for sure but a far cry from a transformation of society.

Despite the variation in usage among movement participants, the concept of just transition was not as hotly or openly contested by activists within the LCM as we would expect. Rather, the varied meanings were strategically and fluidly deployed depending on social context. However, one outstanding point of contention within the proactive frame, and to a lesser extent in the transformative frame, is the extent to which these just transition frames will incorporate climate justice demands such as redressing current and historical social injustices along the lines of race and gender and also toward Indigenous communities.

While prognostic framing serves to build solidarity around a shared solution or solutions to the problem, it is through organizing and mobilizing that the solution is achieved. Each of the three frames uncovered within the LCM serves as a compass to guide the actions of the LCM's operation within the labor–climate landscape. We turn our attention next to a more granular examination of the particular actions the three labor–climate SMOs have taken to achieve their goal of moving labor as a whole away from the Jobs vs. the Environment master frame and toward the Clean Air and Good Jobs frame by way of promoting a just transition for workers and communities.

6

Educate, Agitate, Organize

The Tactical Repertoire of the Labor–Climate Movement

M oving from the process of framing and meaning making to the realm of collective action involves the selection and use of tactics. The target that a movement selects often influences the character and range of tactics employed (Barkan 1979; Manheim 2001; McAdam, Tarrow, and Tilly 2001; Tarrow 1998; Tilly 1995; Walker, Martin, and McCarthy 2008; Wood 2004)—that is, the unique set of strengths, weaknesses, and institutional capacities for response of a particular target may shape the distinctive patterns of action taken by challengers. Just as vulnerabilities that arise within the political opportunity structure can shape the targets selected by movements, the changing vulnerabilities of already-chosen targets can also influence the nature of actions taken by movements.

Take for example the "Battle of Seattle" protests against the WTO in 1999. A study of this protest movement found that the nature of the target—a transnational economic authority—created a unique set of vulnerabilities that shaped the tactical repertoire of protesters, which included labor, environmentalists, Indigenous peoples, and numerous anticapitalist organizations (J. Smith 2001). As individual states became increasingly nested within a complex web of transnational relations and institutions, their vulnerability to social movement challengers increased. In particular, vulnerabilities arose as transnationalism created "new arenas for challengers to question state agendas, draw international attention to domestic practices, and cultivate alliances with powerful actors outside the domestic political arena, including other states" (J. Smith

2001, 16). With the Battle of Seattle, the vulnerabilities arising from the transnational nature of the target inspired distinct actions by challengers, including a global people's assembly, a people's tribunal against global corporate crimes, and an independent media center that broadcast video and posted news from the protests online for the world to view.

Similarly, the tactical repertoires of LCM activists are, in part, contingent on the institutional targets selected. As we shall see, the changing vulnerabilities of the three targets—the state, the mainstream environmental movement, and the labor movement—shape the actions taken by actors and organizations in the LCM. Importantly, these vulnerabilities do not occur in a bubble; they exist within the context of the broader political opportunity structure that sometimes increases, and other times limits, the ability of participants in the LCM to take action. Further, the tactical repertoire of LCM organizations is often limited to actions that align with the prognostic frame the movement actors adopted, and in some cases, the prognostic frame itself was shifted in response to changing opportunities and vulnerabilities.

Time for Some Action: Tactical Repertoires of the Labor-Climate Movement, 2014-2018

Table 6.1 provides the target, level, and name for each of the major actions taken by the three labor–climate SMOs in this study during the years of my participant observation (2014–2018). The actions are organized by their targets, either individually or in combination, listed in the first column of the table. I identified twenty-five actions: four targeting the state, two targeting mainstream environmentalists, seven targeting the labor movement, and twelve targeting multiple targets. With consideration for the actions that had multiple targets, nineteen actions targeted labor, thirteen targeted the state, and nine targeted environmentalists. Of the actions identified, ten were initiated by SPEC, the state-level organization; nine were initiated by USE, the national-level organization; and six by the international organization, LUPE.[1]

Looking at each individual target, the first of the three—the state—was targeted most often at the state level (eleven actions), followed by the national level (three actions) and then the international level (two actions). The state was targeted most often by SPEC (eight actions), followed by USE (three actions) and LUPE (two actions). The second target, mainstream environmentalists, was targeted most often at the state level (eight actions), followed by the national level (five actions) and then the international level (two actions).

TABLE 6.1 TARGETS, LEVELS OF ACTION, AND ACTIONS TAKEN BY THREE LABOR–CLIMATE SMOs, 2014–2018

Target	Level of Action	Action	SMO
The State	State	Establish State Council on Climate	SPEC
The State	State	Climate Change Legislation	SPEC
The State	State	Transit Equity Day	USE
The State	International	Attend Global Climate Negotiations	LUPE
Environmentalists	State, National	Environmentalist Resolutions	USE
Environmentalists	State, National	Labor Workshops for Environmentalists	USE
Labor	State	State AFL-CIO Resolutions	SPEC
Labor	State	Climate Workshops for Labor	SPEC
Labor	*State, National*	*Union Resolutions at All Levels*	USE
Labor	State, National	Union Climate Toolkit	USE
Labor	State, National	Divest/Invest Tutorials	USE
Labor	National	Labor–Climate Conferences	USE
Labor	*National, International*	*Labor–Climate Leadership Workshops*	LUPE
The State, Labor	State	Reduce and Cap Fixed Rate	SPEC
The State, Labor	State	Climate Protection Jobs Study	SPEC
The State, Labor	*State*	*Offshore Wind Campaign*	SPEC
The State, Labor	National	Climate Protection Jobs Study	USE
The State, Labor	State, National, International	Unions against Fracking	LUPE
Environmentalists, Labor	State, National, International	Energy Democracy Video	LUPE
Environmentalists, Labor	State, National, International	Working Papers Series	LUPE
Environmentalists, Labor	International	Just Transition Workshop	LUPE

Target	Level of Action	Action	SMO
TABLE 6.1 TARGETS, LEVELS OF ACTION, AND ACTIONS TAKEN BY THREE LABOR–CLIMATE SMOs, 2014–2018 (*continued*)			
The State, Environmentalists, Labor	State	Expand Energy Efficiency Program	SPEC
The State, Environmentalists, Labor	State	Expand State Renewable Mandates	SPEC
The State, Environmentalists, Labor	State	Discounted Trains to Climate March	SPEC
The State, Environmentalists, Labor	State, National	Mobilized Participants for Climate March	USE

Notes:
The designation "State" as a level of action includes actions taken at the substate level (e.g., local unions, municipalities, etc.).
SPEC is an acronym for State Partnership for Employment and Climate; USE is an acronym for Unions for Sustainable Energy; LUPE is an acronym for Labor Unions for Public Energy (all three names are pseudonyms).
The three signature campaigns described in this chapter are *italicized*.

Environmentalists were equally targeted by all three SMOs (nine actions each). The third target, the labor movement, was targeted most often at the state level (fifteen actions), followed by the national level (ten actions) and then the international level (four actions), and it was targeted most often by SPEC (eight actions), followed by USE (six actions) and then LUPE (five actions). Among the SMOs, SPEC was most likely to target the state and labor (eight actions each), USE was most likely to target labor (six actions), and LUPE was most likely to target labor (five actions).[2]

While this simple accounting offers some interesting insights into the tactics deployed by the LCM, a more intensive examination of the tactical repertoires of each of the three SMOs will shed further light on the complex relationship between targets, tactics, and political opportunity structures. In what follows, I briefly describe the major actions undertaken by each of the three SMOs to provide a sense of their tactical repertoires. I then single out one signature campaign for each SMO to examine in more detail. By "signature campaign," I mean an action or set of related actions that furthers a core goal of the SMO and is highly representative of the work the organization undertook during the time I was a participant. The three signature campaigns I analyze are indicated by italics in Table 6.1. After describing the signature campaign for each SMO, I look more closely at the relationship between the targets, vulnerabilities, collective action frames, and tactics used for each campaign.

Actions Initiated by the State Partnership
for Employment and Climate

Summary of Actions

SPEC initiated two actions targeting the state, two targeting labor, and six aimed at multiple targets. The first action targeting the state involved helping to establish a State Council on Climate Change. This was a tremendously important achievement that helped pave the way for many of the organization's future campaigns and successes. In this case, SPEC, as a representative of labor, faith-based, environmental, and environmental justice organizations concerned with climate change, initiated an effort to revive the state's flagging climate change efforts, which lacked interim targets and concrete plans for achieving the emission-reduction goals set forth in previously established global warming legislation. SPEC reached out to the governor's office and the heads of the various state environmental agencies to raise concerns about the state's falling behind its self-imposed emission-reduction targets. These conversations ultimately led to the Democratic governor issuing an executive order that announced the formation of what I call the State Council on Climate Change, on Earth Day, 2015. The mission of the council is to examine the effectiveness of existing policies and regulations designed to reduce GHG emissions and identify new strategies to meet the state's ambitious target of reducing GHG emissions to 20 percent of 2001 levels by 2050 and establish interim targets as benchmarks. The council is composed of fifteen members from state agencies, quasi-state agencies, business, and nonprofits—including the lead organizer from SPEC. Overall, this action was a success.

With a seat at the table in the State Council on Climate Change, SPEC helped to organize a broad base of public support for aggressive GHG reduction targets through a series of stakeholder meetings and public hearings, which culminated with another action targeting the state: the promotion of various pieces of climate change legislation in 2017 and 2018. One of these bills, which passed in May 2018, set an aggressive interim target of reducing GHG emissions to 55 percent of 2001 levels by 2030, which mirrored the recommendation issued by the State Council on Climate Change four months prior, in January 2018. These ambitious targets would not have been politically viable if not for SPEC's previous work organizing support from a broad range of constituents—including labor, faith, community, and environmental groups—at the aforementioned stakeholder meetings organized by SPEC and the State Council on Climate Change and also through letter-writing campaigns and lobbying efforts.

Despite the tremendous strides made toward the SMO's goal of reducing GHG emissions and creating incentives for more green jobs in some areas of the renewable sector (such as offshore wind), the action can be considered only a partial success because the final legislation also included some measures that threatened jobs in the solar industry.[3] The backpedaling on solar in the final version of the bill led several environmental allies to remove their support for the legislation, which revealed the delicate nature of alliances around legislative measures that are subject to compromise. SPEC vowed to join environmental allies in fighting to undo these negative changes to solar in the next legislative session.

SPEC had two actions that exclusively targeted labor. The first was a set of union resolutions at the biennial state AFL-CIO conventions in 2013 and 2015. The 2013 resolution stated that climate change was a critical issue for labor and established the state AFL-CIO as a member of SPEC. The second, in 2015, reaffirmed the first resolution and urged the state confederation to support the efforts of the State Council on Climate Change to reduce GHG emissions and create well-paying green jobs in the state. The conventions passed both resolutions, making these actions a success. Through the resolution process, SPEC activists learned that many of the unions in the state supported their efforts around climate change, which opened the door for many future conversations about other actions. As we shall see, these secondary networking effects are an important part of the success of SPEC.

The second action targeting labor was a series of labor–climate workshops in which organizers from SPEC met with leaders and members of various local unions in their union halls to talk about climate change, educate them about why it is crucial for labor to be involved with the issue, and provide them with tools to make their unions more active in the struggle for a climate-safe future. The ultimate goal of these workshops was to help build the LCM within the state labor movement and move individual unions from the Jobs vs. the Environment master frame on the left side of the labor–climate spectrum into the Clean Air and Good Jobs counterframe on the right side of the spectrum (see Figure 3.1). This ongoing campaign had not been too successful at the time I completed my fieldwork—only a few unions had actually held workshops for their leaders and members—in part because of the lower priority afforded to this campaign compared with other activities, such as supporting climate change legislation and renewable energy projects. Nonetheless, the workshops contributed to some additional organizational affiliations for the group.

Several additional actions by SPEC had multiple targets. The first, targeting the state and labor, was a campaign to reduce and cap the fixed-charge portion of consumer electrical bills. The fixed charge functions like a poll tax because the amount levied is the same for everyone, regardless of their electricity use. The monopoly energy company in the state had for years been increasing the fixed-charge portion of the bill to shore up their profits in the face of declining consumer demand largely attributable to energy efficiency improvements in homes and businesses and the adoption of rooftop solar panels by many customers. While the fixed charge may have helped the bottom line of the power company, the fee was inherently regressive and punished lower-income consumers the most. Further, this fee reduced incentives for consumers to pursue energy efficiency and rooftop solar (thereby slowing the growth of these green jobs) because the savings became less enticing for consumers who still paid the flat fee every month no matter how little electricity they purchased from the power company. SPEC used this campaign as an opportunity to bridge the frames of labor and environmental activists to mobilize together on a win–win campaign that would help both the environment and low-income workers. After a press conference, a letter-writing campaign, and extensive lobbying, they won a 40 percent reduction in the fixed charge and a legislatively mandated cap of the charge at that amount, making the campaign a success. This campaign also helped to create a track record of cooperation and success between labor and environmental groups that proved to be important for the signature offshore wind campaign described below.

Also targeting the state and labor, SPEC partnered with USE to commission a climate and jobs study. The findings of the study revealed the tremendous economic benefits of pursuing more renewable energy in the state, including more than 6,700 new jobs per year, on average, over business-as-usual projections through 2050. The report was referenced in newspaper op-eds and hearings to support the pieces of climate legislation that were discussed above. It was also used to inform the local building trades unions that SPEC was courting for their campaign to expand offshore wind power.

Focusing on all three targets, SPEC undertook a campaign to expand the state's program to improve energy efficiency in public buildings. These projects would reduce emissions from one of the largest sources of GHGs in urban areas—buildings—and also create well-paying, in-state jobs in the process. SPEC organizers reached out to labor leaders and climate activists to nurture their mutual interest in promoting this campaign through a sign-on letter and various lobbying efforts. Ultimately, this action failed because three consecutive years of state budget crises led the state assembly not only to reject plans for expanding this program but also to shift funds away from other state environmental programs to fill general budget gaps.

At the same time, SPEC targeted unions to support an expansion of the state's renewable energy mandate and targeted environmentalists to support the types of renewables (such as offshore wind) that would create the most in-state jobs. Together, the combined efforts of SPEC and its partners from labor and the environmental movement brought a twofold expansion in the state's commitment to renewable energy by increasing the mandate from 20 to 40 percent of all energy used in the state coming from renewable sources by 2030, making this action a success. This mandate for renewables in conjunction with the aggressive emission-reduction targets described earlier laid a strong foundation for the group's efforts supporting renewable energy projects that would create green jobs in the state. Finally, as was described in detail in Chapter 4, SPEC played a crucial role in organizing participation in the People's Climate March in New York City on September 21, 2014, by winning increased mass transit options to New York and discounted fares for riders on the day of the march. The organization also secured endorsements of the march by fourteen unions and labor organizations in the state, including the only state AFL-CIO to endorse the march.

SPEC's Signature Campaign: Promoting Offshore Wind

On Tuesday, June 13, 2017, I joined a group of labor leaders, climate activists, business leaders, and press correspondents at the Quonset Point ferry slip in North Kingstown, Rhode Island, to take a "field trip." The trip involved a ferry ride to visit the nation's first offshore wind farm, the Block Island Wind Farm, located off the coast of Block Island, which had just begun operating a few months earlier, in December 2016. The trip was organized by a number of organizations, including a labor–environmental alliance, several Rhode Island building trades unions, and a mainstream environmental organization. SPEC helped to promote the event among union leaders in its home state—particularly those from construction unions—and arranged for a few people, including me, to travel to Rhode Island to participate in the tour.

At about 9:30 A.M., I took some motion sickness pills and shared the few extras I had with some fellow labor and climate activists before boarding the ferry for our twenty-mile adventure into the Atlantic. After twenty-five or thirty minutes of sailing the choppy seas, we began to make out the silhouette of the wind farm along the horizon, and for the next thirty minutes we continued to approach the five enormous wind turbines off the coast of Block Island. It is difficult to overstate the breathtaking size of the turbines, especially when you get up close to them. Standing 600 feet tall, the turbines had three enormous blades, each spanning 241 feet. All of the passengers, me included, were awestruck as we scrambled to different parts of the bobbing deck to find the best photo opportunities. The photos, taken mostly from cell phones, were disappointing because the turbines, being situated in the sea, lacked a point of reference in the frame for comparing their size. I share my own photos in Figure 6.1. On the left is a picture of me with three turbines in the background. On the right is a photo looking up at one of the turbines as the sun ducks behind its blades. The blades spun smoothly and steadily on that particular day, which was described by the ship's captain as "slightly breezy." But we learned that they are designed to withstand a Category 3 hurricane and could be turned off and locked if the winds become stronger than that. Once the shock of their size began to wear off, we settled down a bit (but, unfortunately, the seas did not), and the official presentations began.

Figure 6.1 SPEC members, union leaders, and environmentalists toured the nation's first offshore wind farm off Block Island, Rhode Island, on June 13, 2017. *Left*, the author poses with three of the five 600-foot-tall wind turbines in the background. *Right*, a view looking up at a turbine from the ferry while the sun ducks behind the three blades, which are each 241 feet long.

Representatives from various environmental groups, the Rhode Island building trades unions, and the company that operates the wind farm took turns discussing the environmental and economic benefits of the project. For the unions, the discussion focused on the three hundred union construction jobs that were created to make the project a reality and the unknown number of other jobs in land and sea transportation, in logistics, and all along the supply chain that were generated as well. Not only were they well-paying jobs but they also required many new skills that created numerous educational opportunities for building trades workers at union-run training centers and in apprenticeship programs. Union workers drove the steel piles into the ocean floor, poured the concrete piers on which the turbines were mounted, operated the ships and cranes that delivered the components, assembled the turbines at sea, and wired them to the grid. Beyond the initial construction, the wind farm also created several long-term jobs for wind turbine technicians, which, according to the BLS, is the second-fastest growing job in the United States—second only to solar panel installer.

The electricity from the wind farm is transmitted from the turbines to the electric grid on Block Island through a submarine power cable buried under the ocean floor. The five turbines at the wind farm produce more than 125,000 megawatt hours of electricity annually, which is enough to power seventeen thousand homes. This is more than enough electricity to power the entire island with 100 percent renewable power and transmit surplus energy to the grid on the mainland. In fact, since the turbines began operating, the island has shut down its dirty diesel generators, eliminating twenty-one thousand tons of GHG emissions each year—a textbook example of displacement as a means of change. Climate activists on the ship discussed the prospects for GHG emission reductions should other states initiate similar but larger-scale projects.[4] The presentations concluded with a resounding round of applause from attendees, and, after a few more photo opportunities, the ferry turned its bow back toward the mainland and carried some excited, and a few seasick, passengers back to shore.

A few weeks after the Block Island field trip, those of us from SPEC who had visited the wind farm made a presentation at the next meeting of the group. The field trip proved to be an undeniable success: the discussion generated much enthusiasm among meeting participants, who ultimately decided that SPEC would undertake a campaign to promote offshore wind power in the state. The campaign aligned with the group's existing efforts to increase the state's commitment to renewable power use through its seat on the State Council on Climate Change, its work to increase the state's renewable energy mandate, and its promotion of the two climate change bills, all discussed above. The initiation of the campaign was also timely because the group was beginning to consider protective just transition plans for the one nuclear power station in the state, which represents approximately 40 percent of the state's current electricity generation capacity, employs hundreds of union workers annually, and is scheduled to be decommissioned in the coming decades.

In the long run, SPEC's wind power campaign was critical in shifting the organization's framing of solutions to the climate crisis from protective to proactive. Two SPEC members took the opportunity to write an op-ed piece that aligned labor and environmental frames by saying, "[The state] should initiate procurements of offshore wind resources that could, over time, replace much, if not all, of [the nuclear plant's] generating capacity. Construction and maintenance of offshore wind facilities in leased federal waters . . . could provide long-term economic activity and employment opportunities for coastal communities and workers after [the nuclear plant's] retirement." This occasion created a great opportunity to overcome some of the divisions between labor activists and mainstream environmentalists.

The group officially launched its campaign for wind power by organizing a Forum on Offshore Wind, held on September 20, 2017. The forum was cosponsored by several building trades union locals and climate change groups in the state and was hosted by the local electrical workers' union at their union hall. SPEC used the event as a launching pad for building enthusiasm for offshore wind by gathering over 130 individual and group endorsements on a statement urging the state to integrate offshore wind into its climate and energy strategies. SPEC organized LCM activists to lobby state legislators and write letters urging state agencies to make offshore wind energy a key part of the state's climate plan and to be a part of a just transition when the nuclear power plant faces its final years of operation. In November 2017, the state's Department of Environmental Protection responded by announcing plans to procure offshore wind energy the following year, and in January 2018, the department issued a request for proposals for up to 240 megawatts of wind power.

As the state awaited bids from wind power companies, SPEC continued to publish editorial pieces and lobby lawmakers to ensure that the projects would help create good jobs in the state. In a newsletter from May 2018, SPEC stated:

> As it takes this first step, [the state] can learn from other states that have taken the lead in pursuit of local jobs and supply-chain investment from offshore wind development. [The state] needs to develop a robust offshore wind strategy that leverages our modern port facilities and skilled labor pool in securing local investments from this rapidly ex-

panding regional industry. We will continue to work with the building trades unions and other allies to ensure that offshore wind development brings jobs and economic opportunities to [the state's] workers and communities.

Later that month, three developers submitted proposals to supply 200 megawatts of offshore wind power to the state, and in June 2018 the state awarded its first contract to one of the developers. Announcing the award, the governor said, "We have an obligation to our children and grandchildren to invest in energy projects that reduce the impacts of harmful emissions; that's why [the state] is making investments in the technologies of the future, not of the past."

The project, which will be sited in federal waters, will bring hundreds of local jobs, millions of tax dollars, and enough clean energy to provide power to one hundred thousand homes in the state. In particular, the plan included $15 million of investments to upgrade the state pier so it could serve as a primary staging area for future work on other offshore wind projects in the region. In an interview with a local media outlet, an organizer from SPEC said, "Whether it's on the docks, in the water, or on the factory floor, [the state] has the skilled labor needed to jumpstart this new industry bringing clean energy to the region." However, despite this victory, SPEC noted that state law currently limits offshore wind procurement to only about 250 megawatts per year, so they will continue to advocate in the state legislature to expand these limits in order to keep this industry growing enough to displace fossil fuels in the future.

SPEC's Targets, Vulnerabilities, Opportunities, Frames, and Tactics

The two targets in this signature campaign—the state and labor—each presented a set of vulnerabilities. For the state, the economy was still hobbling along in the wake of the Great Recession and in particular had been facing annual budget crises resulting from revenue shortages. Private investments in a new offshore wind industry would create jobs and generate an influx of tax revenue for the cash-strapped state government. Additionally, the sitting governor had a low approval rating of 29 percent, making him the least popular Democratic governor in the United States and the third-least-popular governor overall. However, the few areas of strong support from the Democratic base were his leadership on the issues of gun control, gay rights, and climate change. Promoting offshore wind provided an opportunity for him again to show his chops on this issue and perhaps edge up his approval rating.

An additional vulnerability stemmed from the pending closure of the state's lone nuclear power plant. Many legislators from both parties were considering an unpopular piece of legislation to offer financial assistance to the company that owned and operated the nuclear power plant, which had shown no evidence of being in financial need. The bill was widely seen as a form of corporate welfare to help shore up profit margins for shareholders. Offshore wind provided an alternative solution that could ensure a carbon-free future energy source as well as create local jobs for the displaced workers from the plant, many of whom are building trades union members and have transferable skills. At the very least, supporting offshore wind could serve as a smokescreen for politicians who could point to their pro-environmental efforts with one hand while also helping the company that owned and operated the nuclear power plant with the other hand—which they ultimately did.

In terms of vulnerabilities in the second target—the labor movement—the building trades unions in the state had not fully recovered from the Great Recession. Construction unions, who were still experiencing higher than average unemployment rates among their members, were looking for ways to drum up employment and reverse their waning economic fortunes. The prospects of participating in a coalition with other labor groups, as well as environmental and faith groups, under the banner of Clean Air and Good Jobs to promote a project that could generate employment for their members aligned well with their standing mission.

The existing political opportunity structure was also favorable for a number of reasons. First, the state had a history of bipartisan support for climate protection measures and already had legislation on the books calling for the government to take action to reduce GHG emissions. In fact, the state was among the first in the nation to pass global warming legislation, in the early 1990s. As for labor, aside from the particular vulnerability of high unemployment, the building trades' standard operating procedure is always all-of-the-above when it comes to supporting construction projects that would create jobs for their members. As the old adage among trade unionists goes, construction unions will support a project to build a ladder to the moon and then support a project to dismantle it the day after it is completed. But in this case, their opportunism worked in favor of the LCM activists.

Also helping to make the opportunity structure favorable was SPEC's history of collaborative efforts with unions and environmental organizations in the state. This type of "indigenous organizational strength" refers to the importance of tapping into preexisting organizational strengths among potential social movement constituencies.[5] In this case, the opportunity to promote offshore wind in the wake of the successful project at Block Island may have been missed if SPEC had not had a preexisting organizational network of labor, faith-based, environmental, and community groups it had previously worked with on other campaigns, such as the reduction and capping of the fixed electric rate. The offshore wind forum that was organized by SPEC early in the campaign, which brought together stakeholders from these various constituent groups, proved to be a key juncture in the campaign's success. This activation of the preexisting network provided the essential components of the campaign's success: members, solidarity, communication networks, and leaders.

Taken together, the vulnerabilities and the existing opportunity structure in the state allowed SPEC to engage in a more traditional political campaign, with tactics that included public forums, editorials, petitions, letter-writing campaigns, lobbying efforts, and press conferences. Had the state been in better financial shape, had a conservative governor (or a more popular Democratic governor who was not seeking to shore up support from his base) been in office, or for some other reason had the state been less politically inclined to entertain the demands of SPEC and its allies, the tactics would surely have been different and may have included more confrontational forms of action, including protests or direct actions. However, in this case, the existing political opportunity structure and vulnerabilities of the state and labor allowed for a tactical repertoire that resembled traditional reform efforts.

Prior to the offshore wind campaign, some in SPEC were considering how to build support for protective just transition measures for workers at the nuclear power plant as speculation began emerging about the plant's closure. Luckily for SPEC, the newly operational Block Island Wind Farm was a success and was garnering national attention as a possible model for future projects to reduce GHG emissions. Stumbling on this opportunity to support offshore wind projects led activists to shift their prognostic framing from protective to proactive by supporting the development of offshore wind as both a means to address climate change and an orderly transition from jobs in nuclear to jobs in offshore wind. This shift supports the claim in Chapter 5 that the state-level organization would shift between the protective and proactive frames depending on the target. This also suggests two things about framing and political opportunity: frames are not necessarily cast in stone but can be fluid, and changes in the underlying political opportunity structure or vulnerabilities of targets can influence social movement frames. Together, these insights raise the possibility of a frame-shifting process in which SMOs not only modify their tactical repertoires in response to changing opportunity structures but also may shift their frames to find the optimal alignment of framing, opportunity, and tactics. This also potentially prefigures a general shift in framing within labor as a whole to a more progressive stance on climate change that rejects the Jobs vs. the Environment master frame, given the right political opportunity.

Actions Initiated by Unions for a Sustainable Economy

Summary of Actions

The national-level organization in this study, USE, engaged in one action that targeted the state, two that targeted environmentalists, four that targeted labor, and two others with multiple targets. Targeting the state, USE partnered with transportation unions and civil rights groups around the country to organize a Transit Equity Day on February 5, 2018. Participants in fifteen cities around the United States celebrated the birthday of Rosa Parks by holding rallies and issuing press releases promoting the need for safe, fair, and affordable public transit—a goal that reduces GHG emissions, creates good jobs, and addresses social injustices by helping marginalized workers, who often cannot afford housing close to their jobs. Activists in some cities boarded buses and circulated voter guides that outlined where elected officials and candidates stood on public transportation issues. This ongoing campaign had a small but successful first day of action. The organization planned to do more in the future and has indeed made it an annual event.

Targeting environmentalists, USE drafted and circulated a resolution template that environmentalist organizations could modify and adopt in order to state their support for workers. The template would be used to draft resolutions encouraging environmental groups to engage in frame extension and hopefully expand their organizational ranges by incorporating labor rights into their missions. The resolution template, titled "A Labor Rights Statement of Support," read in part: "RESOLVED, We pledge to work together for job creation in a climate-friendly economy; fight together for full employment in an economy that uses union labor. For example, American steel made by USW members must be used to make wind turbines erected by union building trades workers." To date, this campaign has gained only limited traction, but USE members hope to further promote the resolution among environmental groups.

USE also developed a labor workshop to educate environmental organizations about the labor movement and ways to partner with labor on the issue of climate change. The stated purpose of the training, which is advertised on USE's website and offered on request to environmental organizations, is to "strengthen the capacity of leaders of environmental organizations to more effectively develop alliances with labor unions and workers; develop strategies to navigate political differences; expand and deepen the understanding of environmental organizations about how and why organized labor is an essential element of environmental and climate justice work; and examine the opportunities and challenges of working with the labor movement." The first training was held in March 2018 with national-level leaders from four prominent environmental organizations and was by all accounts a success.

Targeting labor, USE engaged in many actions, including the promotion of various union resolutions that I discuss in greater detail as a signature campaign in the next subsection. USE also developed a labor–climate action toolkit for union members and leaders to engage on the issue of climate change within their unions. The toolkit includes a template for a union resolution on climate change, some suggestions for ways to bring climate change into the daily work of the union, important facts, and answers to frequently asked questions. The toolkit is available on the USE website and has been shared with union activists throughout the United States. It is unclear how successful this action has been in persuading labor leaders and union members to engage with the issue of climate change.

USE has also created a guide and offers tutorials on how to start "divest/ invest campaigns" within unions. These resources are designed to help unions consider whether they should divest from fossil fuels. For example, the guide states:

> Working people collectively own an enormous amount of capital in our pensions. As a sector, pensions are the largest source of investment in financial holdings, even larger than standard investment houses and banks! Pensions constitute over $40 trillion! Our pension funds are invested in stocks and bonds that may not be serving our interests as working people and may be harming our families' futures. Imagine what we might be able to support and build, imagine the great jobs we could create, if we use more of our pension funds to directly benefit our members and our families.

Several activists from USE who helped develop this guide were also involved with the divestment efforts in New York City that ultimately led to Mayor Bill de Blasio's announcement on January 10, 2018, that New York City would divest the $5 billion of its public pension funds invested in fossil fuel stocks and reinvest them in renewable energy. Although this campaign is ongoing, the success in New York can be counted as a win for the movement.

A central activity of USE that targets labor is their series of labor–climate conferences held biannually at the national level and intermittently at the regional level. The conferences are modeled after the "convergences" used by activists from U.S. Labor against the War (USLAW)—an antiwar movement within the labor movement. In the lead-up to the U.S. invasion of Iraq in 2003, USLAW created opportunities for antiwar activists within labor to "converge" as they built their campaign around an issue they believed the national leadership was either not addressing or even on the wrong side of—the Iraq War. Ultimately, USLAW successfully organized within the labor movement for the adoption of a national AFL-CIO resolution opposing the Iraq War (AFL-CIO 2005). USE's first labor–climate conference, held in January 2016, saw the creation of a set of guiding principles and the formation of a new network within the labor movement whose goal was to lead labor as a whole in a progressive direction on a climate change agenda. The first few of these conferences brought together between 75 and 150 union leaders and activists from around the country (or region for regional meetings) to share their experiences and develop strategies for moving labor from the Jobs vs. the Environment side of the labor–climate spectrum to the Clean Air and Good Jobs counterframe. Having grown the ranks of the movement, this action has been a success.

Targeting both the state and labor, USE commissioned a national climate jobs study in 2015 that found that the United States could reduce GHG emissions to 20 percent of 1990 levels by 2050 while adding a half million jobs and saving consumers billions of dollars on their electrical, heating, and transportation costs. This frame-amplifying study concludes that "[while] protecting the climate has often been portrayed as a threat to American workers' jobs and the US economy, this report shows that a clean energy future will produce more jobs than 'business as usual' with fossil fuels and save money to boot." The study has been circulated to union leaders and politicians and used by union climate activists to urge their unions to support renewable energy and their state governments to adopt strong climate protection policies. To date, however, there is no clear evidence that the study has succeeded in persuading any labor leaders to move toward the Clean Air and Good Jobs counterframe.

Finally, addressing all three targets, USE activists helped to mobilize union participation in the People's Climate Marches in New York City in 2014 and Washington, DC, in 2017. Some members organized buses for their unions or groups of unions from their local areas to come together and demand Clean Air and Good Jobs. The adoption of the Paris Climate Accord is often attributed in part to the demonstration of public concern at the first People's Climate March in New York, which would make this action a success.

USE's Signature Campaign: Resolving to Make Climate a Labor Issue

On Tuesday, October 24, 2017, a resolution titled "Climate Change, Energy and Union Jobs" came to the floor of the AFL-CIO's twenty-eighth quadrennial national convention in St. Louis (AFL-CIO 2017). Delegates lined up at the microphones, awaiting their two minutes to speak in favor of or against the proposed resolution. Judging by the words and tone of the first speaker, it did not sound promising for supporters of the resolution: "I'm a little more than concerned and very much disappointed to have to fight and defend my craft within the house of labor," exclaimed the president of a national building trades union. "Unicorns and Easter bunnies are more real than the United States being powered by renewable," he went on, and "the postal workers and the nurses to the left of me, and maybe appropriately to the left of me . . . have no equity in the work but continue the attack on other [elements of] organized labor." By "equity," he meant that the members of those other unions were not going to be the ones losing their jobs if fossil fuel use were curbed. He also expressed anger that his union did not have a say in the drafting of the resolution and concluded by stating that "the folks that are coming after [my union] and the building trades need to be ashamed."

So, what was the resolution all about, and where did it come from? In general, the resolution portrayed the proactive frame that USE most often adopted, as was noted in Chapter 5. In particular, it acknowledged the scientific consensus about the reality and urgency of climate change, stated that the problem disproportionately affects workers and communities of color, demanded that workers who are negatively affected by climate mitigation be protected, acknowledged that climate protection efforts will create millions of jobs, insisted that labor must have a seat at the table in developing plans to address the issue, and urged the U.S. government to remain a party to the Paris Climate Accord. The origin of the resolution dates back to the first national labor–climate conference held by USE in January 2016.

Coming out of that first labor–climate conference, USE activists set a number of short- and medium-term goals, including building their base of support within labor by educating union members and passing proactive resolutions on climate change at all levels of the labor movement. While sometimes frustratingly contentious in drawing up, resolutions are important tools within labor organizations that compel union leaders to act in an official capacity on particular issues, including climate issues. The resolution process is a democratic mechanism for members to express their opinions on an issue or, in some cases, for leaders to ensure the membership agrees with actions they plan to take on behalf of the organization. The resolutions pursued by USE activists would serve as vehicles for expanding the organizational range of unions, extending their frames to include climate change as a union issue. Unlike the offshore wind campaign that was executed directly by SPEC as an organization, USE's resolution campaign involved individual activists, in consultation with USE leaders, acting as a movement within the movement to pass resolutions within their own local unions, national unions, and state labor federations.

Throughout 2017, at least fifteen different climate change resolutions drafted by USE activists wended their way through the cumbersome democratic machinery of local and national unions and, in most cases, although often with revisions, were ultimately adopted. The organizations that adopted these resolutions were most often education unions, healthcare unions, service sector unions, public sector unions, and transportation unions, which is why they are situated squarely on the Clean Air and Good Jobs side of the labor-climate spectrum in Chapter 3. A few local building trades unions, mostly electrical workers in large urban areas on the two coasts, had also adopted pro–climate protection resolutions. Depending on the industry of the union, the resolutions varied greatly in terms of their framing of the problem and solution, ranging from protective to transformative, and many, as a result of revisions, shifted from transformative to proactive or from proactive to protective in order to win approval.

One memorable campaign involved a climate change resolution drafted by James, a leader in a state manufacturing union and participant in both SPEC and USE. The resolution was adopted by his local union and then submitted to the national union's convention for consideration in September 2016. However, the proactive resolution, which had sailed through the acceptance process in his local union, faced an uphill fight in the national organization. While the resolution was being reviewed and debated by the national convention's Resolutions Committee in the lead-up to the convention, several revisions were made to accommodate the less supportive views of many members who were employed in fossil fuel industries in other parts of the country. The major modification—the addition of a plank stating that the national union would fight vigorously to protect fossil fuel jobs until a truly viable transition plan was in place—effectively shifted the framing of the resolution from the proactive to the protective just transition frame. The distinction between James's local union, which manufactured fuel cells, and his national union, which had over one hundred thousand members employed in the fossil fuel industry, highlights the finding in Chapter 5 that manufacturing unions often wavered between protective and proactive just transition frames depending on the nature of goods manufactured by the particular union. Even with the change in language, the Resolutions Committee still recommended that the convention not adopt the resolution.

When the resolution came to the convention floor for discussion, six of the seven speakers who lined up to voice their opinion spoke against the resolution. James, who spoke last, was the only person to rise in favor of the resolution. As with the other speakers before him, his image was projected on the giant video screen above the speaker's podium for the whole convention to see. With only two minutes to make his case, his impassioned speech appealed to the hearts and minds of his fellow union delegates. First, the mind: he delivered a succinct but compelling litany of scientific evidence supporting the reality of climate change. Then the heart: James lifted up his tablet computer to reveal a picture of his grandson, which projected from over his head throughout the convention hall, and his voice choked with emotion: "This is [my grandson], and he is counting on me to make sure he has a livable world when he grows up." He then asked all of the delegates in the hall to take out their cell phone and look at a photo of their kids or grandkids before casting their votes, "because those kids will be asking what we had done to help stop the destructive aspects of climate change." As James stepped down from the podium, the hall was silent. When the vote was taken, the resolution passed 607 to 503. It was the first time ever at one of that union's conventions that a floor vote went against the recommendation of the Resolutions Committee and ultimately the union leadership.

James had spoken passionately for a resolution that seemed doomed to fail, but his words snatched victory from the jaws of defeat. With facts, emotion, and his own humanity, he turned the convention body around and truly won the hearts and minds of his fellow union members. In so doing, he also extended the frame of his manufacturing union from the oppositional stance to the protective just transition frame. While the resolution passed by the national organization was not as sweeping as the one that had been passed by James's local union, his national union for the first time declared that it "recognizes climate change as a real threat to our quality of life, our livelihoods and even our lives, and declares that addressing the destructive nature of climate change is a priority for our Union going forward." This incremental success within one particular union exemplifies the many small battles waged by the LCM as activists seek to move labor as a whole on the issue of climate change without causing outright division within the house of labor.

At the opposite end of the spectrum, a national healthcare union adopted a more radical climate change resolution that unabashedly embraced the transformative just transition frame by calling for public ownership and control of the energy sector. In the case of this healthcare union, the "Resolution on Resisting Climate Change Denial and Promoting a Just Transition to Public Renewable Power with Justice for Workers and Our Communities" read, in part:

> Be it resolved, that [the union] will join with unions and allied organizations to promote democratic, public ownership and control of electrical power generation and distribution as essential to energy transition, sustainable development, and an end to energy poverty worldwide; and be it further resolved, that [the union] supports a "just transition" for workers in the fossil fuel and carbon-intensive sectors into permanent jobs in sustainable energy, "green" industries, and public service with full labor rights, and will advocate for a "Superfund" for workers and communities negatively affected by the necessary transition from fossil fuels; and . . . be it further resolved that [the union] supports the demands of frontline communities for environmental justice, including access to newly created jobs in the renewable energy sector.

This resolution not only embodies the core tenets of the transformative frame—public ownership and environmental justice—but also calls for a Superfund for workers, which reinforces the nested nature of the three just transition frames.

I return now to the climate change resolution that was being debated at the national AFL-CIO convention first described at the start of this section and which differs from the resolution passed by James's manufacturing union. In the days leading to the AFL-CIO convention, USE circulated an "Open Letter from Union Members and Our Families to American Labor Leaders." The letter urged national leaders to "take a strong stand on climate change," stating that working people, poor people, and frontline communities, including Tribal communities, are most heavily affected by the effects of climate change. "From more powerful hurricanes to wildfires, from rising sea levels to crop-destroying droughts and floods," these communities feel the devastation first and worst, the letter stated. For this reason, it claimed, union members and their families have the biggest stake in moving as rapidly as possible from a fossil fuel–based society to a sustainable energy society. In conclusion, it posed the rhetorical question "Who will speak for the global majority of working people and poor people if organized labor does not?" The letter was shared widely on the Internet and signed by hundreds of local union leaders and labor activists from around the country.

Meanwhile, the Resolutions Committee for the national convention was compiling, discussing, and making recommendations on the hundred-plus resolutions on various issues that had been submitted. The climate change resolution that was ultimately debated and voted on, like James's resolution at the manufacturing union convention, followed from a series of revisions and compromises. In this particular case, the key compromise involved the combination of five different climate change resolutions that were submitted and the input of several building trades union leaders on the Resolutions Committee who had strong objections to several of the resolutions that were submitted. Four of the five submissions originated from USE activists in a healthcare union, a transportation union, and two state labor federations, respectively; the fifth came independently from a public sector union that ultimately coordinated with the other four unions. Each of the resolutions had, per convention rules, been previously adopted by the union that submitted them.

The major compromise in the final version of the climate resolution, which greatly disheartened many USE activists, was the inclusion of a plank calling for the support of "clean coal" and advanced nuclear technology in addition to renewables as part of the solution to climate change. The revised resolution read, in part: "The AFL-CIO supports incentives and robust funding for research programs to bring new energy technologies to market, including renewables, carbon capture, and advanced nuclear technologies." This plank was the result of efforts by several building trades and extraction unions that sought to keep alive the AFL-CIO's support for so-called "clean coal"—which in effect would allow the less progressive elements of labor to continue their business-as-usual, all-of-the-above energy strategy despite the federation's proclamation about the threat of climate change. Solutions such as CCS are generally understood as unrealistic possibilities that are not offered as real solutions but simply as red herrings to justify opposition to a renewable energy transition. Despite disappointment with this modification, USE activists acknowledged that without this compromise, the resolution stood little chance of passing, and thus they were willing in this instance to engage in a process of "frame contraction"—shifting from a decidedly proactive stance promoting displacement of fossil fuels to a more moderate layering of green infrastructure over the existing carbon-based energy system with a set of protections in place for affected workers.

After the first speaker finished his diatribe about "unicorns and Easter bunnies," the next nine speakers spoke in support of the resolution, including three national leaders from building trades unions, one national leader of a manufacturing union, one national leader of a service sector union, one national leader from a public sector union, and three leaders from state and regional labor federations. Each of the building trades leaders cited the inclusion of language supporting carbon capture and advanced nuclear energy options in the resolution as the determining factor that brought them from opposing to supporting the resolution.

Other supporters made moral arguments or passionate pleas, as James had done at his manufacturing union's convention. For example, speaking in support of the resolution, a national leader from a service sector union said:

> Our members in the past two months alone have called on our emergency relief fund [because of Hurricanes Maria and Harvey] more than in its entire 16 years of existence. Many have lost pay and work, lost homes. These are working people's issues, and this is our future. I'm proud of this resolution that puts labor at the heart of the discussion about energy policy so [that] we can have high labor standards, create good union jobs, maintain good unions jobs and respect the work of all of the workers of this country while providing us with environmental sustainability for all of our futures and personally for my 8-year-old son.

A national leader of a utility workers' union with many members in the public sector talked about the potential for new jobs if labor supported a green infrastructure plan: "Our transmission system is 100 years old. If Thomas Edison could come back today, he would be amazed by LED lights and cell phones, but if he saw our transmission system he'd say, 'Nothing new there.' There's a lot of work that's needed, and our members and the building trades and everyone else in the room can make good off of this. Good union jobs."

The national president of a manufacturing union talked about the need for renewable energy technology to be manufactured in the United States with American-made steel as a means of both protecting the climate and creating good jobs. He went on to say that he and many of his members who grew up in steel towns always heard, "Hey, kid, you gotta choose between good jobs and a clean environment." He added, "Bullshit. It's not either/or, it's both or neither. And that's been our position." This particular speaker also served as the chair of the Resolutions Committee and coordinated much of the behind-the-scenes work that led to the revised resolution and the committee's recommendation that the convention vote to adopt it. When the call for the vote came up, AFL-CIO president Richard Trumka asked, "All in favor?" and the response was a resounding "Aye." Then, "All opposed?" There was nary a "nay" to be heard.

In one regard, the resolution signaled a marked departure from the federation's previous stance on climate change. It acknowledged the threat and demanded labor be at the table in efforts to reduce GHG emissions and create good, green jobs. However, through the compromise language about CCS, it also left the door open for pro–fossil fuel unions to continue their efforts to save or resurrect coal jobs. It also did not recognize any scientifically informed targets or timetables for GHG reductions. The resolution did signal a shift of labor from fossil fuel entrenchment toward protective layering as a preferred mode of change. By supporting the resolution, USE also shifted its frame accordingly to meet the federation in the middle. Despite its limitations, the resolution nonetheless signals the arrival of the LCM in the house of labor and lays bare the dividing line between the Jobs vs. the Environment frame and the Clean Air and Good Jobs counterframe within labor as a whole.

USE's Targets, Vulnerabilities, Opportunities, Frames, and Tactics

The union resolution campaign had one primary target: the labor movement. At the time of this campaign, in 2017, there was an opportunity in that the AFL-CIO would be holding its quadrennial convention later that year. Through the resolutions process at conventions, the federation becomes vulnerable to democratic forces within the movement to press for changes in political stances or the general direction of the organization. Additionally, the national leadership is forced to be in the room for several days with constituents from all of the different unions that are members of the federation and must try to balance the interests of these very different unions from all industries. An added vulnerability in this particular convention year was the increased sense of urgency about climate change after President Trump announced in June that he would move to have the United States exit the Paris Climate Accord—an international agreement that nearly all of the countries of the world signed pledging to reduce GHG emissions. Although largely seen as inadequate by climate change activists, the agreement was the first major global agreement to address climate change, and U.S. leadership was crucial in bringing the original agreement together. This move by the Trump administration sparked a strong reaction from many unions affiliated with the AFL-CIO, who quickly passed resolutions and made public statements that the United States must remain a party to the agreement. Even the AFL-CIO president, Richard Trumka, issued a statement calling the withdrawal from the Paris Climate Accord a "failure of American leadership." This put the issue front and center just a few months before the national convention began, and the base of support for labor–climate action was primed and ready to make their voices heard. USE took advantage of this energy by circulating their open letter to labor leaders.

The key features of the political opportunity structure in this case were by and large not working in favor of the LCM at the national level. However, the political landscape was varied and shifting for the other resolution campaigns pursued at the subnational level or within particular unions. At the national level, the building trades have always had a disproportionate say in the political positions and general direction of the AFL-CIO. This is due in part to the historically greater influence held by the craft unions of the AFL compared with the industrial unions of the CIO when the two federations merged in 1955 (Chaison 1980). The building trades unions also have their own subfederation, the NABTU, which gives them a powerful collective voice within the AFL-CIO and strong veto power because they can threaten to leave the federation, which would have tremendous economic consequences for the organization. Further, the largest service workers' union, the largest transportation workers' union, and the largest teachers' union are not members of the AFL-CIO, leaving only the smaller unions in these sectors belonging to the federation.[6]

Together, this meant that the powerful building trades unions, many of which met with President Trump after his election to discuss fossil fuel infrastructure projects, had a disproportionate voice within the federation despite the vulnerabilities emerging in this particular year. It is important to note that these same unions also dominate the powerful AFL-CIO Energy Committee, which shapes the confederation's policy on climate. Further, as was noted earlier, many building trades unions emphasize that climate mitigation strategies harm only their members—thus, other unions who "don't have skin in the game" should stand down on the issue or, better still, stand in solidarity to protect unionized fossil fuel jobs. Many unions buy into the "no skin in the game" argument or just do not want to find themselves in the crosshairs of the building trades unions, who have been known to be pretty vindictive.[7] In other words, the strong anti-climate voice of the building trades unions generally "neutralizes" voices of other unions that might otherwise speak out in favor of climate activism. However, the "no skin in the game" position—or the "equity" argument, as it has been called—fails to acknowledge that climate change is a threat to *all* working people and that there should be a greater solidarity to protect all workers and future generations from the devastating effects of unmitigated climate change.

At the subnational level, state federations in the Northeast and some on the West Coast were much easier targets for climate change resolutions. In the Northeast, the fossil fuel industry is not a major source of employment, aside from natural gas power pants. Moreover, many of the unions that fall on the Jobs vs. the Environment side of the labor–climate spectrum nationally tend to be more progressive in these regions because of the generally liberal political climate in places like New England and California—but also because these states, which have begun to invest in energy efficiency and re-newable energy, have started to see the economic benefits of climate protec-tion (Brownstein 2016).[8]

Another important aspect of the political opportunity structure in this case has to do with the status of the LCM as a movement within the labor move-ment. While this status gives LCM activists an official voice within the union polity through the democratic process, it also limits their tactical repertoire. From the outset, USE and other LCM activists stated that they do not wish to undermine solidarity or sow disunity within the labor movement and thus would not pursue protest actions against their own labor leaders. The underly-ing logic is that it would show weakness within the movement and open up many already-vulnerable unions to further attacks from employers and conser-vative politicians. Instead, LCM activists opted for a strategy to win the hearts and minds of their fellow union members, as James had done with his eloquent plea at the national convention of his manufacturing union. They wanted to expand the understanding and practice of solidarity by creating a cultural shift away from job consciousness toward class consciousness within the labor move-ment. Through the resolution process, LCM activists hope to win over their union sisters and brothers whose structural location in the political economy makes them either neutral or averse to climate protection—to persuade them to look past the short term and act in favor of their long-term interests.

Given the political opportunity structure and vulnerabilities at the time, the tactical repertoire of USE was constrained to pursuing resolutions in plac-es where they were most likely to be received favorably and, when in a divided house such as the national convention, where some of the strongest unions advocating for climate protection were no longer members, to engaging in compromise so as not to sow disunity within labor as a whole. The unwilling-ness of USE activists to protest against their union leadership left them with a standard political repertoire of tactics that included pressing to put climate change on the agenda for discussion and then offering persuasive, impassioned pleas in public forums. Despite the unfavorable political opportunity struc-ture at the national level, the vulnerability of the national AFL-CIO through the resolution process nonetheless created space for USE activists to move labor as a whole in a more progressive direction on climate change.

In regard to framing, the resolutions adopted by various unions and fed-erations around the country ranged from being protective to transformative. The five that were ultimately submitted to the national AFL-CIO convention represented a mix of these frames as well. Ultimately, through the compila-tion of these resolutions and the revision process under the Resolutions Com-mittee, the final product put forth was protective, with a focus on an all-of-the-above model for economic growth, pursuing layering as the mode of change. In particular, the final resolution stated that the federation would "fight politically and legislatively to secure and maintain employment, pensions and health care for workers affected by changes in the energy market" and would support "incentives and robust funding for research programs to bring new energy technologies to market, including renewables, carbon capture, and advanced nuclear technologies."

Actions Initiated by Labor Unions for Public Energy

Summary of Actions

LUPE, the international-level organization in this study, had one campaign that targeted the state, one that targeted labor, and four aimed at multiple targets. Targeting the state, LUPE representatives regularly attended the United Nations Framework Convention on Climate Change's Conference of the Parties (COP) meetings—commonly referred to as UN climate talks or simply COPs. LUPE participants regularly joined with activists at COP meetings to protest the tepid action of states in response to the urgent crisis of climate change.

LUPE also targeted labor at the climate talks by organizing a number of union panels and strategy sessions in the days before and during COP23 in Bonn, Germany, in 2017, including two on just transition, titled "The Just Transition: Stop Lying and Start Doing" and "Just Transition and Speeding Up the Development of Renewable Energies." They also convened a strategy roundtable on the need for reclaiming public ownership and control over the energy sector; that event was attended by more than forty representatives of roughly twenty-five unions from thirteen countries—Argentina, Australia, Belgium, Brazil, Canada, Dominican Republic, Germany, Italy, Netherlands, Norway, Philippines, the United Kingdom, and the United States—as well as several allies from the environmental movement. The meeting provided an opportunity for LUPE members to share their perspective on the struggle for the future of global energy systems with other unions that were not (yet) part of the network. The outcome of these actions was mixed, with some union leaders embracing the transformative frame and becoming involved with LUPE while others shunned the proposals as unrealistic. Also targeting labor, LUPE has conducted a series of multiday, intensive labor–climate leadership workshops in the United States, which are described in greater detail as a signature campaign in the next subsection.

Targeting both the state and labor, LUPE started a campaign titled "Unions against Fracking." The campaign emerged during the UN climate talks (COP20) in Lima, Peru, in December 2014, when a number of unions at a LUPE event began to discuss the need for the international union movement to join the growing opposition to hydraulic fracturing. As a part of the campaign, LUPE issued a public statement calling for a moratorium on fracking, which read in part:

> Water contamination is a known result of drilling. The high-volume use of carcinogenic chemicals such as silica also poses a threat to health, particularly to workers on drilling sites and who handle the wastewater from fracking. . . . We are also concerned about the impact of fugitive methane from drilling sites on global warming. Recent drill-site and atmospheric studies show high levels of methane leakage—suggesting that shale gas is worse than coal in terms of its impact on the atmosphere.

LUPE gathered endorsements of the statement from thirty-seven labor organizations, including sixteen global, national, or regional union federations and twenty-one individual unions and local-level affiliates. The outcome of this action has been mixed: organizing unions to publicly take a stance on fracking was a partial success, but the statement thus far has largely been unheard.

Targeting environmentalists and labor, LUPE has engaged in a number of campaigns to win the hearts and minds of workers, unions, and environmentalists. The first involved the production of a four-minute animated video about climate change, labor, and the need for a just transition involving public ownership and control of the energy sector. The video, which has been viewed more than eighteen thousand times on the Internet and used in LUPE training sessions (described in the next subsection), lays out the case for a rapid, orderly switch to renewable energy. The video directly challenges the dominant free market ideology undergirding capitalist society by making the case that an orderly transition to a sustainable energy system is achievable only by bringing the energy sector back into public hands and removing the profit motive from the decision-making process. This action has largely been a success because the video, which is compelling, continues to serve as an effective vehicle for the organization to introduce and promote their transformative vision of just transition.

In addition to the educational video, LUPE regularly releases policy papers or working papers on topics related to climate change, labor, and just transition. These papers are targeted at the state, labor leaders, and environmentalists, with the hope of persuading other activists and policy makers to pursue a transformative just transition that involves public control of the energy sector. Paper topics include just transition, public investment in renewables, an assessment of the failure of the current market-driven approach to addressing climate change, health impacts of climate change, facts about "clean coal," facts about fracking, and more. The papers are shared widely online, via email, or in print with LUPE members. The papers are often used as discussion anchors for quarterly meetings of the organization or for special union workshops on particular topics. One such workshop in 2018 centered on the topic of just transition. The meeting, which was held in the union hall of a large service sector union, included participants from labor, environmental organizations, environmental justice groups, and Indigenous rights organizations who shared their often-differing understandings of the term "just transition" (most of which aligned with one of the three LCM just transition frames presented in Chapter 5). The meeting was part educational and part network building; many activists created new connections for future actions in support of a just transition. The papers have had mixed success because, as many have noted, they are well researched, but they are too long and technical for those who are not policy wonks or they require more time than busy labor leaders can devote to reading. The just transition workshop, however, was a success and a great way to bring one of the papers to life.

LUPE's Signature Campaign: Educating for a Transformative Just Transition

On March 2, 2016, I joined a group of twenty-five labor leaders from around the United States in New York City for a three-day workshop on labor and climate change, organized by LUPE. This was the first of what would become an ongoing series of labor–climate leadership workshops with the stated goal of "helping participants acquire a solid grasp of the key issues—scientific, technical, political and historical—of climate change and climate policy." The workshops were designed for union officers, committee members, and staff to help them play a more effective role within their unions in the struggle for climate protection and a just transition to renewable energy. With this in mind, organizers from LUPE deliberately targeted individuals to be invited to the workshops on the basis of a combination of criteria, including recommendations from previous participants, the strategic importance of their position within the labor movement, the likelihood they would attend and learn something from the workshop, and their ability to take what they had learned back home and make changes within their own unions. In attendance at this first workshop were seven transportation union leaders, five service sector union leaders, four education union leaders, four building trades union leaders, two healthcare union leaders, one manufacturing union leader, one leader from a union federation, and one leader from a labor–climate coalition group.

The instructors at the workshop included leaders from LUPE, university labor educators, and leaders from environmental justice groups and labor–climate coalitions, along with prominent climate scientist Robert Howarth from Cornell University. For most of the union leaders in the room, meeting an actual climate scientist and being taught the fundamentals of climate change, including its causes and consequences, was an enlightening experience. For example, Hakim, a local leader of a transportation union, said to me, "It's one thing to hear about the 97 percent of scientists who agree [about climate change], but it's totally different when one of those scientists is standing in front of you and showing you charts and data. It gets very real, quickly."

Howarth's area of expertise and major contribution to climate research focuses on methane gas, which had not previously been considered a major contributor to global warming. His research shows that massive methane gas leaks from fracking operations, natural gas pipelines, and gas-burning power plants are a major source of GHGs in the atmosphere (see, for example, Howarth, Santoro, and Ingraffea 2011). This finding undermined the logic behind many existing climate mitigation plans, espoused by mainstream environmentalists and building trades unions, that pursued natural gas as a carbon-free "bridge fuel" for power generation until some unspecified future date when renewable sources such as wind and solar could produce the majority of electricity.

In addition to information about climate science, the workshops gave a history of the role of unions in the climate debate over the years, both in the United States and internationally through UN climate talks. The workshops also addressed how unions from all sectors could engage with climate policy and activism in ways that could "build union strength on the job and in the community, engage members, and promote union values." The aim was to help build a community of climate leaders inside the labor movement to register a collective impact at the local, national, and international levels. To this end, the workshop leaders spent considerable time discussing current debates within the climate community, assessing the effectiveness of existing policies, and, important to the ideology and mission of LUPE, advocating for intentional change and public ownership and control of the energy sector as the best possible means of achieving the goal of Clean Air and Good Jobs.

At the time I left the field, LUPE had conducted four of these workshops, drawing over one hundred union leaders from a broad cross section of industries. Unlike the majority of LUPE's work, the labor–climate leadership workshops focused on U.S. (and occasionally Canadian) labor leaders rather than on the international labor movement. This was due in part to the logistics of travel for a two- or three-day workshop. But it was also mostly by design because the U.S. labor movement is most conservative on the issue of climate change. While the research for this book has emphasized some progressive voices within the U.S. labor movement on the issue of climate change, it is important to emphasize that on a world scale, the U.S. labor movement as a whole, much like the U.S. government, is a "climate change laggard," trailing behind other unions throughout the world. Having attended three workshops—once as an attendee, once as an observer, and once as a guest facilitator—I was able to immerse myself in the learning experience of many union leaders. Not all attendees fully embraced the intentional-change agenda of promoting a transformative just transition, but many did, which for LUPE activists constituted a successful action.

Additionally, after returning home from the workshop, a small number of the supportive participants persuaded their unions to affiliate with LUPE. Of the sixty-plus unions that make up LUPE, sixteen are from the United States. Of those sixteen, four are education unions, three are healthcare unions, three are service sector unions, two are transportation unions, two are building trades unions, and one is a manufacturing union. The building trades unions were electrical workers' locals, one from the Northeast and one from the West Coast—similar to the locals that adopted climate change resolutions with USE. These union categories align well with the unions on the Clean Air and Good Jobs half of the labor–climate spectrum (see Figure 3.1).

LUPE's Targets, Vulnerabilities, Opportunities, Frames, and Tactics

LUPE's education campaign sought to promote the transformative vision for addressing the climate crisis within the U.S. labor movement, and the primary target of its labor–climate leadership workshops was the unions in the U.S. that were slow to embrace climate change activism. There were no clear vulnerabilities of the target, per se, over the period of the four workshops. However, in the wake of President Trump's announcement that he was pulling the United States out of the Paris Climate Accord, many unions felt pressure from their members to make statements or take action; thus, the leadership workshop held shortly after that announcement was a good opportunity for union leaders to engage more with the issue.

In this campaign, the political opportunity structure played a larger role in shaping the tactics than did any particular vulnerabilities within labor. The same Clean Air and Good Jobs unions that were likely to pass resolutions with USE were also prime targets for LUPE's outreach for workshop attendance. Those leaders, having already acknowledged the climate crisis as a labor issue, were more likely to be open to attending the workshops. Further, this openness created an opportunity for LUPE to educate the leaders about the transformative frame and hopefully recruit them to their broader campaign for a publicly owned and controlled energy system.

For this campaign, framing was paramount in shaping the tactical repertoire. Unlike the previous two campaigns, the framing here was not fluid. For ideological reasons, the transformative frame was baked into the mission of LUPE, and while they entertained discussions about different policy pathways for addressing climate change, they used their resources to demonstrate that the transformative path would be the most efficient and effective way to deal with the problem. To this end, their prognostic framing shaped their repertoire to include many actions like the labor–climate leadership workshop, which could help build support for their frame within labor.

The Shape of Things to Come

The analysis undertaken in this chapter of the tactical repertoires of the LCM between 2014 and 2018 reveals how the selection of targets—and in particular the vulnerabilities of the targets and the existing political opportunity structure—can shape the tactics used by movements. I found an interesting interaction among collective action frames, political opportunities, and tactics. In the case of the offshore wind campaign, SPEC strategically shifted from a protective to a proactive just transition frame and pursued displacement as the preferred mode of change when the opportunity to develop offshore wind arose. In the case of the union resolution campaign, USE activists acted independently, in consultation with USE leaders, to pursue union resolutions on climate change within their own unions to counter the Jobs vs. the Environment master frame but ultimately won only a compromised resolution at the national AFL-CIO convention. LUPE's campaign targeting the labor movement sought to shape the framing of union leaders who had already acknowledged climate as a labor issue to more actively challenge the dominant free market ideology of capitalist society and gained some limited increases in union support for public ownership and control of the energy sector.

In the years since I completed my participant observation, the United States has seen multiple overlapping extreme weather events, including hurricanes, wildfires, and floods. The country has also witnessed the introduction of the Green New Deal resolution before Congress; the emergence of the COVID-

19 pandemic, which brought the world economy to its knees; and the election of President Joe Biden to replace Donald Trump after one term of undermining progress on climate change and thwarting all attempts to reduce inequality. Each of these changes to the underlying political opportunity structure has influenced the ability of the LCM to promote its vision for Clean Air and Good Jobs, often increasing its resonance with passive bystanders. As I discuss in the next chapter, there have been some encouraging shifts in the labor–climate space, but many challenges remain, including the extent to which a broad-based, multiracial, and cross-class alliance can be formed and sustained to fight for and win a Green New Deal–style solution to the dual crises of climate and inequality.

7

Pandemics, Presidents, and
Public Perceptions

*Changing Opportunity Structures for
the Labor–Climate Movement*

The actions of movement activists often depend on the presence (or absence) of specific political opportunities. When the existing political system is vulnerable to challenge, it creates greater opportunity for movements to push through their desired social change. During the time of my participant observation in the field (2014–2018), the United States transitioned from the Obama administration to the Trump administration, representing a reduction in political opportunity for the LCM at the federal level. At the same time, a number of state and local elections increased opportunities for more localized efforts. In the four years following my field work, we experienced a pandemic, an unprecedented uprising for racial justice, and a slim Democratic majority in Congress with a new party platform embracing many elements of the Green New Deal. This series of events significantly altered the political opportunity structure for the LCM, exposing some vulnerabilities and opening new spaces for leverage in the struggle for sustainability, including formal political opportunities as well as other opportunity structures based on discourse and informal alignments.[1]

In this chapter, the focus switches from the confidential participants to the more specific efforts under way in recent years that have captured news headlines. In particular, I review some of the major shifts in the political opportunity structure for the LCM in recent years, consider how those changes have influenced the actions of the movement, and evaluate whether it made any progress in shifting particular unions or labor as a whole closer to the Clean Air and Good Jobs frame.

Changing Opportunity Structures for the Labor-Climate Movement, 2018-2022

In the years since my participant observation, the world has experienced a number of dramatic changes. Perhaps most notable was the onset of the COVID-19 pandemic hitting the United States in early 2020. Also, the Movement for Black Lives rose to unprecedented levels of social action following the police killing of George Floyd. An overall increase in public support for social spending, including on climate solutions, opened some new political opportunities for LCM activists. Even before these historic events, the introduction of the Green New Deal resolution in Congress in 2019 brought the issues of labor and climate justice to the forefront in political discourse and opened a tremendous organizing space for LCM leaders and activists.

The Green New Deal: Labor and Climate Justice Go Prime Time

The unveiling of House Resolution 109 "Recognizing the Duty of the Federal Government to Create a Green New Deal" by Representative Alexandria Ocasio-Cortez and Senator Ed Markey (U.S. Congress 2019) on February 7, 2019, forced the issues of climate change and inequality to center stage in the media. To the delight of LCM activists, the major planks of the resolution echoed many of the demands that the participants in my study had been making for many years, including various aspects of a just transition. The resolution also once again brought into sharp focus the divide within the labor movement between the Jobs vs. the Environment unions and the Clean Air and Good Jobs unions, as presented by the labor–climate spectrum in Chapter 3. If not for the efforts of the LCM though, this divide might well have been a monolithic wall of opposition to the Green New Deal.

In follow-up interviews with fourteen key study participants between 2019 and 2021, I confirmed that all three SMOs in this study supported the Green New Deal resolution. Jacob, a leader with SPEC, said he was disappointed when the national AFL-CIO announced its opposition to the resolution, citing the anticipated impacts on workers in the fossil fuel economy. "But their decision," he said, "reinforces the need to give attention to the plight of working families and their communities as we transition to a clean energy economy." He went on to describe the "trifocal lens" through which LCM activists should view and evaluate their work: climate action, job creation, and equity. Jake, a national leader with USE, said, "I don't accept the analysis that says if you're for addressing climate change, you can't win the hearts and minds of blue-collar workers in the Midwest." He explained that the Green New Deal resolution includes a federal jobs guarantee, which he said is "very important" because "it tightens labor markets, which drives wages and benefits up, and enables unions to negotiate good contracts that ripple through the economy." Steve, a leader in LUPE, said, "The Green New Deal is potentially transformative in that it paves the way for public control over sectors of the economy that the government substantially funds." He noted that the original draft resolution stated, "There is also a space for the government to take an equity role in projects, as several government and government-affiliated institutions already do." Such a provision would replace public service for profit maximization as the guiding logic of the energy sector, he said.

Efforts to pass union resolutions in support of climate protection in general and of the Green New Deal in particular carried on in the years after my fieldwork ended. One of the most significant resolutions to be adopted was the one by the American Federation of Teachers (AFT) at their national convention in July 2020. Not only did the resolution proclaim support for the Green New Deal but it also called for a just transition for displaced workers, the prioritization of environmental justice for frontline communities, and the use of progressive taxation and demilitarization as a means of paying for the proactive plan. As with other resolution efforts discussed in this study, the AFT resolution began with the work of LCM activists from USE and LUPE working at the local level within their unions in California, Illinois, Massachusetts, New Jersey, New York, Oregon, and Pennsylvania.

Climate justice activists, including those from the CJA and local organizations, have been building toward a Green New Deal at the local level for more than a decade and have extended their frontline-led efforts into the federal Green New Deal space as well. Climate justice activists throughout the United States focused on frontline community solutions during the 2020 election by hosting candidate forums, organizing rallies and direct actions, and engaging community groups and lawmakers on Green New Deal–style policies. With a broad range of allies (including members of the LCM), the CJA launched the People's Bailout, the United Frontline Table, Build Back Fossil Free, and the Green New Deal Network to develop and promote executive orders, push back on bad cabinet choices, introduce legislation, and lay the groundwork for climate justice solutions that acknowledge the interlinked nature of the dual crises of climate and inequality.

Overall, the introduction of the Green New Deal resolution before Congress opened new organizing spaces for the LCM, as well as for environmental and climate justice movements and labor more broadly. While the nature of the Green New Deal remains contested, much like the prognostic frame of a just transition, and especially in the wake of passage of the IRA, there can be no progress without struggle. These hard and soft disagreements represent the space where change becomes possible. As Frederick Douglass famously stated, "Power concedes nothing without a demand."

When Things Fell Apart: The COVID Recession and Social Spending

Since (and even long before) the first laboratory-confirmed case of COVID-19 hit America on January 21, 2020, U.S. residents have experienced the high cost of decades of privatization, deregulation, cuts to the social safety net, and a general prioritization of corporate interests over human needs. Through lack of paid sick time, inadequate unemployment benefits, uneven access to healthcare, and unequal broadband access for students, the pandemic exposed and exacerbated the deep structural inequalities that define our contemporary society. Death and severe illness from the disease disproportionately affected the most vulnerable in society: the elderly, the poor, disabled people, and people of color. In other words, the same populations that have suffered environmental injustice for decades felt the worst effects of the pandemic. At the date of this writing, more than one million Americans have died, and the numbers continue to rise.

Unemployment also skyrocketed as a result of economic shutdowns to stop the spread of the virus, with nearly twenty-five million claiming benefits in May 2020, representing 20 percent of the U.S. labor force—more than double the unemployment rate of the Great Recession. After decades of neoliberal governance exacerbated by the harmful actions of the Trump administration, vital government agencies were underfunded, understaffed, or put under the charge of political lackies who did not believe in the missions of the agencies they were tasked with running. The production of vital healthcare equipment had been outsourced in pursuit of cheaper labor and lax environmental regulations, putting U.S. healthcare providers at the mercy of global supply chains. These ideologically driven actions left the federal government incapable of marshaling the health and safety equipment needed to help critically ill Americans and protect the courageous first responders and healthcare workers trying to save them.

And yet the death, fear, and economic ruin caused by the COVID pandemic, many LCM activists contend, are only a taste of what will happen if we do not take dramatic and immediate steps to address climate change. Continued global warming could lead to multiple, simultaneous climate disasters occurring on a regular basis. Category 5 hurricanes hitting the Gulf Coast at the same time as massive wildfires in the West, extreme flooding in the Midwest, and heat waves in the Northeast could place the country in a near-constant state of emergency, further exacerbating existing inequalities along race, class, and gender lines. The federal government's inadequate capacity and tepid response during the pandemic have not only raised public alarm but also increased the public's appetite and demand for social spending to an extent that has not been seen in recent history. From enhanced unemployment benefits and moratoriums on rent to paid sick leave and free vaccinations, the American public has come to realize the value of a robust public response to address collective social problems and market failures.

The collective experience of the economic fallout from the pandemic is analogous to what countless groups of workers and local communities have experienced after plant closures in recent decades. In other words, the American public writ large has experienced an unjust transition and understands more than ever how uncontrollable forces can cause economic and social ruin. But with proper social supports in place, the pain can be eased. These experiences could lead to a rise in support from bystanders for policies designed to protect workers who are dislocated by climate change or decarbonization efforts. The work of the LCM makes clear the connections between the pandemic experience and that of workers as a result of these impacts as well as mitigation efforts. Publications from USE compared the current moment with the Great Depression, citing five distinctive though deeply interpenetrating crises: climate, pandemic, depression, racial inequality, and democracy. The solution? A comprehensive program like the New Deal—a Green New Deal.

From "PPE Now!" to #Striketober: Increasing Public Support for Unions

The pandemic also increased public support for unions and raised general awareness of the value of having a collective voice for working people. Gallup polls show public support for unions at record high levels since the onset of the pandemic. From the start, essential workers such as those in grocery stores, warehouses, and assembly lines were some of the most vulnerable, typically working with woefully inadequate safety protections and often at wages that do not fairly reflect the value their work adds to society each day. Under the Trump administration, the Occupational Safety and Health Administration was missing in action, refusing to issue an emergency infectious disease standard for healthcare workers. Guidance issued from the Centers for Disease

Control and Prevention was uneven and inadequate at best, and compliance was largely voluntary. A unified message for the workplace was altogether lacking, giving employers leeway to disregard the guidance in the pursuit of profits.

In the face of federal government inaction and an inadequate response by many employers, unions and organized workers across the United States used their collective voice to demand better COVID-19-related health and safety protections (Greenhouse 2020). From nurses to warehouse workers, fast-food workers, and librarians, workers fought for and in many cases won battles for personal protective equipment (PPE), cleaner workplaces, hazard pay, and, where possible, the ability to telecommute. Unions joined with worker centers and other allies to support better conditions for nonunion workers, including immigrant workers in precarious work arrangements. They fought for furlough plans to keep fellow workers in their jobs rather than having them be laid off. To win these protections, workers signed letters, organized sick-outs, filed grievances, engaged in bargaining, and, in some cases, conducted work stoppages. These actions contributed to the issuance of executive orders by several governors, mostly in Democratic-led states, to protect workers. One such example, Executive Order #122 in New Jersey—a measure fought for by the Protect Workers Coalition, a diverse coalition of workers, worker centers, community groups, advocacy organizations, and labor unions—required essential employers to have infectious control practices, social-distancing measures, and face-mask requirements and to notify workers of any known exposure to COVID-19 at the worksite.

Economists from Columbia University, using data from a national survey of essential workers, found that union members reported better COVID-19 workplace practices and outcomes than nonmembers did (Hertel-Fernandez et al. 2020). Even adjusting for demographic and workplace factors, union members were more likely to report using PPE regularly at work, receiving PPE and other disinfecting or sanitizing resources from their employers, receiving paid sick leave, and being tested for COVID-19. A report by the Economic Policy Institute cited how unionized workers secured enhanced safety measures, additional premium pay, paid sick time, and a say in the terms of furloughs or work-share arrangements to save jobs during the pandemic (McNicholas et al. 2020).

Taken together, the increased support for social spending, the strong support for unions and collective action, and the generalized experience of an unjust transition resulting from the COVID-related recession marked a significant shift in the political opportunity structure for LCM activists seeking collective solutions that centered the interests of workers.

Black Lives Matter: The Murder of George Floyd and the Uprising for Racial Justice

The grief and anger surrounding the deaths of George Floyd, Breonna Taylor, Tony McDade, Ahmaud Arbery, Jamel Floyd, and thousands of other Black citizens whose lives have been taken by the police, white supremacists, and the carceral state reached a boiling point in the summer of 2020. Demands for justice, safety, and freedom in many places, such as Kenosha, Wisconsin, were met with state-sanctioned resistance. The police killing of Black Americans that triggered the unprecedented uprising of civil protest is only the latest in a long history of violence against Black communities and movements to confront and stop this violence (see, for example, Hayes 2021). However, the confluence of several highly visible killings, captured on video, brought many citizens of all racial backgrounds to a moral tipping point, and the outrage bubbled over into the streets in cities across the country.

The protests also arrived at a time when the COVID-19 pandemic was disproportionately affecting Black, brown, and Indigenous communities. COVID death and infection rates are significantly higher in communities of color, in part as a consequence of a history of occupational segregation. Essential workers of color who went to work in the midst of the pandemic were often treated as expendable. Limited protections, including a lack of paid sick days, inadequate PPE, and poor sanitation measures, exacerbated an already-dangerous situation. Employer retaliation was a common response when workers demanded a safe working environment. In addition to the risks on the job, COVID-19 resulted in mass unemployment, also disproportionately affecting historically marginalized workers. For example, Black communities faced an unemployment rate of nearly 50 percent, and 60 percent of those laid off during the height of the pandemic were women.

The Movement for Black Lives played a notable role in shaping the views of some participants in the LCM as it garnered tremendous national attention and new levels of public support during the spring and summer of 2020. Many LCM participants had a standing concern about racial justice issues, but the Black Lives Matter protests during the summer of 2020 sharpened that understanding for many and brought the issue closer to the top of their list of organizing priorities. Equally important, the uprisings raised awareness among many of the targets of the LCM—namely, labor as a whole, the state, and the mainstream environmental movement. The increased focus on and understanding of structural racism by each of these groups has contributed to a greater possibility of frame alignment around issues of climate justice and the need for prioritizing the remediation of historical disadvantages and injustices experienced by members of frontline and vulnerable communities of color.

Black and brown workers have always experienced structural racism, but the brutal execution of George Floyd by white police officers and the massive response drawing in bystander publics in cities and towns across the country at levels not seen since the 1960s touched many labor leaders in new ways. While not specifically about climate change or transitions, the protests sensitized some who were not already aware to the ubiquity of systemic racism. A few participants described their increased understanding of the ways racist decision-making in the past had created unequal environmental benefits and burdens for communities along the lines of race and ethnicity. For some labor leaders, the protests opened doors to conversations about the history of environmental injustice, and a number of environmental organizations realized the significance of integrating both social and environmental justice into their priorities. Building a broad-based, multiracial, and cross-class movement for labor and climate justice will require further frame alignment across each of the movements operating within the climate space—the LCM, labor, the mainstream environmental movement, and the environmental justice and climate justice movements.

Building Back Better? The Biden Administration and a Changed Political Landscape

Due in part to the demand for a greater government response to the pandemic, voters elected Joseph Biden as the forty-sixth president of the United States in 2020. Notwithstanding the extreme political divide among the electorate—fueled largely by the Big Lie that the election had been fraudulent and deprived Trump of a victory, which led to the violent January 6 insurrection and attempted coup at the Capitol—the election of Biden represented a potential break from a decades-long trend of full-blown neoliberalism in governance. The extent to which Biden is or is not progressive, Keynesian-leaning, or possibly "the next FDR" in his approach to governance is open to debate, but the fact that he ran on a package of massive government spending and public investment, funded largely through progressive income taxation, and promises to be the be "the most pro-union President" in a generation marks a dramatic shift in the political landscape at the federal level.[2] For many progressives and members of the LCM, Biden was a second or third choice for president, behind Senator Bernie Sanders or Senator Elizabeth Warren, but once the primary election was over, they worked to help defeat the climate-denying, antidemocratic administration of Donald Trump while simultaneously working on the inside to shift the Biden labor and climate policy agenda to the left.

Seeing Biden's reluctance to offer full-throated support for the Green New Deal as proposed by Ocasio-Cortez and Markey (U.S. Congress 2019) but noting his support for many of its individual provisions, several LCM leaders joined ranks with other labor leaders to ensure that his signature Build Back Better plan addressed labor–climate concerns. Activists from labor, the mainstream environmental movement, environmental justice and climate justice organizations, and the LCM began formulating policy proposals and collective action plans long before Election Day in hopes of influencing the shape of the first hundred days should Biden succeed in ousting President Trump. By the time he took office, Biden's Build Back Better framework contained many aspects of these demands.

Although the Build Back Better package as a whole was not achieved, a series of bills have been passed and efforts to do more are still underway (at the time of this writing). One piece of legislation—the $1.2 trillion Infrastructure Investment and Jobs Act—was passed by Congress in November 2021. The legislation was intended to help communities across the country rebuild their roads and bridges, railways, and public transit systems, and it promised to add an average of twenty million jobs over the next decade. In a win for environmental and climate justice, the act lifted the ban on local hire provisions for construction projects that was put in place under the Reagan administration. This provision is a historic advance for racial justice resulting from decades of activism to empower cities to put their local residents to work. The act also included an important push for the U.S. Department of Transportation to do targeted hiring so that agencies could push for more diversity in construction projects. Additionally, the act provided $2.5 billion in funding to support the transition to emissions-free electric school buses, a win for both environmental justice and labor because many of the buses will be union made in the United States by UAW and USW members. While supportive of these provisions, most in the LCM were disappointed that the administration and Congress had peeled the infrastructure component away from the larger BBB plan, forfeiting much of their political leverage to pass the ambitious social plans that were part of the broader agenda.

A second piece of legislation came in the form of the Inflation Reduction Act (IRA) of 2022. The IRA allocates approximately $370 billion over a period of ten years, about 75 percent of which is in the form of market incentives (rather than direct investments or regulatory mandates) to advance the transition to "clean energy." Much smaller energy investments focus on tackling pollution in poorer communities and promoting conservation and rural development. The bill considers clean energy to be inclusive of renewables, nuclear power, biofuels, hydrogen, and carbon capture and sequestration (CCS) and it lacks any regulations limiting the production and use of fossil fuels. This silence on the phaseout of fossil fuels, the inclusion of CCS as a solution to the climate crisis, and the reliance on market incentives to advance renewables did not please most within the LCM. But most frustrating was the last-minute dealing with Senator Joseph Manchin III of West Virginia, who demanded a side deal that mandates that renewable energy siting permits cannot be approved during any year unless accompanied by opening two million acres of land or sixty million acres of ocean to oil and gas leasing bids.

Blue greens and labor as a whole were very supportive of the IRA and celebratory of its passage, not just because of its climate provisions, but also because of provisions to reduce healthcare and prescription medicine costs and collect uncollected tax revenue from the rich. USE, the CJA, and other environmental and climate justice activists expressed immediate displeasure with the climate justice provisions of the bill. The CJA issued a statement proclaiming the IRA was "NOT a climate justice bill," saying: "We can't allow frontline communities to be sacrificed by catering to the profit interests of the dying and outdated dirty energy industry (CJA 2022)." USE issued a statement saying that:

> The fossil fuel industry, the Republican Party, conservative fossil-fuel Democrats, and right-wing ideologues combined to block the climate, labor, and social justice programs of the Green New Deal and Build Back Better resulting in compromise legislation, the Inflation Reduction Act.

Despite being critical of the fossil fuel provisions and the relatively small amounts of money earmarked for reducing pollution in frontline communities, USE did acknowledge that the IRA represented the most significant climate legislation ever passed into U.S. law. The statement noted an opportunity for the LCM to shape the federal subsidies provided for nonfossil energy development and manufacturing and help to advance a Green New Deal from below. The potential for job creation, an estimated 1 to 1.5 million jobs, was also applauded and seen as an important piece of a protective just transition for workers being displaced from declining industries.

Perhaps most encouraging though, was the broad-based and concerted effort by LCM activists, environmentalists, and climate justice activists to prevent Senator Manchin's "dirty side deal" from being included in a must-pass budget continuing resolution. Over 650 frontline communities, environmental justice, and other organizations signed on to a letter to the Senate and House Democratic leadership calling for them to "unequivocally reject any effort to promote fossil fuels, advance unproven technologies, and weaken our core environmental laws" and to "stand with the communities who continue to bear the brunt of harm from fossil fuels and act to prevent wholesale climate disaster (People vs. Fossil Fuels 2022)." Activists from USE and SPEC issued a call for unions and other labor organizations to stand with frontline environmental justice communities whose wellbeing and very existence was threatened by the proposal. "We call on unions and other labor organizations to stand with their own members who require protection from rapacious corporations who are eager to take advantage of this proposal in order to destroy the communities of which workers are part." The side deal was ultimately defeated when Senator Manchin withdrew the proposal in September 2022, but there is no guarantee that he will not try again to get it passed by attaching to other future legislation.

While the Infrastructure Investment and Jobs Act and the IRA do not espouse the fully proactive or transformative vison the LCM had hoped for in a Green New Deal, they represent a significant step forward from the climate denial and anti-unionism of the previous administration. Their passage reinforces the sense among LCM activists that they at least have a receptive audience in the White House, and many remain hopeful that more real action in pursuit of the Clean Air and Good Jobs counterframe can be made during this window of political opportunity.

Rising Down: The Changing Costs and Benefits of Renewables versus Fossil Fuels

Accompanying the changes to the political opportunity structure described thus far is a change in economic structure—namely, a decline in costs of renewable energy sources relative to fossil fuels. The International Renewable Energy Agency (IRENA) found renewable power to be rising down, becoming increasingly cheaper than any new electricity capacity based on fossil fuels (IRENA 2020). More than half of the renewable capacity added in 2019 achieved lower power costs than the cheapest new coal plants. The report also highlighted that new renewable power-generation projects increasingly undercut existing coal-fired plants. On average, new solar and onshore wind power cost less than keeping many existing coal plants in operation. Up to 1,200 gigawatts of existing coal capacity can cost more to generate than actually building and operating the same amount of new utility-scale solar. Replacing the costliest 500 gigawatts of coal with solar and wind could cut power-system costs by up to $23 billion per year and reduce annual GHG emissions by around 1.8 gigatons of carbon dioxide (CO_2), equivalent to 5 percent of total global CO_2 emissions in 2019.

Around the same time the International Energy Agency noted that the costs of generating electricity from low-carbon technologies such as wind and solar are falling, making these technologies cost competitive with fossil fuel power generation (International Energy Agency and Nuclear Energy Agency 2021). The report was based on expected 2025 plant-level costs reported by 243 plants in twenty-four countries, ranging in energy source from coal and natural gas to solar and wind to nuclear energy. Through a survey, the agency found that, in most of the represented countries, costs for renewable energy are expected to be lower than those of coal- or gas-powered plants. In the United States, onshore wind and solar power are expected to be the least expensive to operate, followed by natural gas, offshore wind, nuclear, and then coal. The report reveals that the cost of solar photovoltaic electricity has fallen 85 percent since 2010, and the costs of both onshore and offshore wind electricity have been cut by about half during the same period. Both renewable sources are now cost competitive with fossil fuel electricity. And the more that renewable energy technologies are deployed, the cheaper they become. In part responding to these economic trends, consumer demand for renewable energy is also on the rise. While not nearly enough, solar and wind increased from 1.7 percent of global electricity generation in 2010 to 8.7 percent in 2020, considerably higher than predicted by economic models (Jaeger 2021). Further, evidence suggests that the spread of renewable energy is socially contagious. Studies have found that installing solar panels on one's roof increases the odds that neighbors will install their own panels as well (Plumer 2016).

The rise of hybrid, plug-in hybrid, and fully electric vehicles (EVs) has also begun to make a small dent in the combustion-engine auto market. While EVs and hybrids still represent just a fraction of all sales, market projections anticipate those sales to increase significantly in coming years, especially as battery capacity improves (increasing vehicle range) and a robust charging infrastructure is established (which is a piece of the infrastructure spending package passed by Congress in 2021). The cost of running a hybrid or fully electric vehicle is just a fraction of what it takes to operate and maintain a combustion-engine vehicle over the life of the product. These increased demands for renewable energy and noncombustion-engine vehicles represent a clear threat to the fossil fuel regime, possibly undermining one of its major pillars of support—fossil fuel consumers. It also signals further decline in employment in fossil fuel industries, including extraction and production of coal, oil, and gas products.

Glen, a leader from a fossil fuel union on the West Coast, described two realities that will drive the change: the economic reality and the political reality.[3] The economic reality is that the declining cost of renewables, the increasing range of EVs, and better access to charging infrastructure will undermine demand for combustion engines—and that means less demand for gas and oil, which his members refine. "If you're smart enough or pragmatic enough to realize that you can power an electric vehicle for like 20 percent of the cost of gas right now," he said, it is only a matter of time. "I might've been the first one to park an electric vehicle in the refinery parking lot, but I'm certainly not going to be the last." On top of the economic reality is the political reality, which is that voters increasingly support efforts to cut carbon emissions and reduce fossil fuel dependence—particularly in blue states such as Glen's. "The fact [is] that we seem to have a clear majority of voters who want to address this problem—maybe confused about the best way to go about it, but they want to address this problem," he said. This topic is discussed in greater detail below.

These economic and political realities are underpinned by the environmental reality that we ultimately must stop burning fossil fuels if there is to be any hope of preventing the most cataclysmic climate change outcomes. For Glen though, it was crucial to think of the climate crisis in terms of the economic and political reality when speaking with his fellow union members. Like others I spoke with, he indicated that the word "transition" is not well received by members of his union, and the idea of saving the environment or saving the world may appeal to some but not to the majority. The real motivator, he said, is understanding that this change is coming down the pipeline "whether we like it or not." And we need to prepare for that inevitable reality. "Ultimately, of course, we want all workers and all citizens to understand how we can achieve the benefits while avoiding the horrible consequences . . . but they don't have to know all the details down to the nitty gritty if they simply understand that it's in their best interest to be part of the solution instead of part of the problem."

The Moral Tipping Point? Increasing Public Awareness and Demand for Climate Action

At the risk of stating the obvious: climate change is an issue that affects everyone. However, not all those affected by climate change are aggrieved. At least not yet. But that may be changing. Through the consumption of relatively inexpensive fossil fuels, the residents of the world's richest nations have enjoyed tremendous economic growth and development since the late nineteenth century. These benefits, of course, have not been evenly distributed.

As with other areas in the capitalist political economy, a small but influential group has reaped the lion's share of the rewards of the climate-altering, fossil fuel economy in the form of corporate profits and affluent lifestyles. Many workers benefited as well, but the history of racial exclusion and gender discrimination in America meant that some were denied the opportunity to work in many of the fossil fuel occupations, which, as a result of generations of collective bargaining, are among the highest-paid blue-collar jobs in the country today. The disparities are even greater on a global scale, and those living in the nations from which fossil fuels and other wealth-generating resources are often extracted may lack reliable electricity and transportation.

Tragically, the affluence of the developed world can in many instances be clearly linked to the exploitation of labor and the environment that occurs in less-developed countries. The uneven distribution of rewards from the fossil fuel regime are mirrored in the highly unequal experiences of the negative effects of climate change. Up to this point, the consequences of a warming world have disproportionately affected the poor and the working classes—hence the rise of the climate justice movement. One need only recall the images that dominated television news and the Internet in the wake of Hurricane Katrina in New Orleans or more recently of Hurricanes Harvey and Maria in Puerto Rico to understand the relationship between poverty and climate carnage.

However, climate change's reach is extending and beginning to affect the lives of middle-class and affluent citizens as well. Stronger, more frequent, and slower-moving storms have devastated affluent coastal properties on the East Coast. Wildfires have ravaged countless suburbs on the West Coast. Droughts and floods have shocked agricultural centers and wreaked havoc on food prices and supplies throughout the world, including staple commodities such as wheat and luxury items like wine (Wheeler and von Braun 2013). Millionaires and billionaires, many of whom have been driving and profiting from the crisis, are building and purchasing "doomsday bunkers" for themselves and their families to survive in a post-climate-apocalypse world. Others are launching private rockets and designing plans for colonizing Mars.

However, the greatest consequences of climate change by far are saved for one final victim: the future generations who are not currently present to have a voice in the decisions that will affect their lives. Elevated sea levels, extreme heat, refugee crises, food and water shortages, and armed conflict over resources and borders are just some of the potential consequences that tomorrow's citizens will inherit. Lawsuits by youth activists, such as those brought forth by Our Children's Trust, have argued that inaction on climate issues by state and federal governments is violating the fundamental right to life, liberty, and property of future generations, as well as the public trust doctrine, by knowingly engaging in actions that create a dangerous climate situation (Schwartz 2017). The outcomes of these lawsuits are as yet unknown, but the conservative tilt of the Supreme Court and the influx of a large number of conservative federal judges resulting from appointments by President Trump do not bode well for a favorable decision for the future inhabitants of Planet Earth.

Swedish teenage activist Greta Thunberg inspired a global youth climate strike movement with her Fridays for Future protests outside the Swedish Parliament. Taking her message all the way to the UN climate talks in 2018, she scolded top world leaders for not being "mature enough" to tell it like it is. "Our civilization," she stated "is being sacrificed for the opportunity of a small amount of people to continue making enormous amounts of money. Our biosphere is being sacrificed so that rich people in countries like mine can live in luxury. It is the sufferings of the many which pay for the luxuries of the few. . . . You say you love your children above all else, and yet you are stealing their future in front of their very eyes" (Mesey 2018). She went on to deliver a powerful and scathing rebuke of past and present efforts by neoliberal governments to address the climate crisis and to put them on notice that change will happen whether they are part of it or not:

> Until you start focusing on what needs to be done rather than what is politically possible, there is no hope. We cannot solve the crisis without treating it like a crisis. We need to keep the fossil fuels in the ground and we need to focus on equity. If solutions within this system are so impossible to find, maybe we should change the system itself. We have not come here to beg world leaders to care. You have ignored us in the past and you will ignore us again. You have run out of excuses and we are running out of time. We have come here to let you know that change is coming whether you like it or not. The real power belongs to the people. (Mesey 2018)

In the United States, the youth-led Sunrise Movement emerged around the same time, using disruptive direct-action tactics to demand a Green New Deal for America, including a just transition for workers and vulnerable, frontline communities.

Together, these visibly aggrieved groups—the poor and the youth—though growing, still represent a minority of the population in the United States. Like other movements in the past such as the civil rights, women's, and marriage equality movements, the nascent LCM will need to broaden its base to enlist others beyond the communities that are directly hurt by the effects of climate change and current mitigation proposals.[4] This includes the many unions not in the fossil fuel industry that have either remained silent on the issue or merely offered lip service and have provided little tangible help to build pro-worker solutions to the crisis. Only by reaching a critical mass of support, including workers from all industries, can the movement achieve its ultimate goal of promoting a just transition to a sustainable future.

The good news is that the growing concern with climate change and injustice might be approaching a moral tipping point. Drawing on a nationally representative survey, researchers at the Yale Program on Climate Change Communication (Cook et al. 2019) found that public belief in climate change rose steadily from 65 percent in 2015 to 73 percent in 2020 and that the percentage who believe it is caused by humans increased from 51 percent to 60 percent during the same period. Importantly, the realization that most scientists agree about the human causation of global warming increased from 40 percent to 57 percent over the same period. The study also found that large majorities of registered voters across the political spectrum support a range of specific policies that promote clean energy and reduce GHG emissions and dependence on fossil fuels, suggesting that as climate change moves from an abstract diagnosis to concrete remedies, a larger number of citizens will be "all in" on addressing the problem. For example, over 85 percent of registered voters support increasing funding for renewable energy research, generating renewable power on public lands, and providing tax rebates to people who purchase energy efficient vehicles. More than 70 percent—including 85 percent of Democrats, 75 percent of independent voters, and 52 percent of Republicans—believe that when there is a conflict between environmental protection and economic growth, environmental protection is more important.

These figures starkly intimate that the Jobs vs. the Environment master frame, the ideology that has undermined progress on climate change over the years, is on the verge of collapse—if not in the agendas and policies of mainstream political parties, then in the hearts and minds of ordinary citizens. Focusing just on unions and workers, I coauthored a study in 2016 that examined the relationship between unionization and environmental attitudes and behaviors in the General Social Survey and the American National Election Studies between 1980 and 2012 (Vachon and Brecher 2016). We found union members, on average, to be more likely than the general population and other nonunion workers to display pro-environmental attitudes and behaviors, including a belief in climate change. A survey by progressive think tank Data for Progress gauged support for the Green New Deal among 1,012 U.S. voters between March 30 and April 3, 2019. The poll found that 62 percent of union members supported the Green New Deal, compared with just over 50 percent of nonunion respondents, again reflecting an untapped pool of climate justice "activists in waiting" among the ranks of labor (McElwee et al. 2019).

These ongoing attitudinal shifts on climate change in the United States can be attributed in part to the educational and framing efforts of authors, filmmakers, and social movements like the LCM. For example, Al Gore's film *An Inconvenient Truth* (Guggenheim 2006) opened the eyes of many people to the real dangers of global warming. The documentary film *From the Ashes* (Bonfiglio 2017) put a human face on the devastating results of environmental policies that do not include a just transition for workers. Naomi Klein's compelling film *This Changes Everything* (Lewis 2016) presents sobering images of the devastating consequences of climate change for the lives of vulnerable populations living in "weak states" such as India, for Indigenous peoples living near the tar sands in Alberta, or those on the frontlines of fossil fuel disasters such as an oil pipeline spill in Montana.

The film effectively demonstrates that those negative outcomes are a by-product of a lifestyle lived in rich countries that is placing many of the negative externalities of environmental destruction on less affluent populations living under governments that are ineffective or unconcerned about environmental justice. Similar to northern white people watching the repression of southern Black people during the civil rights movement, for citizens of affluent countries, watching the movie could incite "moral outrage" when they realize how their own comfort and affluence is harming the lives of these vulnerable populations. This is one of the potential moral tipping points of the LCM. The engagement of bystander publics and the activation of conscience constituencies on the issue of climate change and the effects it has on frontline communities could expand the terrain of political opportunity, opening up numerous vulnerabilities for the movement to attack.

Finding Movement in Labor: Labor-Climate Responses to Changing Opportunity Structures

I contend that existing political opportunity structures at the local, state, and national levels—shaped in large part by the underlying structural features of American capitalism outlined in Chapters 2 and 3—can either enhance or constrain the ability of movements such as the LCM to effectively promote change. However, as I argued in Chapters 4, 5, and 6, social movement participants such as those in the LCM are not merely carriers of ideas that grow automatically out of existing structural arrangements; they also act as signifying agents actively engaged in the collective production and maintenance of meaning for their constituents, antagonists, and bystanders. That's not to say that structural factors no longer matter—far from it—but rather that social agents can act within, or choose to challenge, existing structures. And as social structures evolve, the actions of social movements can also be expected to change and adapt to the opening or closing of opportunities.

Given the shifts in the political opportunity structure detailed above—the rise of COVID-19, the increased demand for social spending, massive social justice protests, the election of a pro-union and pro-climate president, the declining costs of renewables, and growing public support for climate action—have unions moved in their position on the labor–climate spectrum? Has the LCM, through framing and targeted actions, shifted unions and environmentalists away from the Jobs vs. the Environment master frame and closer to the Clean Air and Good Jobs counterframe? Are unions, mainstream environmentalists, or the government embracing just transition as a solution to the dual crises of climate and inequality?

The short answer is yes, there has been some movement. However, it has not been meteoric and is still not nearly enough to ensure just solutions for workers and communities as we transition from fossil fuels toward a climate-safe future. A few rays of light and signs of progress include the release of various economic studies and transition plans by several fossil fuel unions who previously would not even discuss the idea of transition, only job protection. Other signs of hope appear in the passage of the federal IRA and various state-level just transition legislative initiatives, including the Climate and Equitable Jobs Act in Illinois, the Climate and Community Investment Act in Connecticut, and the creation of the Colorado Office of Just Transition. There are also countless efforts by unions and LCM activists to forge sustainable and equitable climate solutions at the local level, which have come to be seen as constituting a "Green New Deal from Below." For some, the Green New Deal may not come entirely from the top down but could instead be the result of democracy from below and the culmination of thousands of local initiatives that, taken together, could constitute a large-scale change over time.

What follows are some of the ways in which the LCM has mobilized for social change, made gains in light of changes in the political opportunity structure between 2018 and 2022, and chiseled away a little bit more from the major pillars of support for the fossil fuel regime.

Climate Strike! Organizing with Youth to Promote a Federal Green New Deal

LCM leaders have been advocating for World War II–style governmental solutions to the climate crisis for years, and some even helped to shape aspects of the congressional Green New Deal resolution, laying the groundwork for its arrival. They also immediately used its release on the public stage as an opportunity to open up conversations about climate change in union halls and houses of labor across the United States. Many were able to have resolutions in support of the Green New Deal adopted by a significant number of local, state, and national labor bodies—including the AFT. The expansiveness of the Green New Deal, containing elements of protective, proactive, and transformative just transitions, allowed for LCM activists to coalesce around supporting it.

In the summer of 2019, SEIU worked with the youth Sunrise Movement to coordinate a series of town halls across the United States to generate excitement for the Green New Deal and educate their members about the urgency of the climate crisis and the reasons they as union members needed to help shape climate policy. The town halls were part of an organizing buildup for a global student climate strike on September 20, 2019. LCM activists from dozens of unions urged their organizations to participate in the strike. USE held biweekly videoconference calls to encourage unions and other labor organizations to support and participate in the action and to coordinate their work. The calls involved regular reports on organizing efforts and strike support by more than a dozen unions and allied organizations. The calls also played a significant role in encouraging unions to participate and to gain information and inspiration from one another. In the end, AFSCME, AFT, NYSNA, UE, 1199SEIU United Healthcare Workers East, several central labor councils, and numerous local unions associated with the CWA, UAW, UFCW, and others participated in the strike. Even bigger plans were under way for Earth Day 2020, but they were forced to an online format after the arrival of a second major change to the political opportunity structure—the COVID-19 pandemic.

Connecting the Dots: COVID and Climate

The intersection of workplace issues and equity issues during the first year of the COVID-19 pandemic brought together many movements, including labor and climate activists, to support efforts such as the Coronavirus Aid, Relief, and Economic Security (CARES) Act, the stimulus package, and enhanced unemployment benefits. A "labor–climate COVID solidarity" listserv was created for activists from USE and allied labor and climate justice organizations to share resources and ideas as well as calls for solidarity and action. Some demands were limited to the pandemic and its immediate effects, such as the need for PPE, free coronavirus treatment and testing for all, and wage supplements for essential workers. Others proposed major social reforms, such as universal healthcare, fifteen-dollar minimum wages, large-scale infrastructure investment, the phasing out of fossil fuels, and many others. LCM activists connected the dots and portrayed the Green New Deal as a vehicle for a wide array of forces and programs to integrate solutions to our overlapping crises.

Some LCM activists began calling for an Emergency Green New Deal, which could start with a federal jobs program to put unemployed Americans to work wherever they could be safely deployed, in jobs such as healthcare, education, social work, and food supply work—occupations that are a central part of a sustainable economy. Jacob from SPEC argued that the jobs program could be expanded and made permanent as part of the broader Green New Deal plan to address climate change and inequality by "building the kinds of infrastructure and institutions that can ensure our collective health and safety." LCM activists also joined more than three hundred environmental, justice, and labor organizations and SMOs to develop and sign on to the Five Principles for Just COVID-19 Relief and Stimulus, per their website at https://www.fiveprinciples.org: (1) make health the top priority, for all people, with no exceptions; (2) provide economic relief directly to the people; (3) rescue workers and communities, not corporate executives; (4) make a down payment on a regenerative economy, while preventing future crises; and (5) protect our democratic process while protecting one another.

Making Build Back Better Better

After being inaugurated in January 2021, Biden set his plan to Build Back Better into motion. The Build Back Better framework, which was the core of his presidential campaign, was divided into three parts for the purpose of developing and passing legislation: (1) the American Rescue Plan, a COVID-19 relief package; (2) the American Jobs Plan, a proposal to fund infrastructure and reduce the effects of climate change; and (3) the American Families Plan, a social policy proposal that includes spending on welfare and social services. The American Rescue Plan was signed into law in March 2021, and the Infrastructure Investment and Jobs Act and the IRA, which were break-off pieces from the American Jobs Act, were passed in November 2021 and August 2022, respectively. The remaining elements of Build Back Better are still being debated in Congress.

From the start, many LCM participants wanted to make Build Back Better better by ensuring strong GHG emission-reduction targets and strong protections for workers and vulnerable communities. Some aligned with environmental and climate justice activists to develop the THRIVE agenda, which stands for Transform, Heal, and Renew by Investing in a Vibrant Economy. THRIVE, which has been portrayed as the first piece of a federal Green New Deal, was spearheaded by a newly formed coalition called the Green New Deal Network, which comprises fifteen national organizations (mostly environmental and climate justice organizations) and one major national union partner—the SEIU. Packaged as a plan for an equitable economic recovery from the pandemic that would simultaneously cut fossil fuel emissions in half by 2030, THRIVE would invest over $10 trillion to expand wind and solar power, EVs, clean water, and public transit, creating millions of union jobs that have strong wage and benefit guarantees and are guided by a board with union and community representatives. Research by the Sierra Club found that an investment of $1 trillion every year for ten years under THRIVE would create and sustain more than fifteen million jobs in the United States while cutting climate pollution in half (Beachy 2021).

THRIVE was first introduced as a congressional resolution in September 2020 and then as an act alongside the American Jobs Act in April 2021, after the new Democratic majority was in Congress. At the time of its introduction, the plan was backed by hundreds of grassroots and labor groups, including AFT, APWU, ATU, CWA, SEIU, UE, and UFCW. Although the fate of THRIVE remains unknown at the time of this writing, participation by LCM activists in shaping the THRIVE agenda, particularly the pieces focused on a just transition, helped to foster a stronger relationship with climate justice activists, and both movements continue to develop a shared vision for the future.

Some LCM activists went further than THRIVE and affiliated with the Build Back Fossil Free coalition, a group of predominantly environmental and environmental justice organizations that proposed a set of executive actions the Biden administration could take immediately to protect and invest in Black, Indigenous, brown, and working-class communities and end the era of fossil fuel production. The Build Back Fossil Free plan calls for rejecting new fossil fuel projects; eliminating public subsidies to oil, gas, and coal corporations; and launching a national climate mobilization to create jobs and promote justice and opportunity for all. While no national unions are affiliated with this coalition, a handful of local unions and a number of individual activists from the LCM participated—particularly those who are active in climate justice organizations.

With the passage of the infrastructure bill and the IRA, the fate of the remainder of the Build Back Better agenda is unknown, but labor–climate and climate justice activists continue to negotiate the definition of a just transition and cooperate or compete to varying degrees in their development and support for specific policy proposals to be considered as part of a Green New Deal–style solution to the climate crisis. Their joining of forces to oppose Senator Manchin's "dirt side deal" noted above, which would have eased fossil fuel permitting and gutted important environmental regulations, suggests a growing appetite for increased cooperation with climate justice organizations. However, one thing is for certain: without a president in the White House willing to entertain any of these proposals, regardless of the specific details, the opportunity for collaboration and constructive contestation seen in 2021–2022 would not have been possible.

From Opposition to Protection? Fossil Fuel Union Transition Plans

The LCM's relentless message that "change is coming whether you like it or not and labor needs to be in the lead, not reacting after the fact" seems to be resonating more than ever, especially with some fossil fuel unions. A handful of LCM leaders and activists, predominantly from USE, convened a series of meetings with top labor leaders in fossil fuel–producing states to deliver this message and offer technical support and advice. The ensuing release of various studies and transition programs by extraction and energy unions, such as UMWA and Utility Workers Union of America (UWUA), represents a potential shift away from the oppositional frame and movement toward the protective frame.

For example, in April 2021, UMWA issued a statement on the future of coal titled "Preserving Coal Country: Keeping America's Coal Miners, Families and Communities Whole in an Era of Global Energy Transition." It points out the sharp decline in coal industry jobs and notes that the "rise of renewable energy—windmills, solar panels, geothermal energy—is transforming the energy marketplace and the jobs that go with it." The statement also calls for a "true energy transition" built around three goals: "preserve coal jobs, create new jobs, and preserve coalfield *families* and communities" (UMWA 2021, 3).

The strategy to preserve coal jobs relies heavily on CCS technology, and the strategy for new jobs includes a variety of proposals for manufacturing, preferential hiring for former miners, mine land reclamation, prevailing wage requirements, and passage of the Protecting the Right to Organize Act (PRO Act). Perhaps most novel for the Mine Workers union is the strategy to preserve coalfield families and communities, which includes wage replacement or differential if employed; family healthcare coverage; pension credit/401(k) contribution; tuition for miners and their family members to pursue bachelor's degrees, associate's degrees, or technical/career certifications; a national training program for dislocated miners and spouses, geared toward preparing workers for new jobs and to be delivered by career training centers with proven track records of successfully training miners; direct grants to coalfield counties, communities, and school districts to replace lost tax revenues for a twenty-year period; and targeted infrastructure rehabilitation and development funding for coalfield communities—roads, bridges, broadband, schools, and healthcare facilities.

Just a couple of weeks later, on May 4, 2021, UWUA and the Union of Concerned Scientists issued a joint report stating that urgent and bold action on climate change is needed—but that it must be paired with robust, sustained, and comprehensive resources for the workers and communities who have helped power the nation for generations (Richardson and Anderson 2021). With thoughtful planning and sustained resources, the report states, workers and communities that depend on coal for their livelihoods and economic activity can be part of the clean energy future. The report, titled *Supporting the Nation's Coal Workers and Communities in a Changing Energy Landscape*, offers a road map for transitioning coal communities. The analysis estimates the cost of providing a comprehensive set of resources to coal miners and coal-fired power plant workers who will face job losses before reaching retirement age. This includes five years of full salary replacement, including health insurance and employer retirement contributions, as well as flexible options for free education for dislocated workers and their children. These comprehensive resources are estimated to cost $33 billion over twenty-five years or $83 billion over fifteen years—a small fraction of the trillions of dollars that must be invested in the energy system to reach net-zero GHG emissions by midcentury.

Also around the same time, AFSCME Local 3299, the California Federation of Teachers, and USW Local 675 commissioned a study to develop a program for economic recovery and a clean energy transition in California (Pollin et al. 2021). The project, which was endorsed by twenty unions (including several AFSCME locals, SEIU locals, UAW locals, and AFT locals and three fossil fuel unions, including two from the USW), lays out a plan to create good new jobs for fossil fuel workers and others by investing in California's climate goals. USW Local 675 vice president Norman Rogers called for the establishment of an Equitable Transition Fund for fossil fuel workers, covering wage replacement, income and pension guarantees, healthcare benefits, relocation, and peer counseling for professional and personal support. The fund, he argued in an opinion piece in the *Los Angeles Times*, should "provide access to education and training for existing and future jobs that are safe and healthy . . . [and] account for the funding gaps communities face when their tax bases shrink, so schools and libraries can stay open" (Rogers 2021). In the long term, he argued, transitioning the workforce should mean creating stable jobs with good pay and benefits.

A further sign of fracture in the fifth pillar of support for the fossil fuel regime—workers and their unions—came when the BlueGreen Alliance released its "Solidarity for Climate Action" platform in June 2019. The platform addresses the dual crises of climate change and income inequality in a number of ways, including calling for rapid reductions of GHG emissions to put America on a pathway toward reducing its emissions to net zero by 2050.[5] The plan calls for massive immediate investments in clean and renewable technology and energy efficiency across all sectors, along with investments in rebuilding and modernizing America's infrastructure to make communities more resilient. The platform also calls for efforts to increase union density across the country through strong support for the right to organize, including in the clean technology sectors. In announcing the platform's release, D. Michael Langford, president of the UWUA, said, "With the right approach, we can take significant steps that put America on the path to net-zero emissions, while creating high-quality jobs that bolster the middle class."

Most LCM activists remain skeptical of the plans issued by the UMWA and the BlueGreen Alliance because the plans leave the door open to reliance on unproven CCS technologies and thus remain unclear about how aggressive the carbon-emission demands would actually be in the end. Some believe that the continued support for CCS (and nuclear) in each of these reports represents a doubling down on the same strategy that the AFL-CIO has been pursuing for decades, kicking the can down the road. Others fear that the continued acquiescence to neoliberal thinking and an assumption that markets will solve the problems spells doom for the climate.[6] However, many acknowledge that the LCM's constant messaging that "change is happening whether we like it or not" has inspired some progress among even the unions situated farthest toward the Jobs vs. the Environment side of the labor–climate spectrum. "That we are seeing the Mine Workers issuing a statement that details what a transition, they call it a true energy transition, should look like in terms of protections for workers and communities is a step forward from where we were even just a few years ago," says Jake, a leader in USE. Other LCM activists I spoke with acknowledged these reports together as representing a baby step forward and agreed that much more work is needed to move these unions further along, from what I call a protective frame to a more proactive frame, and that time to do so is running short.

Promoting Proactive Just Transitions at the State Level: Labor–Climate Legislative Action

In mid-September 2021, Illinois passed the Climate and Equitable Jobs Act—a law to move the state to 100 percent clean energy by 2050 while creating thousands of new clean energy jobs. The legislation is the product of a multiyear effort by labor, environmental, and LCM activists in the state and months of negotiations between the Clean Energy Jobs Coalition (an alliance of environmentalists, climate activists, faith-based activists, and environmental justice activists), the renewable developers' Path to 100 Coalition, and the recently formed labor coalition Climate Jobs Illinois. According to the coalition, the law "sets the strongest clean energy labor standards in the country" and "promises to raise the bar for other states seeking to enact new labor and employment policies for building and maintaining clean energy developments."

According to an organizer with USE, "What happened in Illinois is the result of years of deep organizing work, hard conversations, real compromises, and a collective commitment to responsibly addressing climate, jobs and equity. There's a lot to learn from the Illinois experience—and a lot on the line to ensure that everyone is held accountable for successful implementation of this ambitious bill." Pat Devaney, secretary-treasurer of the Illinois AFL-CIO, said, "We have a lot of jobs in the energy sector and particularly in fossil fuel generation, so for us to come forward with a proactive plan [for transitioning] from fossil generation to clean energy, I think, really says a lot about labor's commitment to combating climate change" (Sainato 2021).

According to Climate Jobs Illinois, the bill will create thousands of new clean energy union jobs, expand union apprenticeships for Black and Latinx communities, increase energy efficiency for public schools, and safeguard thousands of union workers at the state's nuclear plants. The Climate Jobs Illinois Executive Committee includes union representatives from virtually all industries, including the Chicago Regional Council of Carpenters, Illinois Education Association, Illinois Federation of Teachers, the Ironworkers, the Insulators, the IBEW State Council, IBEW Local 134, IUOE Local 150, LIUNA Great Lakes Region, LIUNA Midwest Region, SEIU State Council, and UAW Region 4. Some LCM activists initially critiqued the weakness of the bill in the area of providing for a just transition for workers and communities, however (at the time of this writing) the coalition is working on follow-up legislation that if passed would ensure equity in the transition, including investments in transition assistance programs, workforce development, and more.

In Connecticut, LCM activists spearheaded the development and introduction of Connecticut SB 999 (2021), "An Act Concerning a Just Transition to Climate-Protective Energy Production and Community Investment." The act, passed by the state legislature and signed into law by Governor Ned Lamont on June 14, 2021, will ensure that green jobs created in Connecticut pay fair wages and are filled by skilled Connecticut workers. It also ensures that people in the communities where projects are located have access to the training they need to benefit from those jobs. As a local LCM activist from a manufacturing union told me, "The bill will promote the development of a stable, highly trained clean technology workforce so that Connecticut's workers are not left behind in the transition to a low-carbon economy."

The act, also called the Climate and Community Investment Act, is a climate jobs bill that includes provisions for prevailing wages, community benefits agreements, and workforce development to ensure a just transition to a clean energy economy by protecting the rights of renewable energy industry workers. Regarding workforce development, the act helps working-class families in Connecticut access clean technology careers by requiring developers to partner with approved in-state apprenticeship and pre-apprenticeship programs. Previously, renewable energy developers regularly hired out-of-state workers. The prevailing wage requirement for utility-scale or grid-connected projects guarantees competitive living wages for all workers employed on projects funded in whole or in part by the state. The community benefits agreement provision provides that host communities of renewable energy projects receive benefits from those projects by requiring developers to negotiate community benefits agreements, codifying what is seen as the industry best practice for community outreach. These initiatives, in conjunction with the GHG emission targets enshrined in a previous state law, represent the foundational elements of a proactive transition plan in Connecticut.

In Colorado, in early 2018, a state legislator informed the state labor federation that he was planning to submit a bill to take Colorado to 100 percent renewable energy by 2035. This bill was the impetus for the Colorado labor movement to take the lead on energy and environmental policy rather than resisting or trying to block seemingly unavoidable policy proposals such as this—again reflecting the LCM's message that an energy transition is inevitable and that labor should therefore be at the table or risk instead being on the menu. The decision, which was based on a series of interunion discussions, was also informed by existing relations among unions and environmental justice, faith-based, and national and local environmental groups that started with the People's Climate Movement in 2016. Throughout 2018, several Colorado unions continued their internal deliberations and ultimately decided to commission an independent researcher to conduct a just transition study for the state. The unions also participated in a series of cross-movement discussions with environmentalists and environmental justice activists that were moderated by a professional facilitator. These discussions succeeded in advancing a mutual understanding of the interconnected problems of climate and inequality.

As a result of the study and these cross-movement discussions, the group crafted a just transition bill to accompany the decarbonization bill that was to be introduced at the 2019 session of the General Assembly. The decarbonization bill aimed to reduce GHG emissions by at least 90 percent of the levels of state-wide greenhouse gas emissions that existed in 2005 and would thus affect fossil fuel workers. The just transition bill covered workers in the coal industry and coal communities. While the number of workers affected is only around 2,200, coal is significant in the counties and communities affected, mostly on the Western Slope. Both bills were passed and signed into law in 2019.

The just transition bill set up a Colorado Office of Just Transition (OJT), which became operational in early 2020, and a Just Transition Advisory Committee—consisting of unions, corporations, economic development specialists, representatives of affected counties and disproportionately affected communities, political leaders, and government officers—with a mandate to solicit input for a draft plan for workers and communities. The committee started its work in late 2019 and held two large community meetings just before the COVID-19 pandemic triggered a ban on public meetings, but the work was ultimately completed online, and a draft plan was submitted to the OJT in August 2020. However, although a plan is in place, funding remains an issue to be resolved. The major financial obstacle is the Taxpayer's Bill of Rights, a 1992 constitutional amendment that limits state spending and requires voter consent for new taxes in Colorado. This financial challenge has made it increasingly clear that federal support is likely necessary. However, a stronger OJT, along with the continued commitment of unions, environmentalists, and community activists, can help ensure that just transition remains on Colorado's agenda.

In addition to these successes, other attempts at crafting just transition legislation were initiated but ultimately failed. Perhaps the most notable was the collaborative effort of labor, environmentalists, environmental justice advocates, and Indigenous groups to develop the highly aspirational Initiative 1631 in Washington State in 2018 (see Cha et al. 2021).

Green New Deals from Below: Local Efforts to Forge Proactive or Transformative Transitions

While the LCM continues to promote a Green New Deal at the national level, LCM activists have also participated from below in a wave of local initiatives through community groups, unions, city and state governments, Tribes, and nonfederal institutions designed to contribute to the Green New Deal's goals for climate protection and social justice. Given the closing political opportunity structure at the national level after the election of Trump in 2016, many LCM activists and organizations shifted their focus to state and local campaigns and actions. By the time of COVID-19 and then the election of Joe Biden, many of these campaigns had matured and were on the cusp of bearing fruit. While there are more local efforts than could be described in the limited space here, I will share a few to illustrate the types of local work LCM activists have been doing to promote a Green New Deal from below in the Trump and post-Trump era (Clifton et al. 2021).[7]

In Washington, DC, unionized railroad workers successfully pressured their employers to redesign their diesel locomotives to be more energy efficient, less polluting, and safer for workers. Recology, a unionized zero-waste recycling co-op in the Bay Area initiated by the Teamsters, provides services to 725,000 residential and 110,000 commercial customers in California, Oregon, and Washington. In Connecticut, ATU bus drivers successfully campaigned for conversion to electric buses to reduce GHG emissions while improving driver and passenger health and safety. The NNU and AFT have advanced energy efficiency and clean energy programs in their workplaces—hospitals and schools. SEIU property management Local 32BJ in the New York metropolitan area runs a Green Supers program to provide a professional building service workforce capable of reducing energy use, conserving water, saving money, and providing cleaner and healthier buildings to live in.

Several teacher and faculty unions have been pursuing local Green New Deals at their institutions of employment. For example, after persuading Rutgers University to develop a climate action plan (including plans to electrify the considerable bus fleet and install solar arrays on rooftops and over parking lots), the Climate Justice Committee of the AAUP-AFT local union at Rutgers set its sights on making the university an anchor institution for a partnership with community groups in Camden, Newark, and New Brunswick to build community solar cooperatives. The goal is for the projects to be built with union labor and for the majority-minority communities adjacent to the major campuses, which are sites of environmental injustice historically, to own the new solar installations. Another goal is to pressure the university to create local "resilience hubs" for residents to access potable water, electric charging for vital communication and medical devices, and refrigerators for life-saving medical and dietary needs during the ever more frequent climate-related power outages. An additional goal includes the creation of a pre-apprenticeship program and pipeline for workers from the environmental justice community to access good union careers in the renewable energy sector. The union committee continues to organize with neighborhood associations; climate justice organizations, such as the Ironbound Community Corporation; and local community groups, including the local worker center, New Labor, to pursue these goals.

Notably, the unions mentioned thus far are largely situated on the Clean Air and Good Jobs half of the labor–climate spectrum, but some unions in other industries have been pursuing Green New Deals from below as well. For example, the UMWA is partnering with energy startup SPARKZ to build an electric battery factory in West Virginia, recruiting and training dislocated miners to be the factory's first 350 production workers. IBEW Local 11 and the Los Angeles Chapter of the National Electrical Contractors Association (NECA) established and maintain a Net Zero Plus Electrical Training Institute, which, when it was built, was the country's largest Net Zero Plus commercial retrofit, generating more energy than its own annual energy demand. The project unites energy efficiency practices, new clean energy technologies, improved grid resiliency, and career development. The training center showcases cutting-edge energy efficiency measures and provides training on their installation and maintenance, including classes on electrical vehicle charging, high-efficiency HVAC, battery storage, microgrids, energy dashboards, lighting, and exterior shading. The program aims to "transform commercial markets by employing the newest electrical technologies and training the most skilled workforce in the United States" (Net Zero Plus 2016).

The Climate Jobs National Resource Center, which originated in New York State and then spread into Connecticut, Illinois, Maine, and Texas, is organizing to ensure that addressing climate change creates good union jobs by investing in renewable energy. The campaign seeks to expand support from building trades and other unionists for climate protection by advocating for more climate jobs—but also for labor standards, PLAs, and community benefit agreements to help make sure that climate jobs are good jobs. LCM activists in New York advocated with dozens of grassroots organizations, including NY Renews, a coalition of over 180 environmental, community, and labor organizations, to pass the Climate Leadership and Community Protection Act, which established the nation's strongest GHG emissions limits. The law contains several environmental justice provisions as well, including a mandate that disadvantaged communities must receive no less than 35 percent of the benefits from the state's climate programs. The Climate Jobs Campaign continues to advocate for strong labor standards and PLAs in the budding offshore wind industry.

USW Local 675 worked with Jobs to Move America (JMA), a strategic policy center that aims to transform public spending to advance good jobs

and healthier communities, to organize one of several electric bus manufacturing plants in Los Angeles County. Their partnership came out of a decade-
long effort of several unions working together to develop sustainable businesses that could support good union jobs. JMA uses public procurement agreements
with government entities to leverage incentives for businesses to work with
unions and develop apprenticeships and community benefits programs in their
contracts. The IBEW and SMART have also organized electric vehicle factories with similar strategies. Since the USW members do not have access to
many of the opportunities the building trades have in solar, wind, and other
construction-based occupations, the Proterra Bus contract provides a manufacturing option to displaced refinery workers and a chance for USW membership to grow. Once USW won the organizing drive, the work of winning
the first contract began. JMA helped negotiate the community benefits agreement that commits the employer to hire from marginalized communities.

Stakes Are High and Time Is Short

The IPCC'S Sixth Assessment Report, issued in the summer of 2021, states,
"It is unequivocal that human influence has warmed the atmosphere, ocean,
and land" (Masson-Delmotte et al., 2021). Widespread and rapid changes in
the atmosphere, ocean, cryosphere, and biosphere have already occurred, and
these changes are unprecedented over the span of many centuries to many millennia. Human-induced climate change is already affecting the weather and
climate in every region of the world. Extremes such as heat waves, heavy precipitation, droughts, and tropical cyclones—and their attribution to human
influence—have worsened since the Fifth Assessment Report in 2014.

Many of these changes in the climate system—including increased frequency and intensity of heat extremes, marine heat waves, heavy precipitation,
agricultural and ecological droughts, intense tropical cyclones, and reductions
in Arctic sea ice, snow cover, and permafrost—will become larger, with further global warming. Perhaps most disturbing, many changes resulting from
past and future GHG emissions, especially changes in the ocean, ice sheets,
and global sea level, are irreversible for centuries to millennia. With further
global warming, every region is projected to increasingly experience concur-
rent and multiple climatic impacts. The world will surpass global warming of
1.5°C and possibly 2°C during the twenty-first century unless steep reductions
in CO_2 and other GHG emissions occur in the coming decades. This is the
current scenario. The stakes are high. The seemingly simple solution—rapidly cutting GHG emissions—has proven to be one of the most politically difficult undertakings in living memory.

Sir David Attenborough, speaking before the UN Security Council in February 2021, said climate change is "the biggest threat to security that modern humans have ever faced. . . . If we continue on our current path, we will face the collapse of everything that gives us our security. . . . Civilization will quickly break down" (C. Jenkins 2021). However, the tremendous power of the fossil fuel industry, buttressed by various pillars of support, has ensured continued fossil fuel use at levels equal to or greater than in 1988, the time at which NASA's James Hansen made his prescient speech before Congress. Moreover, the fossil fuel industry has reaped more profits and accrued ever-greater power. In 2014, nineteen of the world's fifty leading corporations were fossil fuel companies, and they accounted for 48 percent of revenue and over 45 percent of profits among the top fifty companies in the Fortune Global 500 (CNN Money 2014). They have used this incredible fortune to wield political power to receive government subsidies to the tune of over $20 billion annually,[8] to elect fossil-friendly politicians who oppose meaningful environmental regulations, and, perhaps most damagingly, to promote climate change skepticism and denial through public misinformation campaigns.[9]

However, there are indications that growing concern with climate change might be approaching a tipping point. Compared with a decade ago, more Americans (nearly two-thirds of U.S. adults) say protecting the environment and dealing with global climate change should be top priorities for the president and Congress, and those who say the same about dealing with global climate change doubled from 26 percent in 2010 to 52 percent in 2020, according to a Pew survey (Funk and Kennedy 2020). Partisanship remains a major factor in these priorities though—85 percent of Democrats and Democratic-leaning independents think protecting the environment should be a top priority, while only 39 percent of Republicans or Republican-leaning voters feel the same way.

Activists in the climate movement, the environmental movement, the climate justice movement, and the LCM have been organizing and promoting solutions to the climate crisis for many years but have made only slow progress despite the steady ticking of the Doomsday Clock. As two LCM activists—John Braxton, from an AFT local, and Peter Knowlton, from the UE union—stated in an op-ed, "It is time for the labor movement at all levels to make climate justice a top priority. We need to heighten discussion at the rank-and-file level—followed by workplace and street actions—to a degree that we have not seen in 80 years. If we don't rise up before the waters and fires do, then all other voices for peace, equity, and justice will be drowned out by an increasingly inhospitable planet" (Knowlton and Braxton 2021).

Recent changes in the political–economic landscape, including the onset of the COVID-19 pandemic and the defeat of Donald Trump at the polls, have marked an opening in the opportunity structure for activists like Braxton and Knowlton. And although labor as a whole has not yet embraced demands for a just transition, a growing number of workers and the general public have come to see climate change as a top priority and are supporting green growth initiatives. As more frequent and extreme weather events create havoc in all regions of the world and across the United States, a greater share of the U.S. population feels the high cost of not doing something about climate change. Whether the LCM and aligned movements can succeed in creating a moral tipping point around the issue of climate justice and a just transition is still an open question. And in the end, the attitudinal shifts that opened up political opportunities for the civil rights, women's, and marriage equality movements of the past did not alone guarantee change. It took deep organizing, direct actions, and massive mobilizations. Much as the impetus for the original New Deal was the collective action and resistance of America's workers, so, too, the prospects for the Green New Deal will rest on a new generation of workers raising their voices to save not only their jobs but the Earth itself.

8

Conclusion

*The Journey from Climate Alienation
to Climate Solidarity*

A t the beginning of this journey, I laid out what I believed to be the five major pillars of support for the fossil fuel regime. The five pillars, as elaborated in Chapter 1, include the fossil fuel industry, fossil-using industries, individual consumers, politicians, and fossil fuel workers and their unions. Together, the entire edifice of support for the fossil fuel regime is built on a foundation of neoliberal, capitalist ideology that undergirds contemporary U.S. society. This dominant ideology shapes our collective understanding of the world and dictates what can and cannot realistically be on the table for political discussion. In particular, direct government action to solve social problems—including climate change—is not on the menu of acceptable options. However, as we shall see, undermining the pillars of support for the fossil fuel regime ultimately requires a serious challenge to this underlying neoliberal ideology.

Having established workers and unions as a pillar of support for the fossil fuel regime, we then explored in Chapters 2 and 3 the history of labor–environmental relations in the United States as well as some structural aspects of the U.S. economy and cultural features of American labor that help explain the varied positions of unions on the issues of climate change and justice. In sum, the relationship between labor and the environment has been complicated and has varied across time and geographic location. At certain historical junctures, particular unions have been opposed to specific environmental policies, such as the timber workers versus the spotted owl, and at others they have been very supportive, such as when the UAW and other unions supported the Clean Air and Clean Water Acts. Four major causes for labor opposition to environmental measures are job protection, lack of an adequate social safety net, the pursuit of economic growth, and constraints on democracy. Six broad means by which unions have come to support environmental measures are occupational health and safety issues, nature conservation efforts, environmental justice, opposition to international trade agreements, green growth initiatives, and the promotion of sustainable development.

Regarding climate change, a clear split within labor comes into focus. The unions with members employed in the fossil fuel industry (e.g., extraction unions and building trades unions) have been most resistant to climate protection measures, while unions whose members' jobs are most directly affected by the negative effects of climate change (e.g., healthcare workers and transportation workers) have been the most supportive. To help illustrate the relative position of unions in relation to one another on the issue of climate change, I constructed a heuristic device I refer to as the labor–climate spectrum. The spectrum ranges from unions espousing the Jobs vs. the Environment master frame on the first half of the scale to those increasingly supporting the emerging counterframe of Clean Air and Good Jobs on the second half.

The unions espousing the Jobs vs. the Environment frame have accepted the dominant free market ideology of U.S. capitalism, which dictates that workers must choose between good jobs and a healthy environment and cannot have both. The unions embracing the Clean Air and Good Jobs frame are challenging the logic of capitalism by using their democratic voice to help provide for a healthy planet and goods jobs, not one or the other. Unions on the Clean Air and Good Jobs side of the spectrum, including those in healthcare, the service sector, the public sector, and education, are typically newer unions in industries that have mostly been organized since the early 1970s and are more likely to display characteristics of social movement unionism, such as pursuing social justice and other gains for the broader working class beyond the workplace, including climate change mitigation. Owing to the variety of products made by manufacturing unions, ranging from gas-guzzling SUVs to clean energy fuel cells, the manufacturing unions as a whole hover around the center of the spectrum, a position that represents the division in their support for the two competing frames.

The more traditional craft unions—those with many members employed in fossil fuel–related industries and who often embrace the characteristics of pure and simple business unionism—are more likely to support the Jobs vs. the Environment master frame and thus have generally been resistant to climate protection measures. The business union approach to unionism, which is rooted in the philosophy of job consciousness, not class consciousness—accepting the fundamental logic of capitalism rather than challenging it—typically eschews the pursuit of any political or economic goals beyond those that directly improve the material interests of their members on the job. However, slightly complicating matters, many unions in the building trades and in manufacturing fall within a group I refer to as the blue–greens, who support investments in green manufacturing and green construction projects but do not back decarbonization efforts and often simultaneously promote fossil fuel projects in pursuit of an all-of-the-above economic growth strategy. While these unions may tout the climate benefits of green projects in their pursuit of gaining broader support for them, their motivation is derived from the instrumental interest in jobs, not from an ideological commitment to the common good. The transportation unions, which have a long history in the U.S. labor movement and a traditional organizational form that resembles that of the craft unions, have proven to be an exception to the rule: they are situated on the Clean Air and Good Jobs side of the spectrum, demonstrating the possibility for traditional unions to shift their relative position to a more progressive location on the spectrum.

The position of the AFL-CIO—the major U.S. union confederation—on the spectrum reveals the nature of the power dynamics within labor as a whole. While the majority of unions are on the Clean Air and Good Jobs side of the spectrum, the AFL-CIO, with its "all of the above" energy policy is situated squarely on the Jobs vs. the Environment side, closer to the conservative building trades and extraction unions than the more progressive public sector, healthcare, and education unions. The structural nature of the federation, which is a voluntary membership organization, has allowed the numerous building trades unions to form a united political block that, through threats of leaving the organization and withdrawing dues contributions, effectively wields veto power over the policy stances of the AFL-CIO. The imbalance in power between the more conservative and more progressive wings of the federation also derives from the history of its formation in 1955, when the former AFL and CIO confederations merged. The merger created a weaker position within the federation's structure for the more class-conscious CIO unions compared with the traditionally job-conscious craft unions of the AFL. McCarthyism also led to a purging of the more radical, communist, and socialist leaders from many CIO unions, effectively making the unions more conservative. As a result of this power imbalance and ensuing disagreements about the direction of the federation, several of the more progressive unions, such as SEIU, opted to quit the AFL-CIO, leaving the more conservative unions with even greater influence in the organization.

Taken together, the various structural factors we examined early in the book, including political, economic, and cultural features of the U.S. economy and labor, have contributed to the unique positions of various unions on the issue of climate change. But structure alone tells only part of the story. In Chapters 4 through 7, I explored the actions of social agents from three SMOs seeking to challenge the status quo and redefine the situation. In particular, I focused on the LCM, a movement of climate activists within U.S. labor promoting pro-climate, pro-worker solutions to the dual crises of climate and inequality. The LCM can be distinguished from other blue–green elements of labor that support green growth by two defining characteristics: (1) LCM activists demand reductions in GHG emissions as determined by current climate science, and (2) LCM organizations are independent from any particular union or labor federation. The goal of the grassroots LCM is to overcome perceived structural constraints and undermine the underlying neoliberal ideology by reframing climate justice as labor justice in order to move labor as a whole away from the Jobs vs. the Environment master frame and toward their preferred counterframe of Clean Air and Good Jobs.

As with all emergent social movements, the first task of the LCM was to define the problem they are seeking to address—a process that is referred to by movement scholars as diagnostic framing. In sum, the LCM elaborated the following multifaceted problem:

- Unmitigated climate change poses a serious threat to all people but particularly workers and people from vulnerable communities.
- Most mitigation strategies currently under consideration pose a threat to the livelihoods and well-being of workers and their communities.
- The mainstream environmental movement is not considering working-class interests in their efforts to address climate change and are often pushing for mitigation strategies that would hurt workers and fuel Jobs vs. the Environment conflicts.
- To its own peril, the labor movement is not actively fighting for real solutions to climate change that actually reduce GHG emissions and incorporate working-class interests into the solution—in fact, in many cases, unions serve as a major pillar of support for continued fossil fuel use.

This diagnosis of the problem led the LCM to identify three distinct targets: the state, the middle-class culture of the environmental movement, and the business union culture of the labor movement. These targets capture both the structural dimensions of power, which are rooted in large-scale patterns of resource exchange, and the cultural dimensions of power, which are based on symbolically potent images and discourses. As we have seen, the structural dimensions are largely ingrained in the political economy of American capitalism, a system that gives tremendous power to nondemocratic institutions (such as corporations) to make major decisions that affect all of society. Rather than serving the public interest, these institutions make decisions solely on the basis of what is most profitable to them and their shareholders, regardless of the impacts on people and the environment.

The cultural dimensions of power include the practices and discourses of major civil society actors, such as environmental organizations and unions. For example, the middle-class culture of most big green environmental organizations fails to consider the impacts of environmental policies on the lives and livelihoods of workers and instead thinks and acts within the confines of the existing capitalist power structure. The myopic vision of the business union culture that is prevalent in much of the U.S. labor movement bars certain unions from engaging with broader working-class issues like climate change, thus failing to pose a real challenge to the existing power structure, in which workers occupy a very weak position.

Having defined the problem and identified distinct targets, the next major framing task for the LCM involved formulating solutions to the problem—a process that movement scholars refer to as prognostic framing. The prognosis shared by most participants in my analysis was to push for a just transition to a more sustainable and equitable energy system and economy, but not all participants agreed on a single definition of "just transition." I identified multiple, distinct uses of the term, ranging from less to more radical in their prognosis. The first, protective just transition, involves the creation of a social safety net in local cases where workers face unemployment as a result of changes such as plant closures that are necessary to decarbonize the economy. The second, proactive just transition, goes further to envision direct participation by labor in the creation of a forward-looking plan to shift the entire economy to a more sustainable energy system with a more universalized social safety net for all workers. The third—and most radical—frame, transformative just transition, involves a massive shift in power from the corporate sector to the public and a reorganization of the economy to put people before profits, including major efforts to eliminate existing social inequalities by bringing the energy sector under social ownership and democratic control. Additionally, I identified a counterframe, oppositional, in which some labor leaders consider the term "just transition" to be toxic because of the negative knee-jerk reaction it causes for many workers who equate it with job loss or the replacement of good jobs with bad jobs.

The first three just transition frames identified—protective, proactive, and transformative—are distinct but interconnected, with each building from the prior frame; that is, the core tenets of protective transition are nested within all three frames, and the core tenets of proactive transition are nested within the last two frames. Transformative just transition, while both protective and proactive, goes beyond the first two and directly challenges the underlying logic of capitalism. In my research, I found that local labor–climate organizations often vacillated between the protective and proactive frames, the national organization most often adopted the proactive frame, and the international organization always espoused the transformative frame. I also found that individual activists would often move freely between these different frames at various points in time, revealing the still-unsettled framing of just transition within the movement.

The LCM engaged in a variety of collective actions to help realize their goal of a just transition as determined through the prognostic framing process. After a close examination of the tactical repertoires and outcomes of multiple campaigns by the three LCM SMOs in this study, I identified several key findings that may be generalizable to studies of other movements. First, I found that the selection of targets and especially the vulnerabilities of those targets interact with the existing political opportunity structure to shape the tactics used by movements. For example, the national-level organization, USE, chose to pursue a union resolution at the national AFL-CIO convention, which happens only once every four years. The timing of this convention, just months after President Trump announced he would withdraw the United States from the Paris Climate Accord, created an opportunity for activists, through the democratic machinations of the convention, to shift the stance of labor as a whole to a more progressive position on climate change. The onset of the COVID-19 pandemic and defeat of Donald Trump at the polls in 2020 also represented dramatic shifts in the political opportunity structure, which LCM activists responded to through actions at the local, state, and national levels, using increased public support for social spending and a receptive ear in the White House to further forge a narrative around just transition within labor and in public policy.

Second, I uncovered a process of frame shifting in which movement activists, in response to changing political opportunity structures, shift fluidly from one prognostic frame to another, expanding and contracting. For example, when SPEC stumbled on an opportunity to support the expansion of offshore wind to both increase renewable energy in the state and create a pipeline to jobs for workers who would be displaced by a plant closure, they shifted fluidly from a protective to a proactive just transition frame. This demonstrates that SMOs not only modify their tactical repertoires in response to changing opportunity structures but also may shift their frames to find the optimal alignment of framing, opportunity, and tactics. This process may be unique to the current case as a result of the nested nature of the three just transition frames, but future research should consider this possibility in different contexts. Importantly, the example of the frame shift in the case of the offshore wind campaign also potentially prefigures a general shift in framing within labor as a whole to a more progressive stance on climate change that rejects the Jobs vs. the Environment master frame.

Third, the analysis highlighted the role of indigenous organizational strength in the successes of the three SMOs as they organized actions in pursuit of Clean Air and Good Jobs. By creating durable, standing relationships between different stakeholder groups such as labor, faith-based, and environmental organizations, the LCM was able to quickly activate a base of support, including experienced leaders, for vital campaigns. For example, by regularly attending international climate talks and presenting the transformative frame, LUPE built an international network of unions and global social movements to support campaigns such as labor–climate leadership trainings and the Unions against Fracking sign-on letter.

This examination of the framing processes and tactical repertoires of the LCM reveals that the selection of targets and collective action frames, in conjunction with the existing political opportunity structure and the level of indigenous organizational strength, can have tremendous influence on the ultimate outcome of the movement. The right combination can lead to the successful promotion of an offshore wind project or state-level just transition policy. The wrong combination can lead to a failure, as was the case with the state-level organization's pursuit of a program to increase energy efficiency in public buildings during a period of budget crisis. However, the majority of examples I explored in this study had mixed outcomes, typically winning incremental changes for labor and climate but often falling short of the more aspirational goals of movement leaders.

In the remainder of this chapter, I make connections between the structural features of the economy and the framing processes of LCM actors to identify the unique modes of change pursued by labor, blue–green groups, and the LCM. I then return to the question of climate justice and consider the possibility for the LCM and the climate justice movement to form a shared vision and build the broad base of support needed to win transformative change. Finally, to bring this journey to a close, I present several possible futures for the LCM.

Just Transition and Modes of Change

The interaction between the various structural factors examined early in the book with the framing processes and collective actions taken by LCM actors creates an array of different approaches for addressing (or not addressing) the climate crisis. As stated in Chapter 1, the transition away from fossil fuels can take many forms. These modes of change exist along a spectrum from an abrupt radical shift to more incremental transitions. Given the current political landscape of America, including the entrenched power of the fossil fuel regime, an abrupt "puncture" in which massive change occurs in a short period of time seems somewhat unlikely but is not beyond the realm of possibility. More likely is one of the several incrementalist approaches theorized by scholars of institutional change (Mahoney and Thelen 2010; Streeck and Thelen 2005; Thelen 2009). Two of the more commonly discussed modes of incrementalist change are layering and displacement.

"Layering" refers to a situation of gradual institutional change through a process of attaching new elements to existing institutions. Important to note: layering does not replace the old but simply adds to it and thus may gradually change the status and structure of the existing institution. Specific institutional arrangements are developed through an accumulation of innovations inspired by competing motives, layering new arrangements on top of preexisting structures (Schickler 2001; see also Peck 1998 and B. Smith 1983). In the case of the current energy system, layering involves the addition of renewable energy sources, such as wind and solar, to the existing fossil fuel–powered energy grid. The addition of rooftop solar and other methods of local electricity generation in some areas are already forcing the existing structure to adapt in small ways. Supporters of the IRA hope that it will help to do the same nationally.

"Displacement" refers to a situation in which "new models emerge and diffuse which call into question existing, previously taken-for-granted organizational forms and practices" (Streeck and Thelen 2005, 19). Displacement differs from abrupt change in that the new institution is introduced alongside the existing institution, gradually displacing it rather than immediately replacing it. Displacement differs from layering because the new institution eventually replaces the old rather than merely adding on to it. As I argued in Chapter 1, displacement of the existing fossil fuel energy system can happen in two primary ways: attrition and intentional change. Through attrition, old fossil infrastructure lives out its life span and only new green infrastructure is built, ultimately displacing all fossil fuels. Intentional change involves the planned phaseout of all fossils and replacement with renewables on a timeline informed by science (which means very rapidly at this late hour).

Figure 8.1 illustrates the relationship between modes of change and the three just transition frames elaborated in this study. In the figure, the first column identifies three nested constituencies—the LCM exists within a broader group of blue–green labor activists, which in turn exists within the labor movement as a whole. The second column lists the preferred growth agenda for social actors, ranging from opposing green growth to promoting an equilibrium economy (or degrowth). Between those extremes are those that support all-of-the-above growth and those that support only green growth. The third column indicates the level of support for science-based GHG emission-reduction targets. The fourth column shows the just transition frames discussed in this study. The last column identifies the mode of change pursued by the constituents on the basis of their unique combination of preferences in columns two, three, and four.

This figure provides several important insights. First, as was elaborated in Chapter 1, the outer boundary for the LCM is determined by support for GHG emission reductions—that is, the line distinguishing the LCM from other labor groups that support green growth initiatives or all-of-the-above growth is their firm support of science-based targets to reduce emissions. Second, the protective framing of just transition is compatible with all forms of growth and can be pursued with or without emission-reduction targets. This joint support for protections could serve as a stepping-stone for labor activists to extend their frame to a more proactive vision of transition. Third, unions supporting all-of-the-above growth are not actually promoting a mode of change; they are merely pursuing the status quo, in which any change that does occur is largely driven by market forces, not by social actors pursuing change. Fourth, the blue–greens support layering as their preferred mode of change. However, as noted earlier, layering may or may not promote change in the end. Some evidence exists that the rise of renewable energy, including its increasingly competitive prices, has had some impact on the status and structure of the fossil fuel sector, which has altered slightly to adapt to the presence of competition. Looking at the LCM, we can see that the preferred mode of change is displacement. Depending on the just transition frame that is adopted, this could mean displacement through attrition or displacement through intentional change. By demanding a proactive plan to decarbonize the economy, only the proactive and transformative frames pursue intentional change.

However, to realize any one of these just transitions, LCM activists must move labor as a whole from stasis to layering and from layering to displacement. This involves not only moving the more progressive unions on the second half of the labor–climate spectrum to take action but also moving the more conservative business unions away from the free market Jobs vs. the Environment

CONSTITUENCY		GROWTH AGENDA	EMISSIONS GOALS	TRANSITION FRAME	MODE OF CHANGE
The U.S. Labor Movement		Non-Green Only	No Targets	Oppositional	Entrenchement
		All of the Above	No Targets	Oppositional/None	Stasis
		All of the Above	No Targets	Protective	Stasis
	Blue–Greens	Green Only	No Targets	Oppositional/None	Layering
		Green Only	No Targets	Protective	Layering
	LCM	Green Only	Science-Based Targets	Protective	Displacement (attrition)
		Green Only	Science-Based Targets	Proactive	Displacement (intentional)
		Green Equilibrium	Science-Based Targets	Transformative	Displacement (intentional)

Figure 8.1 Growth, Emissions, Transition Frames, and Modes of Change

frame and toward the Clean Air and Good Jobs side of the spectrum. Many progressive unions already agree with some form of just transition, but they have taken only minimal action toward making it a reality. Making the energy transition just will also involve a transformation of the mainstream environmental movement to incorporate labor and climate justice into its transition plans. In other words, the LCM must extend the organizational range of labor as well as of environmental organizations to create the greatest degree of frame alignment and build the broad-based support needed to win effective climate protection measures.

Climate Justice Is Labor Justice?

Throughout this journey, we have considered the extent to which the LCM may or may not serve as a bridge between the labor and the climate justice movements by broadening the frame of labor as a whole to support climate justice demands. While those espousing a protective just transition frame generally do not consider the remediation of existing or historic inequalities along the lines of race and gender, those espousing the proactive and transformative frames have to varying degrees incorporated issues of social justice into their demands. The transformative frame in particular is most closely aligned with the definition of "just transition" that is commonly adopted by climate justice activists.

For example, according to the JTA, an organization whose roots are in the environmental justice movement and which was a key participant in early labor–environmental justice efforts, just transition is simultaneously a principle, a process, and a practice. As defined on CJA's (2021) website, the JTA defines "just transition" as "a vision-led, unifying, and place-based set of principles, processes, and practices that build economic and political power to shift from an extractive economy to a regenerative economy." An extractive economy is one driven by the exploitation of resources, people, and capital, while a regenerative economy is one centered on the well-being of workers, communities, and the environment (Cha and Vachon 2021). "The transition itself," the JTA's definition continues, "must be just and equitable, redressing past harms and creating new relationships of power for the future through reparations. If the process of transition is not just, the outcome will never be" (CJA 2021). In other words, "just transition" describes both the destination and the means of getting there. As should be apparent, this understanding of just transition is clearly transformative and involves a host of strategies to transition communities—and indeed the whole economy—to provide dignified, productive, and ecologically sustainable livelihoods, along with democratic governance and ecological resilience.

Labor as a whole has often not been a friend of the climate justice movement. Driven largely by the all-of-the-above growth strategy that is promoted most often by unions from the building trades, the labor movement has often been in direct opposition to the demands of climate justice activists, which is unfortunate because, unlike the mainstream environmental movement, the climate justice movement has espoused a pro-worker stance since its inception. For example, shortly after their formation in 2013, the CJA and allied environmental justice organizations issued an open letter to the leadership of the AFL-CIO, asking for the labor movement to "join hands in the struggle for climate justice, fighting corporate power, deepening democracy, organizing a Just Transition and building a new economy led by workers and communities" (CJA 2013). Unfortunately, the invitation never resulted in a meeting or any form of organized cooperation. A few years later, amid the battles over oil pipelines in the upper Midwest, CJA and allies issued another letter to the AFL-CIO, this time regarding their stance on the Dakota Access oil pipeline, asking the federation, which had proclaimed support for the project, to reverse its decision. The letter read, in part: "We believe that Labor must play a key role in this movement [to build a sustainable future] if it is to continue to represent the aspirations of working people, both on the job and beyond. At the same time, the environmental justice movement cannot halt climate change without organized labor. We need each other to win. Right now, none of us are winning" (CJA 2018).

While the AFL-CIO did not change course on Dakota Access or other pipeline projects that threatened Indigenous lands and peoples, including their water supplies and sacred sites, most participants in the LCM did respond with support. Many unions adopted resolutions in support of the Standing Rock Sioux Tribe and the climate justice protesters opposing the pipeline. USE called for a halt to the Dakota Access pipeline and other climate-destroying fossil fuel infrastructure and demanded the jobs of the future be created by building the climate-safe infrastructure needed to confront the climate crisis. Several members of SPEC traveled to North Dakota to join fellow LCM activists at the Labor for Standing Rock encampment. Other local unions affiliated with SPEC and LUPE took up donations and sent supplies to sustain the pipeline protesters, who were facing increasingly harsh weather conditions as the Dakota winter approached. My own local union passed a resolution opposing the pipeline and purchased a heater that was delivered by one of our members to the protest site.

Beyond the pipeline battles, the labor–climate and climate justice movements have agreed and cooperated on other controversial issues, such as opposing CCS technologies as a solution to the climate crisis. In late 2019, and continuing throughout the first year of the pandemic, I was part of a research team of academics, LCM activists, climate justice leaders, and various community organizations that collected oral histories from workers and community members around the United States who had experienced, were currently experiencing, or anticipated experiencing some form of economic transition, such as displaced fossil fuel and factory workers and workers from historically marginalized and frontline communities (Cha et al. 2021). Overall, the Just Transition Listening Project comprised over one hundred listening sessions, including qualitative interviews and focused discussion groups. We heard stories of how workers and community members from all regions of the country were suffering from a historic decline and lack of access to opportunities and how the COVID-19 pandemic, persistent structural racism, and growing wealth inequality were exacerbating these realities.

We found that transitions are inevitable and constantly happening across the economy and that most past transitions, driven by market forces, corporate entities, or shortsighted public policies, left workers and communities behind with little to no support. We heard that existing governmental transitional policies are fragmented and inadequate, leading to the destruction of human capital as well as deep resentment and opposition to social and environmental policies. Many people affected by past unjust transitions reacted harshly to climate action, creating tensions among labor, community groups, and environmental movements that often erupted into open conflicts. Unsurprisingly, the individual understandings of the climate crisis and economic transitions ranged widely according to one's occupation, class, race, age, political ideology, and previous experiences with labor, environmentalist, or the climate justice movement. However, the experience of suffering was shared universally among all participants.

As the project wound down, it became abundantly clear to all who were involved that a truly solidaristic, multiracial, cross-class movement was needed to address the dual crises of climate and inequality. Past efforts to address just one or the other problem separately served only to further divide workers and communities and undermine solutions to both issues. The seeds of this new movement exist within the labor–climate and the climate justice movements. The LCM in particular occupies a strategically important position because it resides within labor, is not controlled by any union or federation, and often overlaps with the climate justice movement, especially when it comes to demanding scientifically informed emission reductions and opposing the false climate solutions of "clean coal" and carbon capture that are promoted by many blue–greens. By strengthening demands for climate justice and building a bridge between the climate justice movement and the labor movement, the LCM could help build a formidable *labor–climate justice movement* fighting for protections not only for displaced fossil fuel workers and their communities but for historically marginalized workers and communities as well, pursuing the essential features of a Green New Deal, and helping to build a more sustainable, equitable, and democratic world for all.

Possible Futures for the Labor–Climate Movement

The Green New Deal resolution, as introduced to Congress, provides a broad vision for the means to a sustainable and equitable future. It has also opened up a new space for discussion and action within the LCM. In fact, the 2019 annual meeting of the national organization in this study, USE, which focused on labor and the Green New Deal, was by far the best-attended event the group had ever organized. It was also a site where the hard and soft disagreements described throughout this book became visibly apparent. Would labor as a whole support a just transition? What kind of just transition? Would the LCM center racial justice in its efforts to shape the Green New Deal, or would it merely fight to protect displaced fossil fuel workers and thus recreate existing inequalities in the new green economy? Would the LCM demand public ownership and control of the energy sector as the best means to achieve net-zero carbon emissions by 2050, or would it accept market-based solutions to reduce GHG emissions?

In other words, the Green New Deal itself has become a political space where the nested but competing frames of just transition described in this book—protective, proactive, and transformative—are being discussed and debated. Supporters of each frame are attempting to move fellow LCM activists and unions either to the left or the right on the spectrum, ranging from basic social protections for displaced fossil fuel workers to the promotion of transformational change that leads to an entirely new political economy for America. The future of the LCM depends on the outcome of these conversations. On the basis of my analysis in this study, I envision three possible futures for labor and the climate:

- "As the World Burns," a future in which the oppositional frame that resists just transition is pursued and labor does not support a Green New Deal.
- "Between a Rock and a Hard Place," a future in which the protective just transition frame is pursued and labor supports only a watered-down Green New Deal.

- "A Just and Sustainable Future," a future in which a combination of the proactive and transformative frames is pursued and labor supports a Green New Deal as envisioned in the Ocasio-Cortez and Markey resolution (U.S. Congress 2019).

Each will be elaborated below.

As the World Burns

"As the World Burns" represents the scenario where the oppositional just transition frame prevails. In more cynical terms, this is the future we will have if we "leave the environment to the environmentalists" and the interests of unionized workers are excluded from the movement. Jobs vs. the Environment becomes the mantra of the day—even more so than in the present. Under growing public pressure, led by the mainstream environmental movement and the daily experience of climate catastrophe, the government continues to slowly transition away from fossil fuels. But, without a seat at the table for labor, the transition does not include protections for fossil fuel workers, nor does it advocate for union representation in the emerging energy sector. Working from the job-conscious business union perspective, the labor movement engages in a retrograde effort to preserve unionized jobs in the declining fossil fuel industry by putting all of its political capital behind carbon capture technologies and slowly weakens its capacity to have a voice in shaping a more sustainable future.

Having shown themselves to be primarily a barrier to sustainability, the labor movement is greatly weakened. They alienate their traditional allies from other social movements and fail their members in the fossil fuel industry who are losing their jobs and, as a result of their union's resistance to just transition measures, lack a strong social safety net. Further, for being on the wrong side of history and resisting the social forces applying pressure to bend its arc toward justice, labor sees its public support eroding as it comes to be viewed as an impediment to progress rather than a force for good. Simultaneously, the environmental movement alone in pursuit of its class-blind course of action creates even greater animosity toward environmental regulations among an already-skeptical working class. Lacking a progressive labor voice, the more reactionary elements of society lead many workers to align with the fossil fuel industry in opposition to climate protection measures.

In other words, "the world burns" because efforts to address climate change that do not incorporate the interests of workers are doomed to fail. Without broad-based support, efforts to rein in GHG emissions are slow and insufficient, making this future unsustainable and unattainable in the long run. At the end of the day, unchecked capitalism means unchecked exploitation of both nature and labor to increase accumulation. A strategy to liberate the Earth from environmental exploitation therefore must address capitalism's historic penchant for labor exploitation. Thus, without incorporation of labor's call for a just transition that fundamentally challenges neoliberal governance, all roads lead to prolonged struggles over Jobs vs. the Environment, which can only end in climate catastrophe.

Given the divided response to the Green New Deal resolution by various elements of labor, I am encouraged and have hope that the "as the world burns" scenario will not become our collective future. If not for the efforts of the LCM to date, labor as a whole likely would have stood as a monolith in opposition to the Green New Deal and pursued the job-conscious business union approach to climate. Unions that might have otherwise remained neutral, or at least silent, on the issue have taken a stance, and many such as the SEIU and AFT are beginning to take concrete actions based on that stance. In other words, the division over the Green New Deal may at first seem like a problem, but I instead offer that it is the first sign of a crack in this major pillar of support for continued fossil fuel use. However, this does not mean we are free and clear, as we shall see in the second possible scenario.

Between a Rock and a Hard Place

In the "Between a Rock and a Hard Place" scenario, the LCM has won the protective just transition frame. By its very nature, protective just transition is merely reactive, responding to individual plant closures on a case-by-case basis. Even in states that have adopted broad policies to protect fossil fuel workers, many unions continue to fight to protect their jobs first and foremost and accept the protections only as a last resort should they fail to save their jobs. This much is evident in the AFL-CIO resolution on climate change, which supports efforts to address climate change but which also reads in part: "The AFL-CIO will fight politically and legislatively to secure and maintain employment," including the support of dubious proposals such as "clean coal." Further, the building trades unions are one of the most vocal supporters of the fossil fuel regime, and their support stems not only from the desire to protect existing jobs but from the promise of securing future jobs. Thus, the protective frame does little to sway their support from further fossil fuel projects.

Merely providing economic and social protections for displaced workers has done nothing to ensure that the transition away from fossil fuels created good, environmentally sustainable union jobs to replace those lost in the fossil fuel sector. The renewable energy industry, like all other capitalist interests, has incentives to exploit its workforce to maximize profits. For example, the current experiences of workers at companies like SolarCity, where workers perform dangerous rooftop work for low wages, and Tesla, where workers have been illegally fired for unionization efforts, illustrate that businesses doing essentially progressive work are no less capitalist in their treatment of workers and their stance toward unions (Wiessner 2018).

In other words, labor is stuck "Between a Rock and a Hard Place" in this future. On the one hand, they experience a decline in the number of good, unionized jobs in the fossil fuel sector to address climate change—this is the "rock." On the other hand, even though locally displaced fossil fuel workers are offered some protections, labor, without a proactive plan, has no guarantee that the new jobs created in the green economy are good, unionized jobs with living wages, essential benefits, and workplace protections—this is the "hard place." In fact, one of the major reasons many unions have resisted just transition plans is that they see them as essentially replacing "dirty" but well-paying unionized jobs with "green" but low-paying nonunionized ones. And for some capitalist employers, the elimination of unions becomes part of the incentive for supporting a short-term transition to renewables. In terms of realizing climate justice, protecting only the workers who were fortunate enough to have had unionized energy jobs in the first place does little to address existing social inequalities. Further, a decline in union strength by replacing unionized jobs with nonunionized ones means a loss of the best advocates for a full just transition—and the loss of their voice eventually kills the movement.

In sum, the protective just transition frame alone does not go far enough to enlist the full-throated support of labor as a whole in efforts to transition away from fossil fuels. The incentives for workers to continue along the Jobs vs. the Environment path that are built into the neoliberalized American capitalist system remain place. Without a truly broad base of support for strong climate protection, the United States continues on its current slow trajectory of emission reduction and fails to meet even the insufficient goals set forth in the Paris Climate Accord. In other words, we are unable to get to a sustainable world in this future because the worst of climate change comes to pass as the United States approaches and ultimately surpasses an irreversible climate tipping point.

A Just and Sustainable Future

In the scenario offered by "A Just and Sustainable Future," labor as a whole embraces a combination of the proactive and the transformative visions of just transition and by doing so fully enacts the Clean Air and Good Jobs counterframe. By forming local climate action committees, passing union resolutions, raising climate issues in local union bargaining demands, and pursuing other forms of Green New Deals from below, LCM activists in this scenario educate fellow union members and engage in the deep internal organizing necessary to build the critical mass of support needed for labor to adopt the proactive frame. All of the union categories—and, most important, the AFL-CIO—move to the Clean Air and Good Jobs side of the labor–climate spectrum. As part of a broad and inclusive movement with environmental and climate justice and other social movements, the LCM in this scenario pushes beyond the IRA for protective measures for displaced workers, ensures a seat at the table for workers and frontline communities to shape the Green New Deal, and centers issues of racial and social justice for the Indigenous, Black, and brown communities, which have borne the brunt of fossil fuel pollution while reaping few if any of the economic rewards. The more radical activists push for social ownership and democratic control of energy resources and infrastructure at the federal, state, and local levels, with varying degrees of success. While markets still play a role in this future, they are not the driving force or the basis on which all decisions are made; people regain agency over their futures, putting the "political" back in political economy. Most important, labor as a whole begins to espouse the core tenets of social movement unionism—making broad demands that benefit the whole of the working class, engaging in high levels of organizing, both internally and externally, and using innovative tactics to make the Green New Deal a reality.

The Green New Deal that is developed with input from all stakeholders in society stipulates a plan for the managed retreat from fossil fuels with enforceable emission-reduction targets toward the ultimate goal of achieving net-zero GHG emissions in the United States by 2030 and globally by 2050. Early retirement and wage replacement programs, as well as universal provision of healthcare, ensure the economic stability of older fossil fuel workers during the transition. A "green prevailing wage" ensures that fossil fuel workers transitioning to renewable energy jobs are paid at rates equivalent to their former fossil fuel jobs. Tuition-free college education helps younger workers acquire the skills required for the new green economy without bearing the burden of exorbitant debt that prevented so many from returning to school before the Green New Deal. The federal jobs guarantee makes sure that every person who wants a job is gainfully employed at a living wage, with the right to organize a union and bargain collectively with employers. The jobs guarantee helps eliminate the resource constraints and opportunity-hoarding mindset that pits worker against worker, often along racial lines, to compete for a limited number of good jobs. Local hiring and local procurement measures ensure access to local jobs by historically excluded groups and reinvigorate domestic manufacturing. Together, these proactive plans eliminate the major drivers of most Jobs vs. the Environment conflicts.

The construction of renewable energy infrastructure, the expansion of mass transit, and the changeover from combustion to electric-powered vehicles creates millions of jobs in construction, transportation, and manufacturing. The increased valuation of low-carbon "reproductive labor" increases wages and employment in the healthcare, service, and education sectors. The public sector plays a significant role in coordinating and implementing the various components of the Green New Deal. And, as has been the case with most BCG campaigns, labor in this scenario wins greater public support and increased membership after demonstrating that it is on the right side of history and fighting for the benefit of the whole working class. Most important, the next generation of youth will come of age in a society organized around sustainability, equity, justice, and high levels of democratic participation and civic engagement.

As with the original New Deal, realization of the Green New Deal first required the election of an amenable president and Congress, but even then it was possible only as a result of massive organizing by workers and other social groups to engage in large-scale strikes and other forms of civil disobedience. This action began with a wave of internal organizing drives by unions at all levels across the country, engaging rank-and-file members in serious dialogue about the climate crisis and the programs that workers and unions must demand to ensure a climate-safe future for themselves and their children. As with the original New Deal, these individual programs that have become part of the Green New Deal are largely a product of many rounds of experimentation and learning, reconfiguring, and experimenting further (Brecher 2021).

As under the original New Deal, disputes inevitably continue between reformists and radicals—a debate that has existed within the labor movement since its earliest days. Proponents of the transformative frame argue that through proactive "social dialogue," labor at best achieves the status of being a "junior partner to capital." They also argue that the incrementalist gains made by the proactive just transition can easily be lost because the dominant power structures and profit incentives remain in place for powerful actors to regroup to dismantle the Green New Deal, as they did with much of the original New Deal in the decades after World War II. Proponents of the proactive frame aver that the transformational frame is light on details and lacking concrete plans, making it difficult to support. The concrete and tangible demands of the proactive frame are fundamental because they map out a clear path to addressing the dual crises of climate and inequality. However, the transformative frame ensures that social justice for frontline communities is not lost in the social dialogue that typically occurs among labor, capital, and the state regarding the future of economic growth on the treadmill of production. Although light on concrete details, the transformative frame provides much-needed inspiration and motivation for activists—a broad and aspirational vision to strive toward. Within the Green New Deal framework, these two frames coexist, and the debates continue between activists, but at least they have peace of mind knowing that the nation is on track to net-zero carbon emissions, displaced workers are protected by an adequate social safety net, and historically marginalized communities enjoy new opportunities to prosper within a climate-safe society.

Conclusion

Despite NASA scientist James Hansen's best efforts to educate America about the threat of global warming in 1988 (Milman 2018) and subsequent efforts by countless scientists and activists in the years since his presentation before Congress, the United States remains a climate change laggard. Americans continue to burn fossil fuels at an alarming rate. The ascendancy of climate change denier Donald Trump to the presidency with his antienvironmental cabinet in tow suggested that the arc of history may not be bending quickly enough toward climate justice. In fact, in many respects, under the Trump administration the United States moved backward. The withdrawal of the United States from the Paris Climate Accord and the rollback of emission standards for automobiles and regulations of fossil fuel power plants, as well as the repeated efforts to "bring back coal," spell disaster for the atmosphere and the countless precious lifeforms that dwell under it. It is unclear whether the reversal of these measures by the Biden administration will continue beyond his time in office or again be reversed if a Republican takes the presidency again.

However, there have been some early signs of stress fractures in one of the major pillars of support for the fossil fuel regime—workers and unions. Just like the transportation workers, nurses, and educators who experienced Superstorm Sandy, workers in other unions across the United States are beginning to see climate change as a working-class issue. There is not by any means a consensus on the need for unions to play a major role in solving the problem, let alone an agreement on what that solution will be, but discussions on these topics are happening in union halls across the country right now. Labor's presence at the People's Climate March in New York in 2014 and again in Washington, DC, in 2017 illustrate growing engagement with the issue. The endorsement of the Green New Deal by the SEIU, AFT, several state and local labor councils, and many other local unions around the country reveals a crack in this once-shatterproof pillar of support for fossil fueled economic growth. The LCM activists I studied in this project are making a powerful case among their coworkers, among their community members, and in their local and state governments that any real solution to the climate crisis must include a just transition if it is going to garner the broad-based support required to succeed.

Demanding a just transition not only challenges the power of the fossil fuel regime but to varying degrees runs against the dominant free market ideology that permeates American society. Following the structure of various social programs that have been in effect in the United States since the New Deal, the protective frame envisions some form of taxation and redistribution to make society fairer and more equal. The proactive frame goes further by envisioning a social partnership among labor, business, and the government to engage in long- and short-term economic planning and industrial policy setting. Transformative just transition, while admittedly thin on details currently, fundamentally challenges the existing power structure by promoting deep structural changes to eliminate capitalist social relations in the energy sector and beyond.

After I spent four years in the field working with three LCM organizations and four additional years talking with its leaders, it seems clear that the path away from climate alienation and toward climate solidarity, with the reward of a truly just and sustainable future, is the path that is most difficult to travel. To push beyond the Jobs vs. the Environment frame and protect the climate while creating good jobs, labor must support a proactive Green New Deal. However, activists must also continue to imagine and shape a broader transformative vision that directly confronts the system that thrives from the dual exploitation of nature and labor—capitalism. This long, uphill road to a just and sustainable future will require education, agitation, and organization to win the hearts and minds of labor as a whole and achieve "climate solidarity" (Hampton 2015; Brecher 2017). It will also require labor to continue to forge powerful coalitions with other natural allies, including frontline communities, environmental and climate justice organizations, churches, universities, academic and scholarly communities, healthcare professionals, and, yes, mainstream environmentalists as well—just to name a few.

It was in this spirit that, in my capacity as both a union leader and a scholar, I helped to draft and promote several resolutions on climate justice after completing my fieldwork for this project. The first, a resolution on just transition before the annual meeting of the Society for the Study of Social Problems (SSSP) in August 2018, was titled "A Just Transition to Renewable Energy with Justice for Workers and Frontline Communities." The resolution incorporated some of the demands made by the nurses' union that appeared in their proposed resolution to the AFL-CIO but did not make it into the final resolution that was adopted by that body. Fortunately, the resolution process in the SSSP created a space for a vigorous conversation among activist scholars about the intersection of climate change, workers' rights, and environmental justice. It will also help plant the seeds for future networking activities between the academic and labor communities around the issue of climate justice. The resolution passed at the membership meeting of the SSSP on the second day of the conference, and it was agreed that the incoming leadership would be submitting letters to elected officials stating SSSP's support for a just transition to a clean and just economy.

The second resolution, adopted by my current union, the Rutgers University chapter of AAUP-AFT Local 6323, proclaims support for the Green New Deal and the global student climate strikes, which members participated in on September 20, 2019, and also demands that the university work with the union to jointly develop a climate action plan for the university to achieve carbon neutrality by the year 2030. The union brought this demand into contract bargaining two days after the student climate strike. At the time of this writing, a joint task force has been established, and several leading climate scholars from the faculty union are working with members of the university administration and other campus unions to develop a climate action plan. These efforts by the Rutgers union and other progressive AFT locals around the United States ultimately led the AFT to adopt a national resolution in support of the Green New Deal at its national convention in July 2020. I helped with a third resolution on divestment/reinvestment, initiated by David Hughes of Rutgers and the AFT's national climate task force, and cocreated by several AFT locals around the United States, which was adopted at the union's national convention in 2022. The resolution urged the AFT to divest its investments and those of retiree pension and TIAA plans from fossil fuels and reinvest them in support of displaced workers and historically marginalized communities impacted by the fossil fuel industry and the transition away from fossil fuels (Vachon 2022).

While it is unclear which of the three futures I have outlined will come to pass, it is clear that we are in a race to ensure that climate justice reaches a moral tipping point before the Earth reaches a climate tipping point if we want our children and grandchildren to have a world that is as hospitable as ours has been. The question that remains is whether the LCM will choose a proactive path with a transformative vision for tearing down the pillars of support for the fossil fuel regime or instead pursue the narrower protective frame, taking two steps forward, one step back, and eventually falling short of its long-term goal of sustainability.

At a national-level meeting of USE in 2017, a leader from a national union–community coalition was speaking passionately about the need for labor to overcome the Jobs vs. the Environment master frame. She used the analogy of wanting to "have our cake and eat it too" to express that unions must reject the false either-or choice that is presented on the free market menu. After she finished, she received great cheers from the audience of LCM activists. However, the next speaker went further. She stated, "We don't only want to have our cake and eat it too. We want to own the whole damned bakery and we want to manage it democratically!" The room immediately erupted with hoots and howls of approval. The first speaker later expressed her support for the comments of the second, revealing the groundswell of support for transformation that is bubbling just beneath the surface. When asked how such radical changes could be won, the second speaker said simply, "Just like anything else—we make the road by walking. It's just a matter of deciding where we're walking to."

Nearly two hundred years ago, the venerable German philosopher Georg Hegel famously stated in the preface of *Elements of the Philosophy of Right*: "The owl of Minerva takes its flight only when the shades of night are gathering" (1820 [2005], xxi). Referring to the owl that accompanies the goddess of wisdom in Roman mythology and that represents knowledge, wisdom, and perspicacity, the dour and enigmatic Hegel used this metaphor to intone his belief that human understanding of historical events can only be achieved retrospectively, after those events have unfolded. Humankind can comprehend the arc of history only after it has made its bend in the direction of justice or injustice at its preordained velocity and magnitude. The human condition, be it improving or facing precipitous decline, becomes clear only after it has been experienced.

On first glance, Hegel's assertion that historical understanding can be found only in hindsight seems both obvious and harmless. It is self-evident that historical events are better understood in hindsight, with the luxury of time—and the clarity of thought it affords—as one's companion in the construction of knowledge. Yet the implications of this reasoning for human existence are dangerous when applied to climate change. If taken to heart, this assertion bars any claims on the future and renders any questions of the present inveterately obsolete. Lacking the ability to understand its current situation until it has passed, humanity lacks the tools and agency to effect purposeful change. While change happens, it does so without human intentionality, and it is only in hindsight that it can be understood. Unfortunately, understanding a threat to one's survival only after it has taken one's life is no understanding at all— it is a eulogy. When contemplating the consequences of unmitigated climate change, the world cannot complacently indulge in Hegel's fatalistic aplomb. The owl must be wakened and made to fly before dusk.

Notes

1. An iconic example of this is the national boycott of grapes during the United Farmworkers strike, led by Cesar Chavez, against grape farmers in Delano, California, from 1965 through 1970. The strike began when Filipino and Mexican American farmworkers walked off the job, demanding wages equal to the federal minimum wage. When millions of Americans participated in the five-year national boycott of nonunion grapes, destabilizing a key pillar of support for farmworker exploitation, the employers ultimately acquiesced by improving the pay and working conditions of the farmworkers and bargaining a first contract with the union.

2. There are many definitions of social structure in sociology, but in general, they all imply that stable patterns of interaction among the members of a society, institution, or organization constitute its social structure (Allardt 1972).

3. Marshall and Rossman define observation as "the systematic description of events, behaviors, and artifacts in the social setting chosen for study" (1989, 79). Through observation, researchers can describe social settings using all of their senses to create a "written photograph" of the situation under study (Erlandson et al. 1993, 137). Participant observation is a method in which the observer participates in the activities of the people under study, observing things that happen, listening to things that are said, and questioning people, over a defined period of time (Becker and Geer 1957). Participant observation enables researchers to gain a deep understanding of the activities of the people under study by both observing and participating in those activities in their natural setting (Kawulich 2005).

4. Qualitative interviews, sometimes called intensive or in-depth interviews, are typically conversational or semi-structured. The researcher learns about the topic at hand from the respondent through open-ended questions that may not be asked in exactly the same way or in the same order for each respondent. The conversational interview,

as described by Gall, Gall, and Borg (2003, 239), relies on "the spontaneous generation of questions in a natural interaction, typically one that occurs as part of ongoing participant observation fieldwork."

5. Baez (2002, 35) refers to the "convention of confidentiality." This convention is intended to protect research participants from any harm that may come from breach of privacy and is consistent with the Belmont Report's emphasis on "beneficence"—the conviction that researchers must not harm their study participants (National Commission for the Protection of Human Subjects 1978). The convention of confidentiality is espoused in most qualitative sociological research as a means to protect the privacy of study participants, to build trust and rapport with participants, and to maintain ethical standards throughout the research process.

6. In addition to official communications from each organization, I also mined other electronic documents from the various websites associated with each SMO. In some cases, I downloaded official testimony regarding legislation from the *Congressional Record*. Some documents, such as meeting agendas and committee reports, were offered only in print at meetings. As with the participant observation field notes and interview transcripts, all original source documents were read carefully and coded into major themes throughout the process.

7. Figure 1.1 is very stylized and is not intended to be a precise depiction of reality but rather to provide the reader with a general sense of where the LCM is situated in reference to other related movements. Actual relations are too complex to reduce to a simple illustration, but as a heuristic device, this figure offers insight into the important role the labor–climate and climate justice movements could play in building a broad coalition promoting climate solutions that center workers, communities, and justice.

8. I draw from the multi-institutional politics perspective to understand the selection of nonstate targets by movement actors as well as targets that are cultural (Armstrong and Bernstein 2008).

9. The category titles are borrowed from an unpublished presentation to union leaders by Sweeney (2016) and are modified to match the definitions used herein.

CHAPTER 2

1. As noted in Chapter 1, the BlueGreen Alliance is not considered a part of the LCM, on the basis of the criteria used for this study: (1) independence from national labor leadership and (2) promotion of GHG emission-reduction targets in accordance with climate science.

2. In this book, I examine the political dynamics of the LCM that are operating within unions to build a working-class climate activist wing within the U.S. labor movement that will fight for worker-friendly solutions to the climate crisis. For readers interested in learning more about the formation of blue–green coalitions, including the social conditions and processes that draw labor and environmentalists together into lasting partnerships, I recommend reading Obach (2004), Gordon (2004), and Mayer (2009).

3. Although constructed from characteristics of a given phenomenon, an "ideal type" is not meant to correspond to all of the characteristics of any one particular case but rather to emphasize certain elements common to most cases of the given phenomenon.

In other words, ideal types rarely exist in their pure form in the real world but rather are idea-constructs that help put the seeming chaos of social reality in order (Swedberg 2017).

4. Aside from the successes of the IWW early in the twentieth century, revolutionary unionism (and socialist politics) has largely been absent from the American labor movement (Kimeldorf 1999).

5. Chris Rhomberg (2021) has argued that the New Deal labor relations system was only ever applied in the northern states and that a competing southern labor relations system existed simultaneously, and it has been spreading into what used to be New Deal states in recent decades.

6. There is some debate within the literature about the use of the terms "social movement unionism" versus "social justice" unionism, or just "social unionism." However, at the risk of criticism by fellow scholars of labor, I will for the sake of parsimony refer to them in combination as "social movement unionism" throughout the remainder of this book because it reflects the social movement nature of the work being done by the participants in this study (for a critique, see Scipes 2014).

7. Peter Waterman (1991) references Alberto Melucci's "new structural characteristics" (1985, 1996) as being helpful for differentiating social movement unions from more traditional labor organizations. While Waterman acknowledges that Melucci's characteristics may not be all that new—a common critique of new social movements theory (see Calhoun 1993)—he nonetheless accentuates the new social movements' qualities of social movement unionism, including grassroots direct action, democratic structures, and alignment with other movements. Many of the individual characteristics presented here have individually or in various combinations formed the basis for other theoretical constructs (Moody 1997; Robinson 2000; Schiavone 2007).

8. In the case of the Dakota Access pipeline, the project also threatened the land and water of the Standing Rock Sioux Tribal nation. A Labor for Standing Rock group formed on social media and helped to coordinate union member participation in the protests, including at local rallies as well as at the camp at Standing Rock. Many unions also donated material resources such as camping gear to support the "water protectors" as the cold winter months approached.

CHAPTER 3

1. Readers should note that while the diagram presented in this chapter can provide us with some useful information, it is intended to be a heuristic device only. One illustration cannot possibly capture the complexity of the relationships among unions regarding climate change, but it can help paint a broad picture of the nature of relations. The placement of each category on the spectrum is also based on aggregated data and cannot capture the local variations within union categories. Elsewhere, I develop a more elaborate "labor–climate field," which adds a second axis to account for organizational form—of particular interest there is the relationship between racial and gender diversity within unions and their likelihood of taking more proactive positions on climate change and other big-picture working-class issues (see Vachon 2018).

2. The eight industry categories loosely coincide with the North American Industry Classification System, which is used by the U.S. Census Bureau and most government and business organizations in North America. It is important to note that the

recent trend toward "general unionism" places some particular unions in multiple categories because they represent workers in multiple industries. For example, UAW, known for manufacturing, also represents more than seventy thousand teachers and researchers in higher education. For this research, I categorize unionized groups of workers on the basis of their industries of employment rather than their union's name. Owing to data limitations, this list includes only those industries from which unions or union members participated in at least one of the three LCM organizations examined in this study.

3. All statistical data on unions in this chapter come from Hirsch and Macpherson (2017).

4. All statistical data on employment and demographics in this chapter come from the BLS (U.S. BLS 2018a, 2018b).

5. Many building trades union members, such as power plant operators or cabinet builders, are employed in standard jobs, but in general, the construction industry uses the hiring hall structure to connect workers and employers and to manage employee benefits.

6. The placement of each union category onto the spectrum is based on aggregated data and cannot capture the types of local variation within union categories; this is particularly true for unions in the manufacturing industry, where workers' interests can vary depending on the nature of the products they produce. Manufacturing unions are also some of the most diversified, general unions because of organizing in new industries after deindustrialization in the 1970s and 1980s.

7. Many transportation unions also have members in the public sector, but as with teachers, I classify them into their own category of union.

8. Currently, collective bargaining by teachers is prohibited in Georgia, North Carolina, South Carolina, Texas, and Virginia; permitted in Alabama, Arkansas, Arizona, Colorado, Idaho, Kentucky, Louisiana, Mississippi, Missouri, Ohio, Utah, West Virginia, and Wyoming; and required in the remaining thirty-two states.

9. The long-distance trucking industry, once highly unionized by the Teamsters, has transformed dramatically in recent decades as a result of deregulation and reclassification of many drivers from employees to independent contractors or "owner–operators"—a classification that makes them ineligible for unionization. For more information, see *The Big Rig* by Steve Viscelli (2016).

10. Two key exceptions are International Ladies' Garment Workers' Union (IL-GWU) and Brotherhood of Sleeping Car Porters (BSCP), which consisted primarily of women and Black men, respectively.

11. Interestingly and ironically, UMWA was one of the first industrial unions and the principal organizer of the CIO but now holds outsize voice within the AFL-CIO and promotes a conservative stance on climate issues.

CHAPTER 4

1. As Manser (2007, 292) points out, this expression misstates what Wilson actually said, which was "What's good for my country is good for General Motors, and vice versa." However, in a classic example where mythology overtakes reality, this emendation is the phrase most remembered and repeated down through the years.

2. In the Gramscian sense, the Clean Air and Good Jobs counterframe is an act of counterhegemony because it provides both a political–economic critique of unregulated free markets and state power as well as a cultural analysis of capitalist hegemony (Carroll and Ratner 1996).

3. Weed's (1997) study of the crime victim rights movement offers a great illustration of the process of frame amplification. The movement took the concept of "victim"—which rests on the perception that a person has been wronged in a fashion that calls for public action—and amplified the frame by tying it to the unjust treatment of crime victims by the very institutions responsible for meting out justice in society. The concept of "revictimization" proved to be a powerful political symbol and rallying point for the movement (Nelson 1984).

4. Benford and Snow (2000) suspect that this is among the most prevalent of framing strategies, although there has been little systematic focus on it in the literature. One example is provided in McCallion and Maines's (1999) study of the liturgical movement within the Catholic Church. Movement activists relied extensively on frame bridging by using the Catholic academic world to link sentiment pools of lay professionals and clergy to the movement.

5. Various peace movement organizations provide a classic example of this process when they claim that the goals of nuclear disarmament and demilitarization are complementary to the causes of ending racism and sexism because pursuing an agenda of demilitarization is not only a means to stop or prevent wars but also to reduce inequalities in society by freeing up resources to invest in infrastructure, jobs, and social programs to counter the ill effects of systemic racism and sexism.

6. Although outlined in Snow and colleagues' (1986) original collective action framework, the concept of frame transformation has not appeared much in social movement research, and the few examples of this process involve religious conversion. Conversion to a new religion involves reconstruction of a meaning system in the context of intense encounters with socializers and a heightened emotionality. Once conversion occurs, the new ideology can function as a frame.

7. A 2018 analysis concludes that at least 4,645 and perhaps more than 5,000 Puerto Ricans died between September 20 and December 31, 2017, as a result of Hurricane Maria (Kishore et al. 2018). This is more than seventy times the official estimate promoted by President Trump and exceeds by at least 1,600 those killed in the terrorist attacks of September 11, 2001. This finding highlights the complicity of the government and the media in masking the real costs of climate change by making frontline communities invisible.

8. In the time since this study was completed, a number of participants in the LCM have begun to embrace a BCG approach that involves bringing climate justice demands directly into collective bargaining campaigns with employers. While the gains that can be made on an employer-by-employer basis are small, the opportunity to educate members and push a pro–climate protection agenda upward within the labor movement is increasingly seen as a worthy cause.

9. See Armstrong and Bernstein (2008) on multi-institutional politics.

10. For a good example of labor directly challenging capital to address climate change, see the story of the Minneapolis janitors in Chapter 3 of this volume. For a general articulation of this tactic, see Vachon and colleagues (2019).

11. Although not shown in the illustration, the labor movement sphere includes the blue–greens, which exist as one of the many constituencies within labor as a whole that are targeted by the LCM.

12. Walker, Martin, and McCarthy (2008) have referred to variants of indirect targeting as "proximate targeting."

CHAPTER 5

1. I borrow the first three category names from an unpublished presentation to global union leaders by Sweeney (2016), in which he referred to just transition as being "protective, proactive, and transformative." The definitions I use for these categories differ in important ways from Sweeney's usage; however, the general themes of worker protection, economic planning, and the need to make radical changes to the political economy remain consistent.

2. For a more detailed treatment of Mazzocchi, the Superfund for workers, and the history of just transition, see Brecher (2015), Leopold (2007), and Stevis, Krause, and Morena (2019).

3. For more examples of local just transitions, see S. Smith (2017).

4. The time frame of this research encompasses the years 2014 through 2018, ending six months before the introduction of the Green New Deal resolution by Representative Ocasio-Cortez and Senator Markey in February 2019 (U.S. Congress 2019).

5. See Demaria and colleagues (2013) for a discussion of levels and goals.

6. Readers should interpret the trends presented in the table with caution because it is not feasible to assume generalizability from such a small sample size; nonetheless, these trends are presented to offer some insight into the leaning of movement participants from various industries.

7. On AFL versus CIO unionism, see, for example, Cornfield and McCammon (2010) and Kimeldorf (1999); on business unionism versus social movement unionism, see, for example, Scipes (2014) and Waterman (1991).

CHAPTER 6

1. Recall that these are pseudonyms and not the actual names of organizations.

2. This count involves the actions I observed and is not necessarily representative of the total number of actions each SMO undertook.

3. The final bill included limitations on net metering and a cap on commercial solar development. Net metering allows customers to reduce the electricity they purchase from utilities when they consume the energy from their solar panels onsite by paying only the net difference between how much energy a consumer produces produce and how much energy they use. Most solar systems are designed to provide close to 100 percent of electricity in order to cancel out utility bills.

4. The Block Island Wind Farm is small compared with others around the world, and the United States has lagged considerably behind other countries in adopting the technology. For example, Denmark was the first country to construct an offshore wind farm, in 1991 (U.S. BLM 2018). At the end of 2016, there were more than 3,500 offshore wind turbines operating off the coasts of Europe. The largest offshore wind farm

currently is the London Array off the coast of the United Kingdom, with 175 turbines generating enough electricity to power 500,000 homes and save 925,000 tons of CO_2 emissions per year (Global Wind Energy Council 2018).

5. The term "indigenous organizational strength" is rooted in social movement scholarship in the contentious politics tradition (McAdam 1982; Tilly 1983).

6. Owing to political and strategic differences, SEIU and the Teamsters left the AFL-CIO in 2005 to help form the Change to Win Coalition, which lasted just a few years as a confederation. The largest teachers' union, the NEA, is not affiliated with the AFL-CIO at the national level, but some NEA locals are affiliated with their state AFL-CIO federations. Various other unions remain unaffiliated with the federation as well, including two of the more radical unions—UE and IWW—both of which are considerably smaller and weakened since the McCarthy era, which followed World War II.

7. For example, the president of a building trades union once threatened to oppose all legislation supporting public transportation after the president of a transportation union announced his opposition to the Keystone XL pipeline.

8. It is important to note that particular renewable projects are more or less viable in certain states and regions. For example, offshore wind construction can be done only along coastal states. However, the viability issue has not correlated with renewable development nearly as much as the political ideology of government has—some of the states with the greatest solar potential happen to be the most conservative and fossil fuel–dependent states, such as Florida, Indiana, Kentucky, and Texas. Texas is second only to California when it comes to solar potential, with 85 percent of buildings in the state ready for solar but having just fourteen thousand rooftop solar installations as of 2018 (Schaal 2018). Unfavorable laws in cities such as El Paso, which actually taxes people for solar installations, create a disincentive for renewable energy use. Other states, with very little renewable potential but more-liberal governments, such as Connecticut and Vermont, have nonetheless pursued renewables aggressively.

CHAPTER 7

1. In simple terms, political opportunities are consistent, but not necessarily formal or permanent, dimensions of the political struggle that encourage people to engage in contentious politics (McCammon et al. 2001; Tarrow 1998). Vulnerabilities often appear at the interstices of different networks of control (Mann 1988), in the overlap of multiple fields (Evans and Kay 2008), or in the contradictions of a multi-institutional social order (Armstrong and Bernstein 2008).

2. Political party control of local, state, and national government plays a significant role in shaping the opportunity structure for the LCM. Democrats have on average been more receptive than Republicans to political demands made by labor and environmentalists, but neither party is receptive to demands that fundamentally challenge the capitalist order or breach the demand constraints imposed by capitalist profitability; this was evident when House Speaker Nancy Pelosi dismissively referred to the Green New Deal as "the green dream, or whatever" after Representative Ocasio-Cortez introduced the resolution to the House of Representatives (Cillizza 2019). Despite the increased favorability of a Democratic government, elected officials are often confronted with competing demands by various interest groups that form their base of support. As

we have seen, the demands by labor activists and environmentalists can sometimes be contradictory, making labor–environmental discourse and alignment among movements another important aspect in shaping the opportunity structure. The more these movements can align their interests and demands, the greater leverage both will have within the political process.

3. This conversation was collected as an oral history interview for the Just Transition Listening Project (Cha et. al 2021).

4. Beyond specific instances of political opportunity that often appear unexpectedly, most social movements that have succeeded in the twentieth century have done so during periods in which the underlying structure they were challenging was already in decline and have been accompanied by a cultural shift that reached a moral tipping point when additional social groups and individuals who did not initiate the movement joined on moral grounds. This implies that social movements don't usually win just because of the efforts of those directly aggrieved but also because of the intervention of bystander publics, or disengaged third parties who are usually drawn into the movement on one side or the other. The concept of a moral tipping point and the engagement of bystanders are important to movement leaders because many social movements begin as minority movements and usually require support from at least a segment of the majority acting as conscience constituents—on moral grounds—to achieve success (McCarthy and Zald 1977).

5. A net-zero target contains within it two responses: stop releasing GHGs by cutting emissions, and remove CO_2 from the atmosphere using "negative emissions technologies," often called carbon sinks (planting new forests, for example). Many climate activists and some LCM activists fear that focusing too much on negative emissions could leave us still reliant on fossil fuels and prone to future risks. Unlike carbon emissions prevented by mitigation, carbon put into forests, soils, or even geological stores could leak back into the atmosphere, where it may bring other environmental or social risks, such as heightened competition for land.

6. Taking a more transformative approach, members of LUPE joined with international trade unionists at the international climate talks in Glasgow, Scotland, in November 2021 to draft and adopt a "Trade Union Program for a Public, Low-Carbon Energy Future." The resolution, the result of the work of a Trade Union Task Force of more than thirty unions, focuses mainly on the power sector and attempts to rally the international labor movement behind an ambitious political effort to bring about a fundamental shift in climate and energy policy—namely, to bring the sector under public ownership and democratic control. This shift, the document states, is needed both to correct the failures of the market model and to ensure that the energy transition is socially just, economically viable, and effective in terms of reaching climate goals (https://bit.ly/3Fo6vFa).

7. See also Jeremy Brecher's blog, *Strike*, which contains an ongoing commentary regarding Green New Deals from below (https://www.labor4sustainability.org/strike).

8. By way of comparison, the U.S. federal government provided $11 billion in subsidies to the renewable energy industry in 2016 (Maloney 2018).

9. As detailed in the report *America Misled: How the Fossil Fuel Industry Deliberately Misled Americans About Climate Change*, the fossil fuel industry has misled Americans on the science of climate change by citing fake experts, placing impossible demands

on the science, cherry-picking data, impugning the integrity of individual scientists and the scientific process, and appealing to conspiracy theories (Cook et al. 2019). Much the same way the tobacco industry sowed public uncertainty about the links between cigarette smoking and cancer, these climate change misinformation campaigns have left the public with the perpetual impression that there are lots of unresolved questions and that scientists are not to be trusted.

References

AFL-CIO. 2005. "Resolution 53: The War in Iraq." July 25. Available at https://aflcio
.org/resolution/war-iraq.
———. 2017. "Resolution 55: Climate Change, Energy and Union Jobs: AFL-CIO."
October 24. Available at https://aflcio.org/resolutions/resolution-55-climate-change
-energy-and-union-jobs.
AFL-CIO Energy Committee. 2019. Letter to the Honorable Edward Markey and the
Honorable Alexandria Ocasio-Cortez. "On Potential Actions to Address Climate
Change." March 8.
AFSCME. 2008. "Resolution No. 46: Global Warming and Green Jobs." July 28–August 1. Available at https://www.afscme.org/members/conventions/resolutions-and
-amendments/2008/resolutions/global-warming-and-green-jobs.
———. 2010. "Resolution No. 4: Climate Change Action Plan." June 28–July 2. Available at https://www.afscme.org/members/conventions/resolutions-and-amendments
/2010/resolutions/climate-change-action-plan.
AFT. 2012. "AFT Resolution: Educating the Membership and the Public on the Urgent Need to Address Climate Change and Environmental Degradation." Available
at https://www.aft.org/resolution/educating-membership-and-public-urgent-need
-address-climate-change-and.
———. 2020. "AFT Resolution in Support of Green New Deal." July 29. Available at
https://www.aft.org/resolution/support-green-new-deal.
Agyeman, Julian, and Bob Evans. 2004. "'Just Sustainability': The Emerging Discourse
of Environmental Justice in Britain?" *Geographical Journal* 170(2): 155–64. Available at https://doi.org/10.1111/j.0016-7398.2004.00117.x.
Akron Beacon Journal. 2012. "Americans against Fracking Formed by 100 Groups." December 7. Available at https://www.beaconjournal.com/story/news/2012/12/07
/americans-against-fracking-formed-by/10719627007.

Allardt, Erik. 1972. "Structural, Institutional, and Cultural Explanations." *Acta Sociologica* 15(1): 54–68. Available at https://doi.org/10.1177/000169937201500105.

Allen, Myles R., David J. Frame, Chris Huntingford, Chris D. Jones, Jason A. Lowe, Malte Meinshausen, and Nicolai Meinshausen. 2009. "Warming Caused by Cumulative Carbon Emissions towards the Trillionth Tonne." *Nature* 458(7242): 1163–66. Available at https://doi.org/10.1038/nature08019.

Altschuler, Glenn, and Stuart Blumin. 2009. *The GI Bill: The New Deal for Veterans.* New York: Oxford University Press.

Armstrong, Elizabeth A., and Mary Bernstein. 2008. "Culture, Power, and Institutions: A Multi-institutional Politics Approach to Social Movements." *Sociological Theory* 26(1): 74–99. Available at https://doi.org/10.1111/j.1467-9558.2008.00319.x.

Aronowitz, Stanley. 1984. *Working Class Hero: A New Strategy for Labor.* New York: Adama Books.

Associated Press. 1989. "Compromise Reached on Spotted Owl." *New York Times Archive*, September 30. Available at https://www.nytimes.com/1989/09/30/us/compromise-reached-on-spotted-owl.html.

ATU. 2016. "Resolution M: Opposing Fossil Fuel Dependency." Labor Network for Sustainability. Available at https://www.labor4sustainability.org/wp-content/uploads/2017/01/ATU-Climate-Change-Resolution.pdf.

Baez, Benjamin. 2002. "Confidentiality in Qualitative Research: Reflections on Secrets, Power and Agency." *Qualitative Research* 2(1): 35–58. Available at https://doi.org/10.1177/1468794102002001638.

Baker, Dean, and Aiden Lee. 2021. *The Employment Impact of Curtailing Fossil Fuel Use.* Report. Center for Economic and Policy Research. Available at https://cepr.net/report/the-employment-impact-of-curtailing-fossil-fuel-use.

Bari, Judi. 1994. *Timber Wars.* Monroe, ME: Common Courage.

Barkan, Steven E. 1979. "Strategic, Tactical and Organizational Dilemmas of the Protest Movement against Nuclear Power." *Social Problems* 27(1): 19–37. Available at https://doi.org/10.2307/800014.

Barrett, Jim. 2001. *Worker Transition and Global Climate Change.* Report. Washington, DC: Pew Research Center.

Bartley, Tim, and Curtis Child. 2014. "Shaming the Corporation: The Social Production of Targets and the Anti-sweatshop Movement." *American Sociological Review* 79(4): 653–79. Available at https://doi.org/10.1177/0003122414540653.

Beachy, Ben. 2021. *How to Build Back Better: A 10-Year Plan for Economic Renewal.* Report. Sierra Club. Available at https://www.sierraclub.org/sites/www.sierraclub.org/files/jobs-renewal-report.pdf.

Beck, Ulrich. 1992. *Risk Society: Towards a New Modernity.* London: Sage.

Becker, Howard, and Blanche Geer. 1957. "Participant Observation and Interviewing: A Comparison." *Human Organization* 16(3): 28–32. Available at https://doi.org/10.17730/humo.16.3.k687822132323013.

Benford, Robert D., and David A. Snow. 2000. "Framing Processes and Social Movements: An Overview and Assessment." *Annual Review of Sociology* 26(1): 611–39. Available at https://doi.org/10.1146/annurev.soc.26.1.611.

Bigelow, Bill. 2016. "Nation's Largest Teachers Union Endorses Teaching 'Climate Justice.'" *HuffPost*, July 16 (updated December 6, 2017). Available at https://www.huffpost.com/entry/nations-largest-teachers_b_11035072.

Bjurström, Andreas, and Merritt Polk. 2011. "Physical and Economic Bias in Climate Change Research: A Scientometric Study of IPCC Third Assessment Report." *Climatic Change* 108(1–2): 1–22. Available at https://doi.org/10.1007/s10584-011 -0018-8.

Bloomberg, Michael R. 2016. "Washington Won't Have Last Word on Climate Change." *Bloomberg News*, November 22. Available at http://www.bloomberg.com/view /articles/2016-11-22/washington-won-t-have-last-word-on-climate-change.

Bluestone, Barry, and Bennett Harrison. 1982. *The Deindustrialization of America: Plant Closings, Community Abandonment, and the Dismantling of Basic Industry.* New York: Basic Books.

Bond, Patrick. 2012. *Politics of Climate Justice: Paralysis Above, Movement Below.* Scotts-ville, South Africa: University of KwaZulu-Natal Press.

Bonfiglio, Michael, dir. 2017. *From the Ashes.* Film. Radical Media.

Boyce, James K. 2002. *The Political Economy of the Environment.* Northampton: Edward Elgar.

Brecher, Jeremy. 2008. "Labor's War on Global Warming." *The Nation*, March 10.

———. 2013. "Stormy Weather: Climate Change and a Divided Labor Movement." *New Labor Forum* 22(1): 75–81. Available at https://doi.org/10.1177/1095796012471308.

———. 2014. "'Jobs vs. the Environment': How to Counter This Divisive Big Lie." *The Nation*, April 22.

———. 2015. "A Superfund for Workers: How to Promote a Just Transition and Break Out of the Jobs vs. Environment Trap." *Dollars and Sense*, November/December.

———. 2017. *Climate Solidarity: Workers vs. Warming.* Waynesboro, VA: Labor Network for Sustainability and Stone Soup Books.

———. 2021. *Common Preservation in a Time of Mutual Destruction.* Oakland, CA: PM Press.

Brecher, Jeremy, Tim Costello, and Brendan Smith. 2000. *Globalization from Below: The Power of Solidarity.* Boston: South End.

Bronfenbrenner, Kate, and Tom Juravich. 1998. "It Takes More Than House Calls to Win: Organizing to Win with a Comprehensive Union-Building Strategy." In *Organizing to Win: New Research on Union Strategies*, edited by Kate Bronfenbrenner, Sheldon Friedman, Richard W. Hurd, Rudolph A. Oswald, and Ronald L. Seeber, 19–36. Ithaca: ILR/Cornell University Press.

Brown, Jenny. 2011. "Oil Pipeline Fight Roils Unions." Labor Notes. Labor Education and Research Project. November 7. Available at https://labornotes.org/2011/11/oil -pipeline-fight-roils-unions.

Brownstein, Ronald. 2016. "The Winds Are Changing for Renewable Energy." *The Atlantic*, July 7.

Buhle, Paul. 1999. *Taking Care of Business: Samuel Gompers, George Meany, Lane Kirkland and the Tragedy of American Labor.* New York: Monthly Review.

Bullard, Robert D. 1993. *Confronting Environmental Racism: Voices from the Grassroots.* Boston: South End.

Burawoy, Michael. 2004. "2004 Presidential Address: For Public Sociology." Author's website. Available at http://burawoy.berkeley.edu/Public%20Sociology,%20Live /Burawoy.pdf.

Calhoun, Craig. 1993. "'New Social Movements' of the Early Nineteenth Century." *Social Science History* 17(3): 385–427. Available at https://doi.org/10.2307/1171431.

Carroll, William K., and Robert S. Ratner. 1996. "Master Frames and Counter-Hegemony: Political Sensibilities in Contemporary Social Movements." *Canadian Review of Sociology/Revue Canadienne De Sociologie* 33(4): 407–35. Available at https://doi.org/10.1111/j.1755-618x.1996.tb00955.x.

Cha, J. Mijin, Vivian Price, Dimitris Stevis, Todd E. Vachon, and Maria Brescia-Weiler. 2021. *Workers and Communities in Transition: Report of the Just Transition Listening Project.* Report. Prepared for the Labor Network for Sustainability and Congressional Briefing.

Cha, J. Mijin, and Todd E. Vachon. 2021. "Climate Change and the Future of Workers: Toward a Just Transition." In *Revaluing Work(ers): Toward a Democratic and Sustainable Future*, edited by Tobias Schulze-Cleven and Todd E. Vachon, 101–20. Ithaca: Cornell University Press.

Chaison, Gary N. 1980. "A Note on Union Merger Trends, 1900–1978." *ILR Review* 34(1): 114–20. Available at https://doi.org/10.1177/001979398003400109.

Cillizza, Chris. 2019. "Nancy Pelosi Just Threw Some Serious Shade at Alexandria Ocasio-Cortez's 'Green New Deal.'" CNN Politics, February 8. Available at https://www.cnn.com/2019/02/07/politics/pelosi-alexandria-ocasio-cortez-green-new-deal/index.html.

CJA. 2013. "Public Letter to AFL-CIO." September 8. Available at https://ecosocialists vancouver.org/sites/default/files/images/AFL-CIO.pdf.

———. 2018. "CJA Letter to AFL-CIO on Dakota Access." May 22. Available at https://climatejusticealliance.org/cja-letter-to-afl-cio-on-dakota-access.

———. 2021. "What Do We Mean by Just Transition?" February 19. Available at https://climatejusticealliance.org/just-transition.

———. 2022. "The Inflation Reduction Act is NOT a Climate Justice Bell." August 6. Available at: https://climatejusticealliance.org/the-inflation-reduction-act-is-not-a-climate-justice-bill/.

Clawson, Dan. 2003. *The Next Upsurge: Labor and the New Social Movements.* Ithaca: Cornell University Press.

Clifton, Rita, Sam Ricketts, Jessica Eckdish, Malkie Wall, Kevin Lee, and Karla Walter. 2021. *The Clean Economy Revolution Will Be Unionized. Center for American Progress.* Report. Available at https://www.americanprogress.org/article/clean-economy-revolution-will-unionized.

CNN Money. 2014. "Fortune: Global 500 2013." Available at https://money.cnn.com/magazines/fortune/global500/2013/full_list.

Collins, Chuck. 2014. "Can We Earn a Living on a Living Planet? The Need for Jobs, and the Ecological Limits to Growth." *American Prospect*, October 13. Available at https://prospect.org/power/must-environmentalists-labor-activists-find-odds-other.

Commons, John R. 1918. *History of Labour in the United States.* New York: Beard Books.

Cook, John, Geoffrey Supran, Stephan Lewandowsky, Naomi Oreskes, and Edward Maibach. 2019. *America Misled: How the Fossil Fuel Industry Deliberately Misled Americans about Climate Change.* Report. Center for Climate Change Communication. Available at https://www.climatechangecommunication.org/wp-content/uploads/2019/10/America_Misled.pdf.

Corbett, Jessica. 2018. "Backed by Ocasio-Cortez, Youth Climate Activists Arrested at Pelosi's Office Demanding Democrats Embrace 'Green New Deal.'" *Common Dreams*, November 13. Available at https://www.commondreams.org/news/2018/11/13/backed-ocasio-cortez-youth-climate-activists-arrested-pelosis-office-demanding.

Corgey, Dean. 2010. "Lack of Union Workers Hurts Offshore Oil Industry." *Houston Chronicle*, June 10. Available at https://www.chron.com/opinion/outlook/article/Lack-of-union-workers-hurts-offshore-oil-industry-1716136.php.

Cornfield, Daniel B., and Holly J. McCammon. 2010. "Approaching Merger: The Converging Public Policy Agendas of the AFL and CIO, 1938–1955." In *Strategic Alliances: Coalition Building and Social Movements*, edited by Nella Van Dyke and Holly J. McCammon, 79–98. Minneapolis: University of Minnesota Press.

Cunniah, Dan. 2010. "Climate Change and Labour: The Need for a Just Transition." *International Journal of Labour Research* 2: 121–23.

Davenport, Coral. 2016. "Donald Trump, in Pittsburgh, Pledges to Boost Both Coal and Gas." *New York Times*, September 23. Available at https://www.nytimes.com/2016/09/23/us/politics/donald-trump-fracking.html.

Demaria, Federico, François Schneider, Filka Sekulova, and Joan Martinez-Alier. 2013. "What Is Degrowth? From an Activist Slogan to a Social Movement." *Environmental Values* 22(2): 191–215. Available at https://doi.org/10.3197/096327113x13581561725194.

DeMoro, RoseAnn. 2015. "Populist Proposals Remind Why Nurses Trust Bernie Sanders to Heal America." National Nurses United. October 31. Available at https://www.nationalnursesunited.org/blog/populist-poposals-remind-why-nurses-trust-bernie-sanders-heal-america.

Dewey, Scott. 1998. "Working for the Environment: Organized Labor and the Origins of Environmentalism in the United States, 1948–1970." *Environmental History* 3(1): 45–63. Available at https://doi.org/10.2307/3985426.

DiMaggio, Paul. 1991 (2012). "Constructing an Organizational Field as a Professional Project: The Case of US Art Museums." In *Institutional Theory in Organizational Studies*, edited by Royston Greenwood, Kerstin Shalin, Roy Sudaby, and Christine Oliver. Thousand Oaks, CA: Sage.

Dodge, Mary Mapes. 1918. *Hans Brinker, or The Silver Skates*. New York: McKay.

Downey, Liam. 2015. *Inequality, Democracy, and the Environment*. New York: New York University Press.

Dunlap, Riley E., and Robert J. Brulle. 2015. *Climate Change and Society: Sociological Perspectives*. New York: Oxford University Press.

Durbin, Kathie. 1998. *Tree Huggers: Victory, Defeat and Renewal in the Northwest Ancient Forest Campaign*. Seattle: Mountaineers Books.

Eidelson, Josh. 2018. "Tesla Workers Start a Drive to Unionize Solar-Panel Factory." Bloomberg Law. December 13. Available at https://news.bloomberglaw.com/daily-labor-report/tesla-workers-start-a-drive-to-unionize-solar-panel-factory-1.

Erlandson, David A., Edward L. Harris, Barbara L. Skipper, and Steve D. Allen. 1993. *Doing Naturalistic Inquiry: A Guide to Methods*. Newbury Park, CA: Sage.

Esping-Anderson, Gosta. 1990. *The Three Worlds of Welfare Capitalism*. Princeton, NJ: Princeton University Press.

Estabrook, Thomas, Charles Levenstein, and John Wooding. 2018. *Labor–Environmental Coalitions: Lessons from a Louisiana Petrochemical Region.* Oxfordshire: Routledge.

Evans, Rhonda, and Tamara Kay. 2008. "How Environmentalists 'Greened' Trade Policy: Strategic Action and the Architecture of Field Overlap." *American Sociological Review* 73(6): 970–91. Available at https://doi.org/10.1177/000312240807300605.

Farnhill, Thomas. 2014. "Environmental Policy-Making at the British Trades Union Congress 1967–2011." *Capitalism, Nature, Socialism* 25(1): 72–95. Available at https://doi.org/10.1080/10455752.2013.879196.

———. 2016. "Characteristics of Environmentally Active Trade Unions in the United Kingdom." *Global Labor Journal* 7: 257–78.

Fatton, Dan. 2017. "Op-Ed: Sink or Swim? Time for Serious Action on Climate in NJ." *NJ Spotlight News*, September 3. Available at https://www.njspotlightnews.org/2017/10/17-10-02-op-ed-or-swim-time-for-serious-action-on-climate-in-nj.

Fine, Janice, and Daniel J. Tichenor. 2009. "A Movement Wrestling: American Labor's Enduring Struggle with Immigration, 1866–2007." *Studies in American Political Development* 23(1): 84–113. Available at https://doi.org/10.1017/s0898588x09000042.

Fletcher, Bill, and Fernando Gapasin. 2008. *Solidarity Divided: The Crisis in Organized Labor and a New Path toward Social Justice.* Berkeley: University of California Press.

Florida, Richard. 2011. "The Geography of How We Get to Work." *The Atlantic*, July 13. Available at https://www.theatlantic.com/national/archive/2011/07/the-geography-of-how-we-get-to-work/240258.

Foster, John Bellamy. 1993. "The Limits of Environmentalism without Class: Lessons from the Ancient Forest Struggle of the Pacific Northwest." *Capitalism Nature Socialism* 4(1): 11–41. Available at https://doi.org/10.1080/10455759309358529.

———. 2000. *Marx's Ecology: Materialism and Nature.* New York: Monthly Review.

Funk, Cary, and Brian Kennedy. 2020. "How Americans See Climate Change and the Environment in 7 Charts." Pew Research Center. July 27. Available at https://www.pewresearch.org/fact-tank/2020/04/21/how-americans-see-climate-change-and-the-environment-in-7-charts.

Gall, Meredith, Joyce Gall, and Walter Borg. 2003. *Educational Research: An Introduction.* Boston: A and B Publications.

Gamson, Josh. 1989. "Silence, Death, and the Invisible Enemy: AIDS Activism and Social Movement 'Newness.'" *Social Problems* 36(4): 351–67. Available at https://doi.org/10.2307/800820.

Geels, Frank W., and Johan Schot. 2007. "Typology of Sociotechnical Transition Pathways." *Research Policy* 36(3): 399–417. Available at https://doi.org/10.1016/j.respol.2007.01.003.

Gerard, Leo. 2017. "Workers Want a Green Economy, Not a Black Environment." *Huff-Post*, June 2. Available at https://www.huffingtonpost.com/entry/workers-want-a-green-economy-not-a-black-environment_us_593068c2e4b09e93d7964899.

Gitelman, Howard M. 1965. "Adolph Strasser and the Origins of Pure and Simple Unionism." *Labor History* 6(1): 71–83. Available at https://doi.org/10.1080/00236566508583956.

Global Wind Energy Council. 2018. "Wind Power Chalks Up More Strong Numbers." November 12. Available at https://gwec.net/wind-power-chalks-up-more-strong -numbers.

Goffman, Erving. 1974. *Frame Analysis: An Essay on the Organization of Experience*. Cambridge, MA: Harvard University Press.

Goodstein, Eban S. 1999. *The Trade-Off Myth: Fact and Fiction about Jobs and the Environment*. Washington, DC: Island.

Gordon, Robert W. 2004. *Environmental Blues: Working-Class Environmentalism and the Labor–Environmental Alliance, 1968–1985*. Detroit: Wayne State University Press.

Gould, Kenneth A., David N. Pellow, and Allan Schnaiberg. 2004. "Interrogating the Treadmill of Production." *Organization and Environment* 17(3): 296–316. Available at https://doi.org/10.1177/1086026604268747.

Gramsci, Antonio. 1971. *Selections from the Prison Notebooks*. London: Lawrence and Wishart.

Greenhouse, Steven. 2020. "Op-Ed: Coronavirus Is Unleashing Righteous Worker Anger and a New Wave of Unionism." *Los Angeles Times*, July 28. Available at https:// www.latimes.com/opinion/story/2020-07-28/coronavirus-workers-unions-em ployers-pandemic.

Guggenheim, David, dir. 2006. *An Inconvenient Truth: A Global Warning*. Film. Paramount.

Hackmann, Heide, Susanne C. Moser, and Asuncion Lera St. Clair. 2014. "The Social Heart of Global Environmental Change." *Nature Climate Change* 4(8): 653–55. Available at https://doi.org/10.1038/nclimate2320.

Haider-Markel, Donald P., and Mark R. Joslyn. 2017. "Not Threat, but Threatening: Potential Causes and Consequences of Gay Innumeracy." *Journal of Homosexuality* 65(11): 1527–42. Available at https://doi.org/10.1080/00918369.2017.1377490.

Hall, Peter A., and David Soskice, eds. 2001. *Varieties of Capitalism: The Institutional Foundations of Comparative Advantage*. Oxford: Oxford University Press.

Hall, Stuart, and Janet Woollacott. 1982. "The Rediscovery of Ideology: Return to the Repressed in Media Studies." In *Culture, Society, and the Media*, edited by Michael Gurevitch, Tony Bennett, and Tony Curran, 56–90. New York: Methuen.

Hampton, Paul. 2015. *Workers and Trade Unions for Climate Solidarity: Tackling Climate Change in a Neoliberal World*. Oxfordshire: Routledge.

Harden, Blaine. 2007. "Conservation Group, Unions Joining Forces." *Washington Post*, January 16. Available at https://www.washingtonpost.com/wp-dyn/content/article /2007/01/15/AR2007011501022.html.

Harvey, David. 2007. *A Brief History of Neoliberalism*. Oxford: Oxford University Press.

Hayes, Christopher. 2021. *The Harlem Uprising: Segregation and Inequality in Postwar New York City*. New York: Columbia University Press.

Hegel, Georg Wilhelm Friedrich. 1820 (2005). *Elements of the Philosophy of Right*. Indianapolis: Hackett.

Hertel-Fernandez, Alexander, Suresh Naidu, Adam Reich, and Patrick Youngblood. 2020. *Understanding the COVID-19 Workplace: Evidence from a Survey of Essential Workers*. Issue Brief. Roosevelt Institute. Available at https://rooseveltinstitute.org

/wp-content/uploads/2020/07/RI_SurveryofEssentialWorkers_IssueBrief_202
006-1.pdf.

Hertsgaard, Mark. 2014. "The People's Climate March Was Huge, but Will It Change
Everything?" *The Nation*, September 21.

Hirsch, Barry T., and David A. Macpherson. 2017. "Union Membership and Coverage
Database." UnionStats. Available at http://www.unionstats.com.

———. 2018. "Union Membership and Coverage Database from the Current Population Survey: A Note." UnionStats. Available at http://unionstats.gsu.edu/Hirsch
-Macpherson_ILRR_CPS-Union-Database.pdf.

Hochschild, Arlie R. 2016. *Strangers in Their Own Land: Anger and Mourning on the
American Right*. New York: New Press.

Howarth, Robert W., Renee Santoro, and Anthony Ingraffea. 2011. "Methane and the
Greenhouse-Gas Footprint of Natural Gas from Shale Formations." *Climatic Change*
106(4): 679–90. Available at https://doi.org/10.1007/s10584-011-0061-5.

Hyde, Allen, and Todd E. Vachon. 2019. "Running with or against the Treadmill? Labor Unions, Institutional Contexts, and Greenhouse Gas Emissions in a Comparative Perspective." *Environmental Sociology* 5(3): 269–82. Available at https://doi.org
/10.1080/23251042.2018.1544107.

Inglehart, Ronald. 1977. "Long Term Trends in Mass Support for European Unifica-
tion." *Government and Opposition* 12(2): 150–77. Available at https://doi.org/10
.1111/j.1477-7053.1977.tb00529.x.

Inglehart, Ronald, and Pippa Norris. 2010. *Rising Tide: Gender Equality and Cultural
Change around the World*. Cambridge: Cambridge University Press.

Institute for Energy Research. 2012. *Hard Facts: An Energy Primer*. Available at https://
www.instituteforenergyresearch.org/wp-content/uploads/2009/04/Hard-Facts
-Final.pdf.

International Energy Agency and Nuclear Energy Agency. 2021. "Projected Costs of
Generating Electricity—2020 Edition." Nuclear Energy Agency. March 5. Available at https://www.oecd-nea.org/jcms/pl_51110/projected-costs-of-generating
-electricity-2020-edition.

IPCC. 2014. *Climate Change 2013: The Physical Science Basis. Fifth Assessment Report of the
Intergovernmental Panel on Climate Change*. Cambridge: Cambridge University Press.

IRENA. 2020. *Renewable Power Generation Costs in 2019*. Available at https://www
.irena.org/-/media/Files/IRENA/Agency/Publication/2020/Jun/IRENA_Power
_Generation_Costs_2019.pdf.

Irons, Meghan E. 2013. "Letter Carrier Complained about Heat before Collapse." *Boston Globe*, July 10.

Jacobs, Tom. 2017. "There Aren't as Many Gay People as You Think." *Pacific Standard*,
October 18.

Jaeger, Joel. 2021. "Explaining the Exponential Growth of Renewable Energy." World
Resources Institute. September 20. Available at https://www.wri.org/insights
/growth-renewable-energy-sector-explained.

Jenkins, Cameron. 2021. "David Attenborough to UN: Climate Change Is Biggest
Threat Modern Humans Have Ever Faced." *The Hill*, February 23. Available at
https://thehill.com/homenews/news/540058-david-attenborough-warns-un-secu
rity-council-on-climate-change-i-dont-envy-you.

Jenkins, J. Craig. 1977. "Radical Transformation of Organizational Goals." *Administrative Science Quarterly* 22(4): 568–86. Available at https://doi.org/10.2307/2392401.

———. 1983. "Resource Mobilization Theory and the Study of Social Movements." *Annual Review of Sociology* 9(1): 527–53. Available at https://doi.org/10.1146/an nurev.so.09.080183.002523.

Jenkins, J. Craig, and Charles Perrow. 1977. "Insurgency of the Powerless: Farm Worker Movements (1946–1972)." *American Sociological Review* 42(2): 249–68. Available at https://doi.org/10.2307/2094604.

Johnston, Paul. 1994. *Success While Others Fail: Social Movement Unionism and the Public Workplace.* Ithaca, NY: Cornell University Press/ILR Press.

Kawulich, Barbara B. 2005. "Participant Observation as a Data Collection Method." *Forum: Qualitative Social Research* 6: 1–22.

Kazis, Richard, and Richard Lee Grossman. 1982. *Fear at Work: Job Blackmail, Labor and the Environment.* New York: Pilgrim.

Kimeldorf, Howard. 1999. *Battling for American Labor: Wobblies, Craft Workers, and the Making of the Union Movement.* Berkeley: University of California Press.

Kishore, Nishant, Domingo Marqués, Ayesha Mahmud, Matthew V. Kiang, Irmary Rodriguez, Arlan Fuller, Peggy Ebner, et al. 2018. "Mortality in Puerto Rico after Hurricane Maria." *New England Journal of Medicine* 379(17): 1801–7. Available at https://doi.org/10.1056/nejmc1810872.

Klein, Naomi. 2007. *The Shock Doctrine: The Rise of Disaster Capitalism.* New York: Macmillan.

———. 2014. *This Changes Everything: Capitalism vs. the Climate.* New York: Simon and Schuster.

Knowlton, Peter, and John Braxton. 2021. "Viewpoint: Climate Justice Must Be a Top Priority for Labor." Labor Notes. September 21. Available at https://labornotes.org /2021/09/viewpoint-climate-justice-must-be-top-priority-labor.

Kojola, Erik. 2015. "(Re)Constructing the Pipeline: Workers, Environmentalists and Ideology in Media Coverage of the Keystone XL Pipeline." *Critical Sociology* 43(6): 893–917. Available at https://doi.org/10.1177/0896920515598564.

Kolbert, Elizabeth. 2014. *The Sixth Extinction: An Unnatural History.* New York: Henry Holt.

Kornbluh, Joyce L. 1964. *Rebel Voices: An Industrial Workers of the World Anthology.* Chicago: Charles H. Kerr.

Lambert, Rob. 1990. "Kilusang Mayo Uno and the Rise of Social Movement Unionism in the Philippines." *Labour and Industry* 3(2–3): 258–80. Available at https://doi .org/10.1080/10301763.1990.10669088.

Lambert, Rob, and Eddie Webster. 1988. "The Re-emergence of Political Unionism in Contemporary South Africa?" In *Popular Struggles in South Africa,* edited by William Cobbett and Robin Cohen, 20–41. London: James Currey.

Larson, Simeon, and Bruce Nissen, eds. 1987. *Theories of the Labor Movement.* Detroit: Wayne State University Press.

Leiserowitz, Anthony A., Robert W. Kates, and Thomas M. Parris. 2005. "Do Global Attitudes and Behaviors Support Sustainable Development?" *Environment: Science and Policy for Sustainable Development* 47(9): 22–38. Available at https://doi.org /10.3200/envt.47.9.22-38.

Leopold, Les. 2007. *The Man Who Hated Work and Loved Labor: The Life and Times of Tony Mazzocchi*. White River Junction, VT: Chelsea Green.

Levin, Kelly. 2018. "New Global CO_2 Emissions Numbers Are In: They're Not Good." World Resources Institute. December 5. Available at https://www.wri.org/blog /2018/12/new-global-co2-emissions-numbers-are-they-re-not-good.

Lewis, Avi, dir. 2016. *This Changes Everything*. Film. Klein Lewis Productions and Louver- ture Films.

Lijphart, Arend. 2020. *The Politics of Accommodation: Pluralism and Democracy in the Netherlands*. Berkeley: University of California Press.

LIUNA. 2016. "LIUNA Re-elects Leadership and Charts Determined, Optimistic Agen- da at Its International Convention." Laborers' International Union of North Ameri- ca. September 26. Available at https://www.liuna.org/news/story/liuna-re-elects-lead ership-and-charts-determined-optimistic-agenda-at-its-international-convention.

Loomis, Erik. 2016. *Empire of Timber: Labor Unions and the Pacific Northwest Forests*. New York: Cambridge University Press.

Lopez, Stephen Henry. 2004. *Reorganizing the Rustbelt: An Inside Study of the American Labor Movement*. Berkeley: University of California Press.

MacGillis, Alec. 2018. "Why Do Americans Stay When Their Town Has No Future?" *Bloomberg Businessweek*, May 23.

Mahoney, James, and Kathleen Ann Thelen, eds. 2010. *Explaining Institutional Change: Ambiguity, Agency, and Power*. New York: Cambridge University Press.

Maloney, Bill. 2018. "Renewable Energy Subsidies—Yes or No?" *Forbes*, March 23.

Manheim, Jarol B. 2001. *The Death of a Thousand Cuts: Corporate Campaigns and the Attack on the Corporation*. Mahwah, NJ: Lawrence Erlbaum.

Mann, Michael. 1988. "Societies as Organized Power Networks." In *The Sources of Social Power*, vol. 1, 1–33. Cambridge: Cambridge University Press.

Manser, Martin H. 2007. *The Facts on File Dictionary of Proverbs*. New York: Infobase.

Marshall, Catherine, and Gretchen B. Rossman. 1989. *Designing Qualitative Research*. Newbury Park, CA: Sage.

Martin, Andrew W. 2008. "The Institutional Logic of Union Organizing and the Ef- fectiveness of Social Movement Repertoires." *American Journal of Sociology* 113(4): 1067–1103. Available at https://doi.org/10.1086/522806.

Marx, Karl, and Friedrich Engels. 2009. *The Economic and Philosophic Manuscripts of 1844 and the Communist Manifesto*. New York: Prometheus Books.

Masson-Delmotte, V., P. Zhai, A. Pirani, S. L. Connors, C. Péan, S. Berger, N. Caud, et al., eds. 2021. *Climate Change 2021: The Physical Science Basis: Contribution of Working Group I to the Sixth Assessment Report of the Intergovernmental Panel on Climate Change*. Cambridge: Cambridge University Press.

Mayer, Brian. 2009. *Blue–Green Coalitions: Fighting for Safe Workplaces and Healthy Communities*. Ithaca, NY: Cornell/ILR Press.

Mazzocchi, Tony. 1993. "A Superfund for Workers." *Earth Island Journal* 9(1): 40–42.

McAdam, Doug. 1982. *Political Process and the Development of Black Insurgency, 1930– 1970*. Chicago: University of Chicago Press.

McAdam, Doug, Sidney Tarrow, and Charles Tilly. 2001. *Dynamics of Contention*. New York: Cambridge University Press.

———. 2003. "Dynamics of Contention." *Social Movement Studies* 2: 99–102.

McAlevey, Jane. 2018a. *No Shortcuts: Organizing for Power in the New Gilded Age.* New York: Oxford University Press.

———. 2018b. "The West Virginia Teachers Strike Shows That Winning Big Requires Creating a Crisis." *The Nation*, March 12.

McCallion, Michael J., and David R. Maines. 1999. "The Liturgical Social Movement in the Vatican II Catholic Church." *Research in Social Movements, Conflict and Change* 21: 125–49.

McCammon, Holly J., Karen E. Campbell, Ellen M. Granberg, and Christine Mowery. 2001. "How Movements Win: Gendered Opportunity Structures and U.S. Women's Suffrage Movements, 1866 to 1919." *American Sociological Review* 66(1): 49–70. Available at https://doi.org/10.2307/2657393.

McCarthy, John D., and Mayer N. Zald. 1977. "Resource Mobilization and Social Movements: A Partial Theory." *American Journal of Sociology* 82(6): 1212–41.

McCartin, Joseph A. 2016. "Bargaining for the Common Good." *Dissent* 63(2): 128–35. Available at https://doi.org/10.1353/dss.2016.0029.

McCright, Aaron M., and Riley E. Dunlap. 2003. "Defeating Kyoto: The Conservative Movement's Impact on U.S. Climate Change Policy." *Social Problems* 50(3): 348–73. Available at https://doi.org/10.1525/sp.2003.50.3.348.

McElwee, Sean, Julian Brave NoiseCat, John L. Ray, and Jason Ganz. 2019. "Memo: The Green New Deal Is Popular." Data for Progress. June 7. Available at https://www.dataforprogress.org/memos/the-green-new-deal-is-popular.

McGeehan, Patrick. 2012. "Nearly 30,000 Jobs Lost Because of Hurricane Sandy." *New York Times*, December 20. Available at https://cityroom.blogs.nytimes.com/2012/12/20/nearly-30000-jobs-lost-due-to-sandy.

McKibben, Bill. 1989. *The End of Nature.* New York: Random House.

McNicholas, Celine, Lynn Rhinehart, Margaret Poydock, Heidi Shierholz, and Daniel Perez. 2020. *Why Unions Are Good for Workers—Especially in a Crisis like COVID-19.* Economic Policy Institute. Available at https://www.epi.org/publication/why-unions-are-good-for-workers-especially-in-a-crisis-like-covid-19-12-policies-that-would-boost-worker-rights-safety-and-wages.

Meadowcroft, James. 2011. "Engaging with the Politics of Sustainability Transitions." *Environmental Innovation and Societal Transitions* 1(1): 70–75. Available at https://doi.org/10.1016/j.eist.2011.02.003.

Melucci, Alberto. 1985. "The Symbolic Challenge of Contemporary Movements." *Social Research* 52: 789–816.

———. 1996. *Challenging Codes: Collective Action in the Information Age.* Cambridge: Cambridge University Press.

Mesey, Christel. 2018. "Greta Thunberg's Speech to the World." *Geneva Business News*, December 21. Available at https://www.gbnews.ch/greta-thunbergs-speech-to-the-world.

Michels, Robert. 1915 (1962). *Political Parties: A Sociological Study of the Oligarchical Tendencies of Modern Democracy.* New York: Hearst's International.

Miller, Char. 2015. "When Firefighters Speak Out on Climate Change, We Ought to Listen Up." *The Guardian*, August 24.

Milman, Oliver. 2018. "Ex-Nasa Scientist: 30 Years On, World Is Failing 'Miserably' to Address Climate Change." *The Guardian*, June 19. Available at https://www

.theguardian.com/environment/2018/jun/19/james-hansen-nasa-scientist-climate
-change-warning.

Moody, Kim. 1997. *Workers in a Lean World: Unions in the International Economy.* New York: Verso.

Munguia, Hayley. 2014. "How Many People Really Showed Up to the People's Climate March?" FiveThirtyEight. September 30. Available at https://fivethirtyeight.com /features/peoples-climate-march-attendance.

National Centers for Environmental Information. n.d. "Billion-Dollar Weather and Climate Disasters." Accessed December 21, 2021. Available at https://www.ncdc .noaa.gov/billions/events/US/1980-2017.

National Commission for the Protection of Human Subjects of Biomedical and Behavioral Research. 1978. *The Belmont Report: Ethical Principles and Guidelines for the Protection of Human Subjects of Research.* Bethesda: National Commission for the Protection of Human Subjects of Biomedical and Behavioral Research.

NEA. n.d. "Community Schools." Accessed December 15, 2021. Available at https:// www.nea.org/student-success/smart-just-policies/community-schools.

Nelson, Barbara J. 1984. *Making an Issue of Child Abuse.* Chicago: University of Chicago Press.

Net Zero Plus. 2016. "Nation's Largest Net Zero Plus™ Commercial Building Retrofit Opens in Los Angeles." Net Zero Plus Electrical Training Institute. June 6. Available at http://nzp-eti.com/author/tesla.

Newell, Peter, and Dustin Mulvaney. 2013. "The Political Economy of the 'Just Transition.'" *Geographical Journal* 179(2): 132–40. Available at https://doi.org/10.1111 /geoj.12008.

NOAA. 2017. "Carbon Cycle Greenhouse Gases." Earth System Research Laboratory, Global Monitoring Division. Available at https://gml.noaa.gov/ccgg/trends.

Obach, Brian K. 2004. *Labor and the Environmental Movement: The Quest for Common Ground.* Cambridge, MA: MIT Press.

Oil Change International. 2015. "Profits for Oil, Gas and Coal Companies Operating in the U.S. and Canada." May 14. Available at http://priceofoil.org/profits-oil-gas -coal-companies-operating-u-s-canada.

Okereke, Chukwumerije. 2010. "Climate Justice and the International Regime." *Wiley Interdisciplinary Reviews: Climate Change* 1(3): 462–74. Available at https://doi.org /10.1002/wcc.52.

Oliver, Pamela, and Hank Johnston. 2000. "What a Good Idea! Ideologies and Frames in Social Movement Research." *Mobilization: An International Quarterly* 5(1): 37–54. Available at https://doi.org/10.17813/maiq.5.1.g54k222086346251.

Oreskes, Naomi. 2004. "The Scientific Consensus on Climate Change." *Science* 306 (5702): 1686.

Parthun, Neil. 2010. "Judi Bari, the IWW and Environmentalism." *The Public*, April 10. Available at http://publici.ucimc.org/judi-bari-the-iww-and-environmentalism.

Patashnik, Eric M. 2008. *Reforms at Risk: What Happens after Major Policy Changes Are Enacted?* Princeton, NJ: Princeton University Press.

Peck, Jamie. 1998. "Geographies of Governance: TECS and the Neo-liberalisation of 'Local Interests.'" *Space and Polity* 2(1): 5–31. Available at https://doi.org/10.1080 /13562579808721768.

People vs. Fossil Fuels. 2022. "Opposition to Fossil Fuel Project Approvals and Permitting Reforms Conditioned on the Inflation Reduction Act." *People vs Fossil Fuels*, August 24. Available at https://peoplevsfossilfuels.org/dirty-deal-letter/.

Perlman, Selig. 1949. *A Theory of the Labor Movement*. New York: A. M. Kelley.

Pettenger, Mary E. 2013. *The Social Construction of Climate Change: Power, Knowledge, Norms, Discourses*. New York: Routledge.

Pires, José, Fernando Martins, Maria Da Conceição Alvim-Ferraz, and Manuel Simões. 2011. "Recent Developments on Carbon Capture and Storage: An Overview." *Chemical Engineering Research and Design* 89(9): 1446–60. Available at https://doi.org /10.1016/j.cherd.2011.01.028.

Piven, Frances Fox, and Richard A. Cloward. 1979. *Poor People's Movements: Why They Succeed, How They Fail*. New York: Vintage.

Plumbers and Fitters Local 392. 2016. "Resolution to Face the Realities of Climate Change." UA Local 393. Available at https://ualocal393.org/resolutions.

Plumer, Brad. 2016. "Solar Power Is Contagious: These Maps Show How It Spreads." *Vox*, May 4. Available at https://www.vox.com/2016/5/4/11590396/solar-power -contagious-maps.

Polanyi, Karl. 1944. *The Great Transformation: The Political and Economic Origins of Our Time*. New York: Reinhart.

Polletta, Francesca. 1998. "'It Was like a Fever . . .': Narrative and Identity in Social Protest." *Social Problems* 45(2): 137–59. Available at https://doi.org/10.2307/3097241.

———. 2008. "Culture and Movements." *Annals of the American Academy of Political and Social Science* 619(1): 78–96. Available at https://doi.org/10.1177/000271620 8320042.

Pollin, Robert, Jeanette Wicks-Lim, Shouvik Chakraborty, Caitlin Kline, and Gregor Semieniuk. 2021. "A Program for Economic Recovery and Clean Energy Transition in California." Political Economy Research Institute, University of Massachusetts Amherst. June 8. Available at https://peri.umass.edu/images/CA-CleanEnergy -6-8-21.pdf.

Ponsot, Beth. 2012. "An Interview with Jill Stein." WNET/PBS. Available at https:// www.pbs.org/wnet/need-to-know/environment/the-green-new-deal/15371.

Pope, Carl. 2008. "The Straight Talk Express Needs a Teamster at the Wheel." *HuffPost*, August 1. Available at https://www.huffpost.com/entry/the-straight-talk-ex press_b_114778?ec_carp=7006123098471081398.

Popovich, Nadja, and Tatiana Schlossberg. 2017. "23 Environmental Rules Rolled Back in Trump's First 100 Days." *New York Times*, May 2. Available at https://www.ny times.com/interactive/2017/05/02/climate/environmental-rules-reversed-trump-100 -days.html.

Räthzel, Nora, and David L. Uzzell. 2013. *Trade Unions in the Green Economy: Working for the Environment*. London: Routledge.

Rector, Josiah. 2014. "Environmental Justice at Work: The UAW, the War on Cancer, and the Right to Equal Protection from Toxic Hazards in Postwar America." *Journal of American History* 101(2): 480–502. Available at https://doi.org/10.1093/jahist/jau380.

———. 2018. "The Spirit of Black Lake: Full Employment, Civil Rights, and the Forgotten Early History of Environmental Justice." *Modern American History* 1(1): 45–66. Available at https://doi.org/10.1017/mah.2017.18.

Rhomberg, Chris. 2021. "Work and Workers in the United States: A Historic Turning Point?" *La Nouvelle Revue Du Travail*, no. 19. Available at https://doi.org/10.4000/nrt.10213.

Richardson, Jeremy, and Lee Anderson. 2021. *Supporting the Nation's Coal Workers and Communities in a Changing Energy Landscape*. Washington, DC: Union of Concerned Scientists.

Robinson, Ian. 2000. "Neoliberal Restructuring and U.S. Unions: Toward Social Movement Unionism?" *Critical Sociology* 26(1–2): 109–38. Available at https://doi.org/10.1177/08969205000260010701.

Rogers, Norman. 2021. "If Our Oil Jobs Are Ending, We Need Safety Nets and Good Replacement Work." *Los Angeles Times*, October 23. Available at https://www.latimes.com/opinion/story/2021-10-23/oil-gas-jobs-clean-energy-california.

Rudel, Thomas K., J. Timmons Roberts, and JoAnn Carmin. 2011. "Political Economy of the Environment." *Annual Review of Sociology* 37(1): 221–38. Available at https://doi.org/10.1146/annurev.soc.012809.102639.

Russill, Chris, and Zoe Nyssa. 2009. "The Tipping Point Trend in Climate Change Communication." *Global Environmental Change* 19(3): 336–44. Available at https://doi.org/10.1016/j.gloenvcha.2009.04.001.

Rutgers AAUP-AFT. 2021. "Resolution in Support of the Green New Deal, Student Climate Strikes, and a Climate Action Plan for Rutgers University." March 9. Available at https://rutgersaaup.org/green-new-deal-support.

Sagan, Carl E. 1980. "One Voice in the Cosmic Fugue." Season 1, episode 2. *Cosmos: A Personal Voyage*. Arlington: PBS.

Sainato, Michael. 2021. "Labor and Environmentalist Movements Team Up and Win Big in Illinois." *Real News Network*, September 28. Available at https://therealnews.com/labor-and-environmentalist-movements-team-up-and-win-big-in-illinois.

Schaal, Eric. 2018. "These States Are Completely Missing Out on Solar Power." Showbiz Cheat Sheet. May 8. Available at https://www.cheatsheet.com/culture/states-cities/these-states-are-completely-missing-out-on-solar-power.html.

Schiavone, Michael. 2007. "Moody's Account of Social Movement Unionism: An Analysis." *Critical Sociology* 33(1–2): 279–309. Available at https://doi.org/10.1163/156916307x168665.

Schickler, Eric. 2001. "Congressional History: New Branches on Mature Trees History." *Legislative Scholar*, newsletter of the Legislative Studies Section of the American Political Science Association, July.

Schlossberg, Tatiana. 2016. "As Trump Signals Climate Action Pullback, Local Leaders Push Forward." *New York Times*, December 16. Available at https://www.nytimes.com/2016/12/16/science/local-government-climate-change-efforts.html.

Schnaiberg, Allan. 1980. *The Environment: From Surplus to Scarcity*. New York: Oxford University Press.

Schwartz, John. 2017. "Students, Cities and States Take the Climate Fight to Court." *New York Times*, August 10. Available at http://www.nytimes.com/2017/08/10/climate/climate-change-lawsuits-courts.html.

Scipes, Kim. 1992. "Understanding the New Labor Movements in the 'Third World': The Emergence of Social Movement Unionism." *Critical Sociology* 19(2): 81–101. Available at https://doi.org/10.1177/089692059201900204.

———. 2014. "Social Movement Unionism or Social Justice Unionism? Disentangling Theoretical Confusion within the Global Labor Movement." *Class, Race and Corporate Power* 2(3): 1–43. Available at https://doi.org/10.25148/crcp.2.3.16092119.

Scoones, Ian, Melissa Leach, Adrian Smith, Sigrid Stagl, Andy Stirling, and John Thompson. 2007. "Dynamic Systems and the Challenge of Sustainability." STEPS Working Paper 1. Brighton, U.K.: STEPS Centre.

Scrase, Ivan, and Adrian Smith. 2009. "The (Non-)Politics of Managing Low Carbon Socio-Technical Transitions." *Environmental Politics* 18(5): 707–26. Available at https://doi.org/10.1080/09644010903157008.

Seidman, Steven. 2002. *Beyond the Closet: The Transformation of Gay and Lesbian Life.* New York: Routledge.

Sharp, Gene. 2005. *Waging Nonviolent Struggle: 20th Century Practice and 21st Century Potential.* Boston: Porter Sargent.

Sheppard, Kate. 2014. "Union Miners Rally at EPA to Protest New Emissions Standards." *HuffPost*, October 7. Available at https://www.huffpost.com/entry/united-mine-workers-epa-emissions_n_5948344.

Silverman, Victor. 2004. "Sustainable Alliances: The Origins of International Labor Environmentalism." *International Labor and Working-Class History* 66: 118–35. Available at https://doi.org/10.1017/s0147547904000201.

———. 2006. "'Green Unions in a Grey World': Labor Environmentalisms and International Institutions." *Organization and Environment* 19(2): 191–213. Available at https://doi.org/10.1177/1086026606288780.

Sink, David. 1991. "Transorganizational Development in Urban Policy Coalitions." *Human Relations* 44(11): 1179–95. Available at https://doi.org/10.1177/001872679 104401103.

Slatin, Craig, Charles Levenstein, Robert Forrant, and John Wooding. 2016. *Environmental Unions: Labor and the Superfund.* Oxfordshire: Routledge.

Smith, Bruce L. R. 1983. "Changing Public–Private Sector Relations: A Look at the United States." *Annals of the American Academy of Political and Social Science* 466(1): 149–64. Available at https://doi.org/10.1177/0002716283466001010.

Smith, Jackie. 2001. "Globalizing Resistance: The Battle of Seattle and the Future of Social Movements." *Mobilization: An International Quarterly* 6(1): 1–19. Available at https://doi.org/10.17813/maiq.6.1.y63133434t8vq608.

Smith, Samantha. 2017. *Just Transition: A Report for the OECD.* International Trade Union Confederation. Available at https://www.oecd.org/environment/cc/g20-climate/collapsecontents/Just-Transition-Centre-report-just-transition.pdf.

Sneiderman, Marilyn, and Secky Fascione. 2018. "Going on Offense during Challenging Times." New Labor Forum. Available at https://newlaborforum.cuny.edu/2018/01/18/going-on-offense-during-challenging-times.

Snell, Darryn, and Peter Fairbrother. 2010. "Unions as Environmental Actors." *Transfer: European Review of Labour and Research* 16(3): 411–24. Available at https://doi.org/10.1177/1024258910373874.

Snow, David A., and Robert D. Benford. 1988. "Ideology, Frame Resonance, and Participant Mobilization." *International Social Movement Research*, 197–217.

Snow, David A., E. Burke Rochford, Steven K. Worden, and Robert D. Benford. 1986. "Frame Alignment Processes, Micromobilization, and Movement Participation."

American Sociological Review 51(4): 464–81. Available at https://doi.org/10.2307/2095581.

Society for the Study of Social Problems. 2018. "2018 Approved Resolutions: The Society for the Study of Social Problems." August. Available at https://www.sssp1.org/file/2018/2018AM/2018_Approved_Resolutions.pdf.

Soule, Sarah A. 1997. "The Student Divestment Movement in the United States and Tactical Diffusion: The Shantytown Protest." *Social Forces* 75(3): 855–82. Available at https://doi.org/10.2307/2580522.

Stepan-Norris, Judith, and Maurice Zeitlin. 2003. *Left Out: Reds and America's Industrial Unions*. New York: Cambridge University Press.

Stevis, Dimitris, and Romain Felli. 2015. "Global Labour Unions and Just Transition to a Green Economy." *International Environmental Agreements: Politics, Law and Economics* 15(1): 29–43. Available at https://doi.org/10.1007/s10784-014-9266-1.

Stevis, Dimitris, Dunja Krause, and Edouard Morena. 2019. "Reclaiming the Role of Labour Environmentalism in Just Transitions." *International Union Rights* 26(4): 3–4. Available at https://doi.org/10.14213/inteuniorigh.26.4.0003.

Stinchcombe, Arthur L. 1965. "Social Structure and Organizations." In *Handbook of Organizations*, edited by James G. March, 142–93. Chicago: Rand-McNally.

Streeck, Wolfgang, and Kathleen Thelen. 2005. *Beyond Continuity: Institutional Change in Advanced Political Economies*. New York: Oxford University Press.

Swedberg, Richard. 2017. "How to Use Max Weber's Ideal Type in Sociological Analysis." *Journal of Classical Sociology* 18(3): 181–96. Available at https://doi.org/10.1177/1468795x17743643.

Sweeney, Sean. 2016. "What Do We Mean by Just Transition?" Unpublished presentation to labor leaders at the International Program for Labor, Climate, and Environment, September 15.

———. 2017. "Standing Rock Solid with the Frackers." *New Labor Forum* 26(1): 94–99. Available at https://doi.org/10.1177/1095796016681547.

Sweeney, Sean, and John Treat. 2018. "Energy Democracy." TUED Working Paper #11. Available at https://unionsforenergydemocracy.org/resources/tued-working-papers/tued-working-paper-11.

Tarrow, Sidney. 1983. "Struggling to Reform: Social Movements and Policy Change during Cycles of Protest." Western Societies Occasional Paper No. 21. Ithaca, NY: Cornell University.

———. 1992. "Mentalities, Political Cultures, and Collective Action Frames." In *Frontiers in Social Movement Theory*, edited by Aldon D. Morris and Carol M. Mueller, 174–202. New Haven, CT: Yale University Press.

———. 1998. *Power in Movement: Social Movements and Contentious Politics*. 2nd ed. Cambridge: Cambridge University Press.

———. 2011. *Power in Movement: Social Movements and Contentious Politics*. 3rd ed. Cambridge: Cambridge University Press.

Thelen, Kathleen. 2009. "Institutional Change in Advanced Political Economies." *British Journal of Industrial Relations* 47(3): 471–98. Available at https://doi.org/10.1111/j.1467-8543.2009.00746.x.

Thornton, Patricia H., and William Ocasio. 2008. "Institutional Logics." In *The Sage Handbook of Organizational Institutionalism*, edited by Royston Greenwood,

Christine Oliver, Thomas B. Lawrence, and Renate E. Meyer, 99–128. Los Angeles: Sage.

Tilly, Charles. 1983. "Speaking Your Mind without Elections, Surveys, or Social Movements." *Public Opinion Quarterly* 47(4): 461. Available at https://doi.org/10.1086/268805.

———. 1995. *Popular Contention in Great Britain, 1758–1834.* Cambridge, MA: Harvard University Press.

———. 2008. *Contentious Performances.* Cambridge: Cambridge University Press.

Touraine, Alain. 1981. *The Voice and the Eye: An Analysis of Social Movements.* Cambridge: Cambridge University Press.

UAW. 1970. "The UAW Steps Up for Earth Day." Gaylord Nelson and Earth Day. Nelson Institute for Environmental Studies, University of Wisconsin System.

Uehlein, Joe. 2010. "Opinion: Earth Day, Labor, and Me." *Common Dreams*, April 19. Available at https://www.commondreams.org/views/2010/04/19/earth-day-labor-and-me.

———. 2011. "Opinion: American Labor; A Sustainable Path." *Common Dreams*, September 1. Available at https://www.commondreams.org/views/2011/09/01/american-labor-sustainable-path.

UMWA. 2021. "Preserving Coal Country: Keeping America's Coal Miners, Families and Communities Whole in an Era of Global Energy Transition." Available at https://umwa.org/wp-content/uploads/2021/04/UMWA-Preserving-Coal-Country-2021.pdf.

Union Sportsmen's Alliance. 2018. "USA's Mission." Available at http://unionsportsmen.org/about/mission.

U.S. Bureau of Labor Statistics (U.S. BLS). 2018a. *Labor Force Statistics from the Current Population Survey.* Available at https://www.bls.gov/cps.

———. 2018b. *Occupational Outlook Handbook.* US Bureau of Labor Statistics, Office of Occupational Statistics and Employment Projections. Washington, DC: Government Printing Office.

U.S. Congress. 2019. "Recognizing the Duty of the Federal Government to Create a Green New Deal." HR 109, 116th Cong., 1st sess., introduced February 7. Available at https://www.congress.gov/116/bills/hres109/BILLS-116hres109ih.pdf.

U.S. Department of Energy (U.S. DOE). 2017a. "2017 U.S. Energy and Employment Report." January 13. Available at https://www.energy.gov/downloads/2017-us-energy-and-employment-report.

———. 2017b. "Global Transportation Energy Consumption: Examination of Scenarios to 2040 Using ITEDD." September. Available at https://www.eia.gov/analysis/studies/transportation/scenarios/pdf/globaltransportation.pdf.

U.S. Environmental Protection Agency (U.S. EPA). 2021. "Greenhouse Gases Overview." Available at https://www.epa.gov/ghgemissions/overview-greenhouse-gases.

U.S. Global Change Research Program. 2017. *Climate Science Special Report: Fourth National Climate Assessment*, vol. 1. Available at https://science2017.globalchange.gov.

U.S. Senate Committee on Interior and Insular Affairs. 1958. "Acreage Limitation (Reclamation Law) Review Hearings before the Subcommittee on Irrigation and Reclamation of the Committee on Interior and Insular Affairs, United States Senate, Eighty-Fifth Congress, Second Session, on S. 1425, S. 2541, and S. 3448, Bills

Pertaining to Acreage Limitation (Reclamation Law), April 30 and May 1, 1958." Washington, DC: U.S. Government Printing Office.

USW. 1990. "Our Children's World." August 30. Available at https://m.usw.org/get-involved/hsande/resources/publications/Our-Childrens-World-1990.pdf.

———. 2006. "Securing Our Children's World: Our Union and the Environment." Available at http://assets.usw.org/resources/hse/Resources/securingourchildren sworld.pdf.

Vachon, Todd E. 2018. "Clean Air and Good Jobs: U.S. Labor and the Struggle for Climate Justice." Unpublished diss. Available at https://opencommons.uconn.edu/dissertations/1958.

———. 2022. "American Federation of Teachers Calls on TIAA and Other Retirement Funds to Divest from Fossil Fuels." *TIAADivest!*, August 8. Available at https://tiaa-divest.org/news/.

Vachon, Todd E., and Jeremy Brecher. 2016. "Are Union Members More or Less Likely to Be Environmentalists? Some Evidence from Two National Surveys." *Labor Studies Journal* 41(2): 185–203. Available at https://doi.org/10.1177/0160449x16643323.

Vachon, Todd E., Gerry Hudson, Judith Leblanc, and Saket Soni. 2019. "How Workers Can Demand Climate Justice." *American Prospect*, September 2. Available at https://prospect.org/labor/workers-can-demand-climate-justice.

Vachon, Todd E., Michael Wallace, and Allen Hyde. 2016. "Union Decline in a Neo-liberal Age: Globalization, Financialization, Regionalization, and Union Density in Eighteen Affluent Democracies." *Socius: Sociological Research for a Dynamic World* 2 (January). Available at https://doi.org/10.1177/2378023116656847.

Van Dyke, Nella, Sarah A. Soule, and Verta A. Taylor. 2004. "The Targets of Social Movements: Beyond a Focus on the State." In *Authority in Contention*, vol. 25, edited by Daniel J. Myers, Daniel M. Cress, and Patrick G. Coy, 27–51. Bingley, U.K.: Emerald Group.

Viscelli, Steve. 2016. *The Big Rig: Trucking and the Decline of the American Dream*. Oakland: University of California Press.

von Holdt, Karl. 2002. "Social Movement Unionism: The Case of South Africa." *Work, Employment and Society* 16(2): 283–304. Available at https://doi.org/10.1177/095001702400426848.

Voss, Kim, and Rachel Sherman. 2000. "Breaking the Iron Law of Oligarchy: Union Revitalization in the American Labor Movement." *American Journal of Sociology* 106(2): 303–49. Available at https://doi.org/10.1086/316963.

Walker, Edward T., Andrew W. Martin, and John D. McCarthy. 2008. "Confronting the State, the Corporation, and the Academy: The Influence of Institutional Targets on Social Movement Repertoires." *American Journal of Sociology* 114(1): 35–76. Available at https://doi.org/10.1086/588737.

Wallace, Michael, Andrew S. Fullerton, and Mustafa E. Gurbuz. 2009. "Union Organizing Effort and Success in the U.S., 1948–2004." *Research in Social Stratification and Mobility* 27(1): 13–34. Available at https://doi.org/10.1016/j.rssm.2008.10.002.

Waterman, Peter. 1991. "Social Movement Unionism: A New Model for a New World." Working Paper No. 110. Amsterdam: International Institute for Research and Education.

Webb, Sidney, and Beatrice Webb. 1897. *Industrial Democracy*. New York: Longmans, Green.

Webley, Kayla. 2012. "Hurricane Sandy by the Numbers: A Superstorm's Statistics, One Month Later." *Time*, November 26. Available at https://nation.time.com /2012/11/26/hurricane-sandy-one-month-later.

Weed, Frank J. 1997. "The Framing of Political Advocacy and Service Responses in the Crime Victim Rights Movement." *Journal of Sociology and Social Welfare* 24(3): 43–61. Available at https://scholarworks.wmich.edu/jssw/vol24/iss3/5.

Wentz, Jessica. 2017. "Trump Appointees at Environmental, Energy and Natural Resource Management Agencies: Not Much Expertise, Plenty of Fossil Fuel Connections." *Climate Law Blog*. Sabin Center for Climate Law Change. April 10. Available at http://blogs.law.columbia.edu/climatechange/2017/04/10.

Wheeler, Tim, and Joachim von Braun. 2013. "Climate Change Impacts on Global Food Security." *Science* 341(6145): 508–13. Available at https://doi.org/10.1126 /science.1239402.

Wiessner, Daniel. 2018. "UAW Accuses Musk of Threatening Tesla Workers over Unionization." Reuters. May 24. Available at https://www.reuters.com/article/us-tesla-union /uaw-accuses-musk-of-threatening-tesla-workers-over-unionization-idUSKCN1 IP2XS.

Wood, Lesley J. 2004. "Breaking the Bank and Taking to the Streets: How Protesters Target Neoliberalism." *Journal of World-Systems Research* 10(1): 69–89. Available at https://doi.org/10.5195/jwsr.2004.313.

Woodly, Deva R. 2015. *The Politics of Common Sense: How Social Movements Use Public Discourse to Change Politics and Win Acceptance*. New York: Oxford University Press.

Wright, Erik Olin, and Joel Rogers. 2015. *American Society: How It Really Works*. New York: W. W. Norton.

York, Richard. 2004. "The Treadmill of (Diversifying) Production." *Organization and Environment* 17(3): 355–62. Available at https://doi.org/10.1177/1086026604268023.

Zalasiewicz, Jan, Mark Williams, Will Steffen, and Paul Crutzen. 2010. "The New World of the Anthropocene." *Environmental Science and Technology* 44(7): 2228–31. Available at https://doi.org/10.1021/es903118j.

Index

Todd E. Vachon is Assistant Professor of Labor Studies and Employment Relations and Director of the Labor Education Action Research Network at Rutgers University. He is the coeditor of *Revaluing Work(ers): Toward a Democratic and Sustainable Future.*

Printed and bound by CPI Group (UK) Ltd, Croydon, CR0 4YY

11/04/2023

03209721-0001